5000 years of tiles

5000 years of tiles

Hans van Lemmen

The British Museum

First published in 2013 by The British Museum Press
A division of The British Museum Company Ltd
38 Russell Square, London WC1B 3QQ
britishmuseum.org/publishing

Hans van Lemmen has asserted the right to be identified as
the author of this work

A catalogue record for this book is available from the
British Library

ISBN: 978-0-7141-5099-4

Designed by Paul Palmer-Edwards at Grade Design
Printed in China by Toppan Leefung Printing Limited

The papers used by The British Museum Press are recyclable products
and the manufacturing processes are expected to conform to the
environmental regulations of the country of origin.

Frontispiece Tube-lined and hand-painted tile panel of a woman holding
a flower with a peacock at her side. Léon V. Solon for Minton's China Works,
Stoke-upon-Trent, Britain, 1900–1905. It was originally made for the Dutch
tile dealer A. M. A. Heystee in Amsterdam, The Netherlands.

Front cover tiles (from left to right) British Museum (p. 63), British Museum
(p. 56), British Museum (p. 234), private collection (p. 241), British Museum
(p. 111), British Museum (p. 169), British Museum (p. 216), British Museum
(p. 197), British Museum (p. 187), British Museum (p. 113), British Museum
(p. 195), private collection (p. 245), British Museum (p. 97), British Museum
(p. 52), British Museum (1980,0307.117), British Museum (p. 136), British Museum
(p. 168), British Museum (p. 80), British Museum (p. 191). (On the front flap)
British Museum (pp. 111, 173 and 41).

CONTENTS

INTRODUCTION

For thousands of years tiles have been used to cover the roofs, walls and floors of buildings. Many are simple sections of baked clay performing a practical purpose, yet others are beautiful objects bearing fascinating designs and intriguing images. Long-favoured by artists and craftsmen throughout the ages as an exciting and versatile medium for artistic expression, they are also assiduously collected as cultural artefacts worthy of academic study and aesthetic appreciation. As such, they are represented in museum collections around the world and there are a number of societies devoted to their study.

This book traces the rich legacy of tiles from pre-history to the present day, revealing how tiles have evolved both in terms of production and as an artistic medium. The way in which tiles have been made and decorated is incredibly diverse and so there is much to be said about the complex accumulation of discoveries, experimentations and inventions that make up the technical history of tiles.

The iconography and decoration of tiles will be explored as these can throw light on the cultures by which the tiles were made. The application of tiles in architectural contexts will also be considered as it is their use as functional and decorative objects that helps us to understand the values placed on tiles by particular cultures at specific periods of time – an aspect which can be overlooked by viewing single tiles in isolation.

And so this book is not only an artistic appreciation of tiles; it places tiles firmly in their cultural, social and historical context, and will highlight significant moments in the making and use of tiles. It will also show how tile art in one time and place has gone on to influence tiles in other periods, highlighting the continuity as well as the creative diversity of tile design throughout the years.

Tiles belong to the larger family of architectural ceramics that includes bricks, terracotta, faience (glazed ware) and mosaic. Fired bricks are normally solid simple building blocks but they can become highly ornamental when they are moulded with relief decoration and covered with coloured glazes. Architectural terracotta and faience are (respectively) large unglazed or glazed hollow building blocks that can have complex shapes and are formed in moulds. Mosaic usually consists of very small pieces of tile (sometimes deliberately broken) put together to make intricate designs and figurative images or just assembled in a random way to create a visually interesting surface.

The word 'tile' is derived from the Latin noun *tegula* which in Roman times meant a roof tile. Tiles are often thought of as thin pieces of square or oblong fired clay but they can be triangular, hexagonal and semi-circular, round and star shaped. They can also be unglazed or glazed. Unglazed tiles are often reddish brown, yellow or white depending on the type of clay from which they have been fashioned and their resistance to water, dirt and heat will depend on how long they have been fired in the kiln. The higher the temperature the more the clay will contract and the harder and more durable they will become. Glazed tiles have a glassy coating that helps protect the body of the tile and although this is in the first instance a purely practical

consideration, glaze also adds the colour which gives tiles their decorative appeal.

Their physical durability and permanency is the main reason why tiles have been so highly valued. A well-made and properly fired tile will last longer than any other type of building material. Wood rots, iron corrodes and stone wears away, but fired clay remains largely unchanged over time. The durability of tiles is also a reason why craftsmen and artists have favoured them as a medium. Not only can tiles be decorated in a myriad of ways, but ceramic colours do not fade once they have been fired.

The breathtaking wealth of examples featured in this book is drawn from collections around the world and includes tiles created for every kind of purpose, but the majority is from the rich collection of the British Museum. The British Museum has been acquiring tiles since the beginning of its history in the eighteenth century and thus its collection spans many cultures and demonstrates numerous techniques and artistic styles. Many large collections were acquired in the nineteenth and early twentieth centuries, while deliberate attempts have been made in more recent decades to add, for example, Gothic Revival tiles to complement the National Reference Collection of medieval tiles.

Our account begins with the tiles in the pre-industrial era and includes Babylonian polychrome bricks, Egyptian faience, Roman terracotta, Chinese roof tiles, Islamic wall tiles, Gothic inlaid floor tiles, Hispano-Moresque lustre tiles and the painted maiolica tiles of the Renaissance and Baroque periods. The Industrial Revolution brought about great changes in the way tiles were made and decorated as mass produced items for the new urban and domestic markets of Europe and America. It is from this time that stylistic changes also gathered pace and the Arts and Crafts Movement, Art Nouveau and Art Deco all left their mark on tile design. Our journey

ABOVE LEFT [fig. 3] Italian tile depicting a rabbit. Tin-glazed earthenware. Italy, *c.*1527. 8.8 x 6.4 cm. British Museum 1885,0508.70. Donated by Sir Augustus Wollaston Franks.

ABOVE RIGHT [fig. 4] Art Nouveau tile with the head of a woman. Dust-pressed earthenware with translucent green glaze. W. Wade & Co., Burslem, England, *c.*1901. 15 x 15 cm. Private collection.

ABOVE [fig. 5] Tile panel with a park landscape and peacocks. Glazed earthenware, painted by the German artist, Lothar Scholz. Germany, 2003. 250 x 250 cm.

will end in the twenty-first century with the tile creations of a selection of prominent international artists, including Eduardo Nery, Frouwien Soenveld and Paul Scott. These contemporary artists show that although the long history of tiles has often been an inspiration to them, they are also able to give their work its own unique creative stamp. They also reveal that tile art and production techniques continue to be as exciting and innovative today as they have been in ages gone by.

ANCIENT BEGINNINGS

I pulled down these gates and laid their foundations at the water table with bitumen and bricks and had them made of bricks with blue stone on which wonderful bulls and dragons were depicted.

Nebuchadnezzar II

Inscription on the Ishtar Gate, 605–562 BC

OPPOSITE [fig. 6] The Ishtar Gate, decorated with glazed bricks showing bulls and dragons. The gate was built in the ancient city of Babylon under the rule of the Neo-Babylonian ruler Nebuchadnezzar II, between 605–562 BC. Since 1928 the gate has been reconstructed and is on permanent display at the Pergamon Museum in Berlin, Germany.

Tiles and bricks were first used in the Middle East when nomadic people began to settle along great rivers like the Nile in Egypt and the Euphrates and Tigris in Mesopotamia. The change from a nomadic lifestyle with no permanent abode to living in settled communities that cultivated crops along the banks of rivers brought about the construction of more permanent dwellings. These fundamental changes in lifestyle were most likely initiated by the changes in the climate when the ice cap began to recede from Europe. The Middle East became much drier, leading people to live near rivers and build permanent settlements. The type of materials used for the construction of buildings normally depended on what was locally available. In Mesopotamia there was hardly any stone or wood, but an abundance of sand, clay and marsh reed was found along the Euphrates and Tigris and these materials proved to be useful for the construction of buildings. Likewise in Egypt, sand, clay and reed were found along the Nile and here stone was also available. Where there were forests such as in Greece, Italy and China, wood was more often used for building material.

Fired clay tiles and bricks, however, are technically a more advanced building material than mud bricks, stone or wood. Although certain tools and skills are needed to work the latter, at the end of the working and shaping process the actual material you started with is still the same. Fired clay needs first to be shaped and then baked in fire until it is hard but when that process is completed it has become a different material that cannot be reconstituted. Well-fired clay is hard and durable and has great compression strength as well as being water and fire resistant. Add to this the developments in glaze technology that allowed potters to give fired clay a glassy coating, improving its functional properties and also allowing the adding of colour

for decoration, and you have a versatile multi-purpose building material which can be used equally on roofs, walls and floors.

Egypt

When people began to form settled communities along the river Nile they developed the political, social and religious institutions necessary for the functioning of a more complex society. Over time a rich and long-lasting Egyptian culture sprang up along the Nile, first as two separate states in Upper and Lower Egypt and then as one nation from about 3000 BC onwards under the dynastic rule of Pharaohs. This rule is historically divided into several different periods: the Old, Middle and New Kingdoms and a late period when Egypt was first under Persian and then Greek rule before it became a Roman Province in 30 BC.

The Nile was the lifeline of Egypt, with its annual inundation allowing crops to grow, but it was also a source of mud and clay which could be made into sun-dried bricks (known as 'adobe') that were used on a large scale as building material for every kind of structure. Sun-dried bricks are simple and cheap to make and were created by mixing mud, a small amount of clay and chopped straw in a simple wooden rectangular mould (fig. 7). The bricks were tipped out and left to dry in the hot sun and were then used for the construction of walls. Adobe bricks are reasonably strong and have good thermal qualities. They are slow to absorb warmth and therefore keep the heat of the sun at bay during the day. At night, when the temperature drops, they act as a kind of storage heater and give out warmth, thus keeping the temperatures inside buildings at fairly consistent levels. Their drawback is that they are susceptible to rain and can only be used effectively in regions with low rainfall. They also cannot withstand earthquakes.

ABOVE LEFT [fig. 7] Making adobe bricks in the Danube Delta, Romania, using a mixture of mud and straw that is pushed into wooden moulds. Afterwards the bricks are left to dry in the sun.

Stone was available in large quantities and, as building techniques evolved, the
Egyptians learned how to quarry and transport stone, which was used for important
buildings. Stone became particularly essential for the building of tombs which
needed to be made from a durable material in order to create lasting dwellings for
the dead. The tombs of the ruling elite were richly furnished with every kind of object
needed for the journey through the afterlife. The walls of the tombs were decorated
with intricate low-relief carvings, wall paintings with various scenes from daily life,
images pertaining to the cult of the dead and sacred texts in the form of hieroglyphs,
but glazed faience tiles were sometimes also part of tombs.

Egyptian faience tiles were not made from ordinary clay, but from a special
composition consisting mainly of crushed quartz with a small amount of sand. When
fired they were covered with a transparent glaze derived from alkali silicates which
could be coloured blue or green with a little copper oxide. Over time more coloured
glazes were developed and by the time of the New Kingdom (1550–1086 BC) some
very fine polychromatic tiles were made for use on walls and as inlays in furniture.
Faience was not only used for making tiles but also for objects like small statuettes,
beads and amulets.

An early example (fig. 8) of the use of faience tiles dates back to the 27th century BC
Old Kingdom, when the pharaoh Djoser (2686–2613 BC) built his great Step Pyramid
in Saqqara, designed by the architect Imhotep. The central burial chamber was
surrounded by four galleries which probably contained the funerary equipment of the
pharaoh. Some of the walls and door jambs were lined with thousands of small blue
faience tiles. Each tile had a slightly convex outer surface and a rectangular
projection on the back for attachment. This projection was pierced horizontally by a
single hole, by means of which the tile could be secured on a copper wire. They were
set into the wall in such a way that they resembled reed bundles or rolled up mats and
the blue glaze mimicked the colour of lapis lazuli, a semi-precious stone that was a
much prized material for the adornment of objects and jewellery. The passages
leading to the royal tomb chamber therefore gave the appearance of being lined
with lapis lazuli.

If faience tiles were first used in royal tombs, they were later also used in royal
palaces. Important tile fragments have come to light at the palaces of the pharaoh
Ramses III (c.1184–1153 BC) at Medinet Habu and Tell el-Yahudiya. They are finely
crafted polychrome faience tiles that resemble human figures and depict foreign
prisoners of war. Some of the captives have been modelled so accurately that their
racial origins can be ascertained, as seen in tiles depicting Libyan captives. These
men are portrayed with uplifted face and one arm bound by a rope, and wear
ornamented chest straps and loincloths, the simple costume of an overlord of the
ancient Libyan tribe (fig. 9). Their tattoos and pierced ears reflect Libyan fashion of
the time. The surface of their bodies is modelled in relief, with moulded pieces like
the face added separately. This focus on Libyan captives shows that the Libyan tribes
were a real threat to the Egyptians in the period of Ramses III, and much wall space
at Ramses III's temple at Medinet Habu depicted battles involving this group. The
prisoner tiles from Tell el-Yahudiya were probably positioned in the same way as
those at Medinet Habu and placed either side of the base of the throne where the
pharaoh appeared before the public as victor and protector of his people while
trampling on his enemies. The tiles from Tell el-Yahudiya are particularly fine,

and rate as some of Egypt's most accomplished tile work, displaying a greater variety of pose, scale and detail than their counterparts from Medinet Habu.

Another type of faience tile found at the palace of Ramses III at Tell el-Yahudiya consisted of rectangular tiles with hieroglyphic inscriptions that were possibly set into a wall, doorframe or throne pedestal (fig. 10). The designs were built up by inlaying different colours into a contrasting base colour. Hieroglyphic script is an ancient form of Egyptian writing based on pictorial symbols, and the tile inscriptions were emblematic of royal and religious power as they carried the cartouche with the name of the pharaoh as well as symbols of gods or goddesses. Decorative faience tiles featuring floral rosettes, lotus flowers and birds were also used to adorn palace interiors (fig. 11), and faience tiles painted with images of gods and pharaohs were used as funerary markers or appear as pectorals placed on the chests of mummies (fig. 12). Although ceramic tiles constitute an important part of Egyptian architectural decoration, based on what has come to light during excavations, their use seems to have been on a relatively small scale compared with what has survived in the form of decorative glazed brickwork in Mesopotamia.

ABOVE LEFT [fig. 9] Tile from the palace of Ramses III at Tell el-Yahudiya showing a Libyan captive. Polychrome faience. Egypt, New Kingdom, 20th Dynasty, reign of Ramses III, 1184–1153 BC 31 x 9.49 cm. British Museum 1871,0619.510.

ABOVE RIGHT [fig. 10] Tile showing the cartouche of Ramses III . The hieroglyphic inscription reads: 'Lord of the Two Lands'. It was probably used as an inlay in a wall, doorframe or throne pedestal at the palace of Ramses III at Tell el-Yahudiya.Faience, with different coloured inlays. Egypt, New Kingdom, 20th Dynasty, reign of Ramses III, 1184–1153 BC. 20.7 x 7.9 cm. British Museum 1871,0619.548.

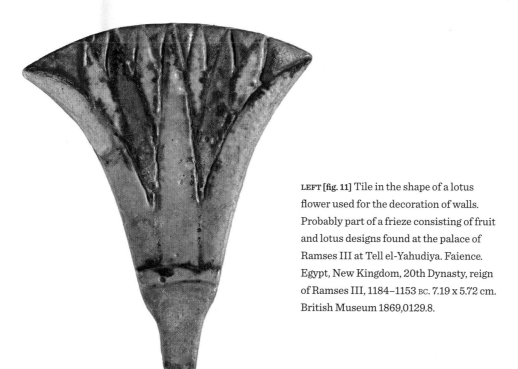

LEFT [fig. 11] Tile in the shape of a lotus flower used for the decoration of walls. Probably part of a frieze consisting of fruit and lotus designs found at the palace of Ramses III at Tell el-Yahudiya. Faience. Egypt, New Kingdom, 20th Dynasty, reign of Ramses III, 1184–1153 BC. 7.19 x 5.72 cm. British Museum 1869,0129.8.

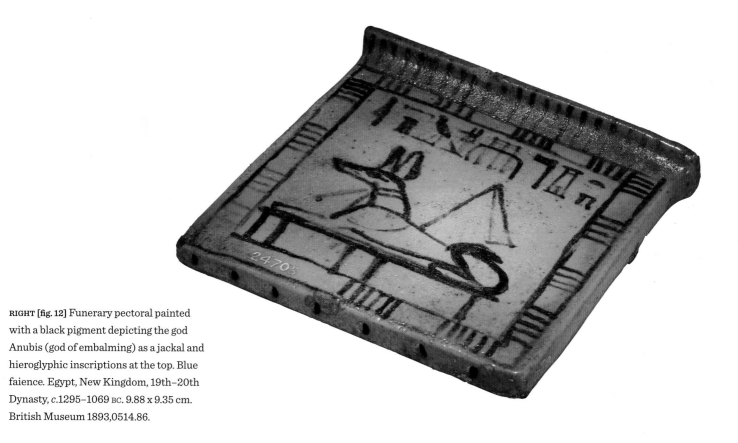

RIGHT [fig. 12] Funerary pectoral painted with a black pigment depicting the god Anubis (god of embalming) as a jackal and hieroglyphic inscriptions at the top. Blue faience. Egypt, New Kingdom, 19th–20th Dynasty, c.1295–1069 BC. 9.88 x 9.35 cm. British Museum 1893,0514.86.

Mesopotamia

The use of sun-dried bricks or adobe was also the main method of building in Mesopotamia where river mud was found in abundance along the Tigris and Euphrates. Here the scarcity of stone may have been an incentive to develop the technology of making kiln-fired bricks to use as an alternative. To strengthen walls made from sun-dried bricks, fired bricks began to be used as an outer protective skin for more important buildings like temples, palaces, and city walls and gates. Making fired bricks is an advanced pottery technique. Fired bricks are solid masses of clay heated in kilns to temperatures of between 950 and 1,150 Celsius, and a well-made fired brick is an extremely durable object. Like sun-dried bricks they were made in wooden moulds but for bricks with relief decorations special moulds had to be made. Unlike the river mud used for sun-dried bricks, the clay for proper bricks needed to be carefully prepared and the building of a kiln, finding suitable fuel and controlling kiln temperatures required a professional level of skill and know-how. This is perhaps the reason why the use of fired bricks came in gradually over time.

The technical complexities involved in making fired bricks may explain why one of the first recorded instances of pieces of fired clay, used as a protective covering for mud-brick walls at the Sumerian city of Uruk in southern Mesopotamia in 3600–

ABOVE [fig. 13] Columns with clay mosaic cones from the Eanna precinct in Uruk, in southern Mesopotamia, dating from 3600–3200 BC. The clay clones were painted in red, black and white and were inserted in such a way that they created geometrical designs on the surface of the columns. The columns are on permanent display at the Pergamon Museum in Berlin, Germany.

ABOVE LEFT [fig. 14] Tile with a guilloche border from the North-West Palace at Nimrud (now in modern Iraq). It is painted in black on a yellow ground showing a king attended by his servants. It probably represents the Neo-Assyrian king Ashurnasirpal II, showing him as a triumphant warrior and hunter. Glazed earthenware. 883–859 BC. H. 30 cm. British Museum N.1035.

ABOVE RIGHT [fig. 15] Three glazed bricks with part of a circular design (possibly a rosette), originally mounted below the crenulations of a fortified building at Nimrud. Rosettes were thought to have magical protective powers. Assyria, dating from the reign of Shalmaneser III, 859–840 BC. Average size of each brick: 27 x 18 cm. British Museum 1987,0131.116.

3200 BC, did not involve bricks but small clay cones (fig. 13). Uruk was one of Mesopotamia's first cities and had an important temple complex at its centre known as the Eanna precinct. Here was found the Limestone Temple, which was connected to a second temple via a courtyard. In this courtyard was a colonnaded terrace with massive pillars made of mud and bundled reeds. To protect them from weathering, thousands of nail-shaped ceramic cones were pushed into an outer bed of clay. The cones have flat tops and were painted red, white or black and arranged in such a way that they formed geometric patterns. What is so significant about this is that here we find, perhaps for the first time, fired clay as a practical protection against the environmental effects of rain and wind, safeguarding the columns from deterioration as well as creating an ornamental surface decoration.

Over time fired bricks also came to be used in Uruk as a building material and for decorative purposes. An example is the temple of Inanna, the goddess of fertility, built by the king Karaindash at the end of the fourteenth century BC. The exterior of the temple was constructed of fired bricks with alternating projections and recessions. In the recessions were brick statues of gods holding vessels from which flowed streams of water.

Assyrian kings used fired bricks for the construction of ziggurats (rectangular terraces of diminishing size), palaces and gateways. Some fine examples have survived from the city of Nimrud in northern Mesopotamia where in the ninth century BC temples and palaces were decorated with both unglazed and glazed fired bricks during the reigns of the Neo-Assyrian kings Ashurnasirpal II (883–859 BC) and Shalmaneser III (859–840 BC). A glazed tile (fig. 14) was found at Nimrud at one of the palaces which shows a king attended by servants and bodyguards, and probably

OPPOSITE [fig. 16] Unglazed brick from the outer face of the ziggurat at Nimrud, completed under the rule of the Neo-Assyrian king Shalmaneser III, 859–840 BC. Cuneiform script is impressed in the clay. The text proclaims the various titles of the king. Earthenware. Assyria, 859–840 BC. 40 x 40 cm. British Museum 1848,1104.28.

represents Ashurnasirpal II who rebuilt Nimrud during his reign. Similar figurative compositions of Assyrian kings attended by their servants can also be found on stone relief carvings of that time.

Bricks with cuneiform script provide important written information about the history of the period. Cuneiform is the oldest known form of writing and dates from around 3200 BC. Text was imprinted with a small stick or reed pen into the soft clay which was then left to harden in the sun, or sometimes fired to become a permanent record of the royal, religious, military or economic history of the various Mesopotamian kingdoms. Cuneiform became the basis for all subsequent Sumerian, Akkadian, Assyrian, Babylonian and Persian writing. It was frequently used to record royal deeds, as on the clay tablets excavated at the ziggurat attached to the temple of the god Ninurta, a prominent building in the city of Nimrud completed during the reign of Shalmaneser III. The outer face of the ziggurat was built of fired bricks with cuneiform inscriptions reciting the sovereign's titles such as 'Shalmaneser, the great king, strong king, king of the world, king of Assyria, son of Ashurnasirpal' (fig. 16).

Adding coloured glazes to fired bricks was the next important technological development and was used with spectacular effect in Assyrian, Neo-Babylonian and Persian architecture. However, kiln-fired bricks always remained expensive to produce, particularly in Mesopotamia where fuel for kilns was in short supply. That is probably why kings regarded brick making as a royal monopoly that was usually

ABOVE [fig. 17] A lion made of glazed bricks from the Processional Way that led to the Ishtar Gate (fig. 6), constructed under the rule of the Neo-Babylonian ruler Nebuchadnezzar II between 605–562 BC. Since 1928 the gate has been reconstructed and is on permanent display at the Pergamon Museum in Berlin, Germany.

commemorated in inscriptions on buildings made of brick. In certain instances they were even depicted themselves on glazed bricks.

Some of the most amazing examples of glazed brickwork were used in the ancient city of Babylon on the river Euphrates. This ancient city was frequently fought over and destroyed but it reached its zenith under the Neo-Babylonian king Nebuchadnezzar II who rebuilt the city during his reign in 605–562 BC. It became known for its fabled Hanging Gardens and the so-called Tower of Babel, as well as for its wonderful palaces and colourful gateways. One of the palaces, known as the Southern Palace, was the administrative centre of the empire and was elaborately decorated with glazed bricks. The walls of the throne room showed palm columns with volute capitals, intricate borders of stylized flowers and rosettes, and a row of lions along the bottom.

The most impressive setting in which glazed bricks was used was the Processional Way leading to the Ishtar Gate situated at the northern side of the city. The Processional Way was about 250 metres long and 20 metres wide, walled on either side, and the walls were decorated with striding lions which were symbols of the goddess Ishtar (fig. 17). The Ishtar Gate was a massive double gate (one placed behind the other) with four square towers sporting battlements. The gates and the towers were faced with glazed bricks showing bulls and dragons (fig. 6). The bull was sacred to the weather god Adad and the dragon was the symbol of the state god Marduk. The main colouration of the animals was orange-yellow and white set against a blue background, creating a striking colour contrast. The Processional Way and the Ishtar Gate were more important than the other city gates because here the Babylonian New Year festival was enacted every year in the honour of the state god Marduk whose image of a dragon was a prominent feature on the Ishtar Gate. This was an important ritual that marked the beginning of the agricultural year and involved the king and city priests.

The bricks used for the Processional Way and the Ishtar Gate were of a special large format. Full bricks measured 33 centimetres wide with a height similar to modern bricks. The relief bricks used for creating the lions, dragons and bulls were press moulded in reusable moulds and there must have been some kind of production line system to create the thousands of moulded bricks needed for the multiple images of the animals. Each lion, for example, was made up of forty-six differently moulded bricks arranged in eleven rows, and when the bricks were moulded great care was taken that joints would not cut across eyes or other parts that would appear aesthetically displeasing. It seems that the bricks were fired before they were glazed which would make them even more expensive to produce as two firings would be needed to complete the whole process. Every brick had a marking to ensure they were assembled in the right way and the bricks were laid in beds of mud with bitumen (a naturally occurring material in the oil rich soil of Mesopotamia) used to seal the joints.

The importance attached to the manufacture and use of glazed bricks under royal patronage is reflected in the glazed bricks with cuneiform inscriptions that formed part of the Ishtar Gate. One such inscription which recorded Nebuchadnezzar's construction of the gate reads: 'and had them made of bricks with blue stone on which wonderful bulls and dragons were depicted.'

The new city of Babylon was not to last; it was conquered by Cyrus the Great of Persia in 539 BC. He did not destroy the city, but over time it became a provincial backwater and was gradually abandoned. It was literally lost in the sands of time until it was discovered by German archaeologists at the end of the nineteenth century. They spent many years excavating it, and much of what they discovered has been meticulously reconstructed at the Pergamon Museum in Berlin, including the front section of the Ishtar Gate and a section of the Processional Way.

After the fall of Babylon, the city of Susa became the new Persian capital. Darius I (521–486 BC) used all the resources of his empire for ambitious building programmes and imported skilled workmen from its furthest reaches for the construction of magnificent palaces. Decorations made of glazed brick using the Babylonian methods were important. The Achaemenid Palace at Susa had a monumental entrance staircase decorated with glazed bricks featuring rows of servants and crenellated battlements with roaring lions, bulls and griffons and decorations like stylized fan-shaped palm and rosettes.

At the East Gate of the Achaemenid Palace was the famous Row of Guards, marching along, each carrying a long spear, a quiver and a string bow. They probably represented the king's bodyguard and were finely executed with moulded glazed relief bricks (fig. 18) with a range of coloured glazes which was greater than used on the Ishtar Gate at Babylon. The bricks were tapered so that they could be laid with a thin joint, making their pictorial effect even more striking.

The Persian Empire in turn succumbed to the Greeks under Alexander the Great who crushed the might of the Persian army under the command of Darius III in 331 BC, and Persia became a Greek province. With the ascendancy of Greek military power and culture also ended the applications of polychromatic glazed brickwork which had been such a special feature of Mesopotamian architectural history.

Greece, Etruria and Rome

The Greeks stand at the beginning of what is now seen as the great classical Greco-Roman era that saw significant developments in art and architecture, engineering, science and philosophy. Greece was historically a collection of independent city

ABOVE [fig. 18] Relief panel with a life-size standing figure of a Persian archer from the East Gate of the Achaemenid Palace, in Susa, built in the reign of Darius I (521–486 BC). It was part of a larger frieze of guards. Moulded bricks covered in a variety of coloured glazes. Persia, 521–486 BC. 198 x 70 cm. British Museum, on loan from Musée du Louvre.

states of which Athens and Sparta on the Greek mainland were the most important. They saw their biggest territorial expansion under Alexander the Great (ruled 336–323 BC) who not only defeated the Persians but also conquered Egypt where he founded the famous city of Alexandria. The Greeks even created colonies in Italy.

The architecture of Ancient Greece is of a trabeated (post and lintel) form, composed of upright beams (posts) supporting horizontal beams (lintels). Although surviving buildings are constructed in stone, it is clear that the origin of the style lies in simple wooden structures, with vertical posts supporting beams that carried a ridged roof. The slightly sloping roof was covered with wooden rafters on which terracotta tiles were fixed to keep out the rain. This introduction of the ceramic roof tile marks one of the important milestones in the history of tiles. It is not clear when the first roof tiles were made but they were probably first used on simple temples made from mud bricks and timber. Since terracotta roofs are heavy, stone walls and columns were introduced for bigger temples to carry the weight of the roof.

ABOVE [fig. 20] Etruscan antefix moulded with a female head set in an elaborate frame. This antefix is of the 'Juno Sospita' type used to adorn the Etruscan temple of Juno Sospita at Lanuvium in Italy. Painted terracotta. Italy, 520–470 BC. 38.1 x 41.91 cm. British Museum 1890,0614.1.

ABOVE [fig. 21] Antefix with the inscription LEG XX and a wild boar, the emblem of the 20th Legion, which was stationed in Chester, England for much of its existence. Terracotta. Roman, 2nd–3rd century AD. H. 21 cm. British Museum 1911,0206.1.

Over time the Greeks developed three types of roof tiles which are now known as the Lakonian, the Corinthian and the Sicilian, taking their names from the areas where they were first used. Lakonian tiles are simply curved tiles laid alternately with the concave side upwards and downwards, which is a simple but effective way to create a terracotta roof. The Corinthian roof system consisted of flat tiles with upturned edges, the gap between two tiles being covered with a narrow oblong triangular-shaped tile. The Sicilian roof system had flat tiles like those of the Corinthian type but in this case the gap between them was covered by semi-circular tiles with the curved side upward. Curved ridge tiles would run along the top of the roof closing the gap between the two sloping sides.

Roofs could have guttering with spouts on each end or the roof could project and throw the water well clear of the wall. The gaps at the end of the tiles along the eaves were often closed with special finishing tiles known as antefixa decorated with simple floral motifs or human faces (fig. 19). On early temples, terracotta statues were used to embellish the triangular pediment and terracotta statues called *acroteria* could be placed on the four corners of the roof.

The Greek way of covering roofs with functional and decorative tiles was adopted by the Etruscans who lived in northern and central Italy before the ascendency of the

ABOVE [fig. 22] Box flue tile decorated with two registers of leaping animals. Terracotta. Roman, 1st–4th century AD. 16.5 x 43 cm. British Museum 1973,0403.72.

RIGHT [fig. 23] Flat roof tile known in Latin as a *tegula*, the etymological source of the English word for tile. Terracotta. Roman, 1st century BC. British Museum 1861,0301.2. Donated by Archaeological Institute for Great Britain and Ireland.

Romans. They used terracotta tiles and decorations much more profusely than the Greeks and some very elaborate antefixa have survived which are minor works of art. Of particular fame were the terracotta antefixa which once adorned the Etruscan temple of Juno Sospita in Lanuvium in the sixth to fifth century BC that show female heads (maenads) with elaborate frames around their heads (fig. 20). They were originally painted in strong colours which must have made them very striking pieces of architectural decoration. When the Romans came to power in the third century BC they adopted many elements of the Greek and Etruscan architectural traditions including the use of functional and ornamental terracotta roof tiles. The Romans, however, used terracotta tiles on a much bigger scale and they used them not only on roofs but also for the construction of walls and on floors.

For roofs the Romans used two types of tile, the *tegula* and the *imbrex*. The *tegula* was a flat tile with upturned flanges (hook-like projections) along the long sides (fig. 23). These were laid side by side on the sloping roof with the flanges pointing upwards. The gaps between the tiles would be covered with a semi-circular *imbrex* tile which would keep the flat *tegulae* in place and keep water out of the roof space. The *imbreces* would form a series of ridges running down the roof and the ends of the ridges that finished above the eaves would be stopped up with a decorative antefix

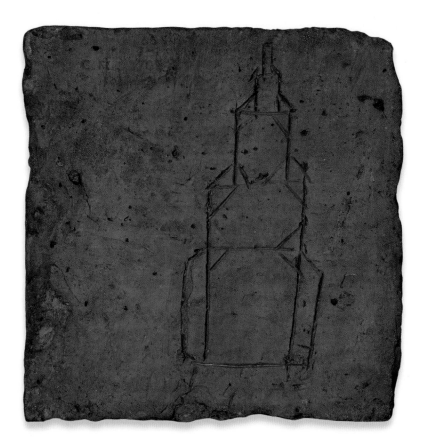

(fig. 21). The gable ridge at the top of the roof would be covered with a larger version of the semi-circular *imbrex*. The tiles were held in place by gravity and pegs or nails were rarely used; this may explain why Roman roofs with terracotta tiles have a low pitch.

The Romans also developed a special type of wall tile known as *tubili* which were four-sided hollow box flue tiles used for the distribution of hot air in Roman villas and bathhouses. Despite the fact the tiles would be built into a wall, the outside was often decorated with relief patterns, usually of an abstract nature but figurative designs are also known (fig. 22). The patterns had a clear practical purpose, acting as an elaborate form of keying for mortar cement.

Plain terracotta tiles were made in large numbers for use in wall construction and on floors. They are the simplest form of tile: squares cut from slabs of red firing clay which were laid out to dry before being fired. They can bear traces of human or animal activity: tiles have survived that show the footprints of dogs or cats that walked over them when the tiles were drying or imprints of boots where people stepped on the tiles accidently. In some instances pieces of writing or small drawings are found which were made when the clay was still soft (fig. 24). Such markings are interesting because they form a link with real Roman life at the time.

The Romans also made figurative terracotta wall plaques for decorations in temples, palaces and up-market villas (fig. 25). The practice originated from temples where such terracotta plaques were used as friezes above or between columns. The terracotta friezes in the precinct of the Temple of Apollo built by the emperor Augustus on the Palatine Hill in Rome show scenes relating to his rule and victories. Many such plaques dating from the first century AD were also used in domestic

RIGHT [fig. 26] Relief tile showing part of a triumphal procession, with two chained captives paraded on a cart who could represent prisoners taken when Emperor Trajan defeated the Dacians in AD 107. Terracotta. Roman, 2nd century AD. 32 x 38 cm. British Museum 1805,0703.342.

settings in atria and peristyles (central courts, entrance halls and colonnades) of villas and the scenes on them often relate to various aspects of Roman life (fig. 26). They can depict sports such as athletes in gymnasia and chariot races, or episodes from Greek mythology, or captive prisoners. These plaques are now commonly called 'Campana plaques' after the nineteenth-century Italian collector Giampietro Campana who amassed a great many of them during his lifetime: examples in many museums come from this collection.

China

As was the case in Egyptian culture, the construction and furnishing of tombs was an important part of Chinese belief in the afterlife and the tombs of ancient emperors could be very grand and elaborate. They were buried with all their earthly possessions which could even include their servants, wives, concubines, guardians and animals. Until the sixth century BC it was common to kill all those who had attended on the emperor in his actual life and bury them in his tomb to continue their service to him in the afterlife, but over time living beings were replaced with terracotta figures of humans and animals. A famous example is the tomb of Qin Shihuangdi, who ruled the Qin dynasty from 246 BC to 210 BC and whose elaborate tomb, near the city of Xi'an, contained thousands of life-sized terracotta soldiers now known as the Terracotta Army. Ceramic wall tiles also became part of this practice, and tiles with low-relief decorations depicting scenes of hunting and harvesting and life at the imperial court have been found in Han tombs of the Wu Family near Jiaxiang in Shandong Province dating from the second century AD. There are other locations where ceramic wall tiles of this kind have also been unearthed such as in tombs of the Song dynasty (AD 960–1279) that show servants attending to their master (fig. 27).

ABOVE [fig. 27] A frieze of six tomb tiles showing a man and a woman sitting at a table in the centre, waited upon by male and female servants. Such images would adorn the walls of tombs of Chinese ruling elite who were still served by their underlings even in the afterlife. Earthenware. China, Song dynasty, AD 960–1279. British Museum OA+.6966.3.

RIGHT [fig. 28] This tile, with a monster mask, was fired in reduction giving it a grey colour but was covered with red pigment afterwards. Traces of the pigment remain. From the Red Pagoda at Mount Qingliang, Henan Province, northern China. This particular tile came from the topmost row of tiles, just under the eaves. Earthenware. Tang dynasty, reign of Taizong, AD 626–49. 43 x 37 cm. British Museum 1983,0725.1.

Moulded earthenware relief tiles were also used on pagodas. Chinese pagoda towers, often part of temple complexes, show the influence of Buddhism and evolved from the stupa (mound-like structure containing Buddhist relics) of the Indian subcontinent. Traditionally they contained relics or statues of Buddha and had religious significance, but later they became part of secular life. They were at first built from wood and then of more durable material like stone or brick. Early Chinese pagodas were round or square but by the tenth century AD they were often constructed as multi-storied polygonal towers and could be elaborately decorated with ornamental brickwork and tiles. The tiles sometimes show the faces of monsters which were used to ward off evil (fig. 28). A good example of the latter is the Red Pagoda at Mount Qingliang in Henan province dating back to the fifth century AD and restored by the Tang Emperor Taizong (ruled AD 626–49), which still has ornate brickwork and relief tiles under the eaves of the pagoda.

The history of Chinese tiles is dominated by glazed roof tiles and there are clear historical reasons for this. Much of traditional Chinese architecture and its construction was based on columns supporting a roof; walls were mere screens dividing up the interior, with no load-bearing function. Wall tiles therefore do not

OPPOSITE [fig. 29] A model of a watchtower with decorative tiled roofs. Clay models like this were found in Han tombs of the ruling elite and give an idea of what very early Chinese buildings looked like since actual wooden buildings of that period have not survived. Earthenware. China, Han dynasty, AD 25–220. H. 86 cm. British Museum 1929,0716.1.

RIGHT [fig. 30] Circular *goutou* tile with the moulded decoration of a five-clawed dragon, covered with a yellow imperial glaze. Earthenware. Probably from either the Hongwu emperor's tomb, east of Nanjing or the Ming Palace, north-east Nanjing, China. Ming dynasty, *c.* AD 1366–1400. Diam. 17.5 cm. British Museum 1933,0317.1.

play a big part in the history of Chinese tiles. Traditional Chinese buildings were constructed on platforms of rammed earth, brick or stone. Wooden columns set in stone bases (this allowed some movement when minor earth tremors struck) carried horizontal wooden beams. The building was crowned by a heavy overhanging tiled roof supported by a wooden bracketing system. The roof protected the building from the weather but its weight also kept it stable in high winds. The character of many Chinese buildings is long and low with strong emphasis on the roof. Temples, palaces and the homes of the wealthy often had roofs with a sweeping curvature that rises at the corners of the roof. Important buildings like imperial palaces were sometimes given double roofs with one placed above the other to signify status.

A long low roof covered with coloured glazed tiles is therefore a specific and notable aspect of Chinese architecture. The Italian traveller Marco Polo (1254–1324) was greatly struck by the beauty of Chinese roofs on his visit to China and in his travel accounts he wrote: 'The roof is all ablaze with scarlet and green and blue and yellow and all the colours that are, so brilliantly varnished that it glitters like crystal and the sparkle of it can be seen from far away.' The fact that Marco Polo was struck by the beautiful coloured glazes of roof tiles also had much to do with the great advances made by Chinese potters in developing various types of ceramic glazes, not just for roof tiles but also for ornamental pottery.

Because Chinese buildings were often constructed of timber no truly ancient examples have survived above ground but pottery models of buildings found in tombs of the Han dynasty (206 BC–AD 220) give us a vivid impression of what early Chinese

architecture looked like, including the shape of the roof (fig. 29). These finely crafted ceramic models show that more than two thousand years ago Chinese roofs were already highly ornamental with decorative round tiles closing the gaps along the eaves and ornamental projections at the four corners of the roof.

The ceramic roof offered both practical and symbolic protection. Pottery guardian figures and fearsome beasts were placed on the roof ridges of important buildings to ward off evil spirits and bring good luck to the inhabitants (figs 31–33). They are placed at the bottom end of the sloping ridges and the number of figures used came to signify the status of a building. Minor or middle ranking buildings may have three to five figures but an imperial building could have up to ten. Pottery guardian figures come in a great variety of shapes and guises ranging from warriors on horseback and figures riding birds, to dragons and Buddhist monks. One recurring roof figure is Prince Min who is often shown riding a cockerel. Min was a notorious figure who was executed in 283 BC and hung on a roof for several days. Afterwards his enemies placed a pottery figure on the roof to protect themselves from his evil spirit returning. Over time he became depicted as riding a cockerel and mythical creatures are placed behind Min to make certain he cannot escape from the roof. The dragon was another roof ornament but since it was the mightiest of all the Chinese mystical animals its supernatural powers and beneficial characteristics were associated with the Chinese emperor and it was therefore reserved for the decoration of imperial buildings.

The colours given to glazed roof tiles were also highly significant. Yellow is the colour of the emperor and like images of dragons could only be used for imperial buildings (fig. 30). This is why the roofs of the Forbidden City in Beijing originally

ABOVE LEFT [fig. 31] Ridge tile modelled in the form of a celestial warrior riding a flying horse. His hands are clenched as if they once held the shaft of a weapon now missing. Its role would have been to protect the building from harm. Glazed earthenware. China, Ming dynasty, c.1490–1620. H. 38.9 cm. British Museum 1962,1019.2. Bequeathed by H. Sidney Richards.

ABOVE RIGHT [fig. 32] Ridge tile with a Buddhist monk in plain apparel, shaven head and elongated earlobes, which are a symbol of long life. It is possible that it represents the historical Buddhist monk Xuan Zang (AD 596–664) who travelled to India on a seventeen-year quest to collect Buddhist scriptures. Glazed earthenware. China, Ming dynasty c.1490–1620. H. 40.5 cm. British Museum 1937,0716.109.

constructed during the Ming dynasty (AD 1368–1644) but subsequently rebuilt are mainly yellow, with some exceptions such as the roof of the library of the Pavilion of Literary Profundity which is black because black was associated with water and thus fire prevention. The roof of the buildings where the crown prince lived was green because green was associated with growth. The colouration of roof tiles is therefore highly symbolic. All these different religious, political and social aspects make the Chinese roof tile a fascinating artefact and that this could be perpetuated over such a long period of time and over such a vast territory is an amazing testimony to the strength and importance of Chinese culture.

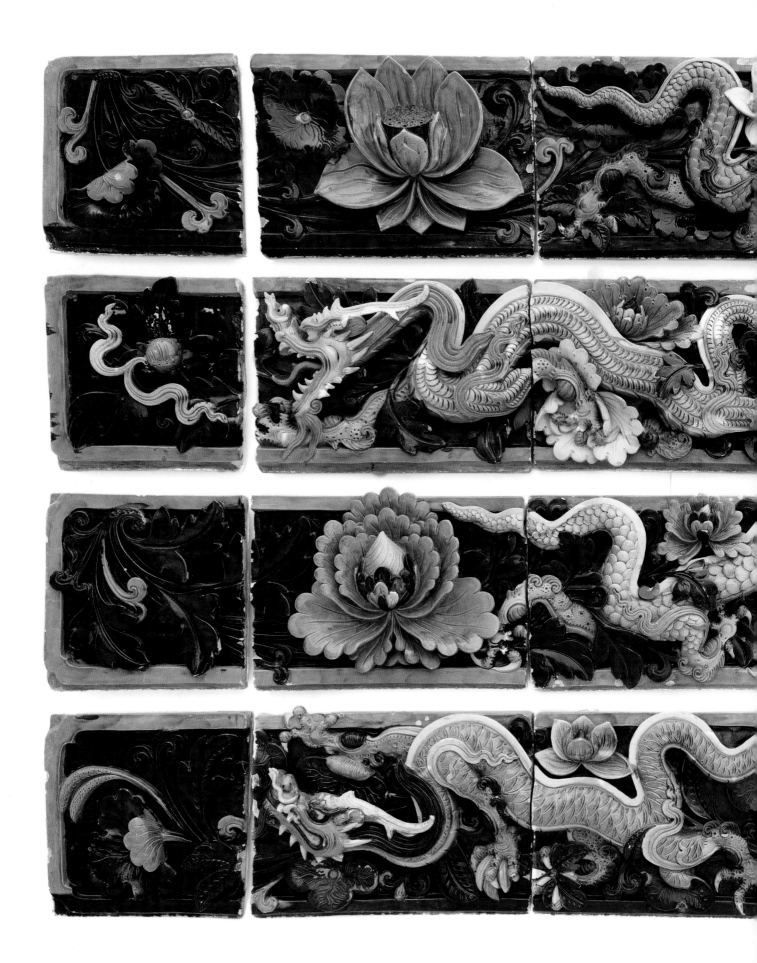

OPPOSITE [fig. 34] Twenty roof tiles. These ceramic tiles once decorated the roof ridges of small buildings in a temple complex in northern China. They were originally arranged into two long rows – one consisting of the yellow dragons and one of the blue. Each frieze today is made up of five tiles, moulded with three-clawed dragons entwined with flower scrolls, including the lotus and the peony. Glazed stoneware. Originally from two buildings, from Shanxi Province, China, Ming dynasty, 15th–16th century. 39 x 244 cm. British Museum 2006,0503.1.1-20. Donated by Sir Joseph Hotung.

ISLAMIC DESIGNS

That which has been evenly fired reflects like red gold and shines like the light of the sun.

Abu'l Qasim

1301

OPPOSITE [fig. 35] Page from a Persian manuscript depicting the epic hero Rustam striking the door of Afrasiyab's palace by night, while his soldiers (in armour) fight with the Turanians (wearing turbans). The facade of the palace is decorated with tiles and the brickwork of the palace and the houses below is accentuated with glazed blue plugs. Opaque watercolour and ink on paper. From a Safavid *Shahnameh*, Isfahan, Iran, c.1610. 22.7 x 15.4 cm. British Museum 1948,1211,0.7.

Since the ninth century AD most countries in which Islamic culture predominates have had a tradition of producing and using tiles for the decoration of important buildings like mosques, palaces, religious colleges, holy shrines and graves. Islamic tiles are found over a wide geographical region covering most of the Middle East, parts of Asia, North Africa and southern Spain.

The religion of Islam was revealed to the world by the Prophet Muhammad in the early seventh century. Two of the most holy places of Islam are the cities of Medina, the Prophet's birthplace, and of Mecca, the location of the Ka'ba, a cubic stone structure which Muslims believe was first built by Adam and then rebuilt by Abraham and his son Ishmael, both revered patriarchal figures. Jerusalem is the third most important city for Islam as it is the site of the Dome of the Rock built in AD 688–91. The building is not a mosque but a shrine for pilgrims built over a sacred stone believed to be the place from which Prophet Muhammad ascended into heaven.

Muhammad's followers eagerly spread his faith and by the time of his death in AD 632 it was established throughout Arabia, and within a century the new faith was carried by invading Muslim armies to most parts of North Africa and Spain as well as Syria, Mesopotamia and Persia, and the frontiers of central Asia and India. The civilization that developed was one of many different peoples with local cultures united by their Islamic faith and the use of the Arabic language and script as well as by the Shari'a, the sacred law of Islam that covers every aspect of the life of a Muslim. The Islamic faith does not allow the depicting of God or other living beings as it was regarded as blasphemous to imitate the inimitable work of God, and this affected the nature of tile decorations in religious buildings such as mosques and holy shrines. In secular buildings, however, it was less strictly adhered to and figurative subjects

on tiles in locations like palaces were not uncommon.

Arabs who launched the Islamic religion often assimilated the architectural traditions of the territories they conquered and adopted them to suit their own needs and purposes. In the first centuries of Islam a mosque was not only a place of worship but also where the Islamic community gathered to conduct religious business and teach the Qu'ran, and once brick or stone built structures became part of Islamic culture, ceramic tiles began to play a role. From the ninth century tiles were used in Islamic architecture and Muslim tile makers developed different methods of manufacture and decoration.

The basic production unit of the Islamic pottery and tile industry was the small family-operated workshop usually located in an area where the necessary raw materials for its craft and a viable market for its ceramic products were available. Small family workshops would often band together in or near a town sharing natural resources, and benefiting from mutual cooperation as well as a healthy level of competition. In these workshops, techniques and trade secrets were passed down from father to son, ensuring technological continuity. Family potters placed high value on strict adherence to the hierarchy of skills and established techniques and designs. This may help explain the inherent conservatism of Islamic pottery and tile manufacture as family potteries were inclined to resist change once proven and successful methods of production and design had been established. When change did come it was often the result of war and conquest when potters were carried off as part of the spoils of war and were forced to work for new masters, or decided to move to safer places where there was a market for their trade.

Islamic potters developed four main tile decoration techniques: lustre decoration, tile mosaic, *cuerda seca* and under-glaze painting which, combined with the use of elaborate abstract and stylized design motifs and the lavish use of tiles in all kinds of buildings, have made Islamic tiles some of the most significant and inspirational in tile history. Some techniques like lustre and under-glaze painting were used for the production of both pottery and tiles, while tile mosaic and *cuerda seca* were techniques developed specifically in relation to tile decoration.

Whatever technique was adopted, all tiles had to be kiln fired to make them suitable for architectural use. Islamic potters used simple round or oval up-draught kilns which because of their rounded shapes were known as 'beehive' kilns. They were on average just under 2 metres wide and up to 3 metres high and consisted of two compartments. The fire box was situated below ground level and the chamber in which the pots and tiles were stacked for firing was above this. The fire box was separated from the upper chamber by a perforated stone or brick floor so that heat could rise up from below and circulate through the upper chamber. This had an aperture at the top which could be capped with a stone to control the temperature. The upper chamber also had ceramic rods sticking out from the kiln wall on which ceramic shelves could be placed to support the ware to be fired. Ware that had to be protected from the direct flames of the kiln would be placed in special ceramic boxes (saggars). The whole process of loading the kiln, firing it, letting it cool down and unloading the ware took about a week. The kilns would be fired with dried wood to minimize the effect of smoke (unless smoke was needed for the firing of lustre ware) and the whole outcome of the potter's or tile maker's endeavours would hang on the successful firing of the kiln. In the absence of any temperature measuring devices it was all down to the practical experience of the men who loaded and fired the kiln.

Lustre tiles

Lustre was a new type of ceramic pioneered by the Islamic potters. It was created by combining metal compounds of silver or copper with a glaze which, when fired, produced a thin iridescent metallic surface that reflected light. Lustre was known before the Islamic potters began to use it for the first time in the ninth century as it was an important technique for glass makers in Egypt who by the fourth century employed copper and silver lustres to decorate glass. Since glass makers and potters both used kilns there would have been contact between them and the idea of applying lustre to ceramics may have emerged from seeing glass makers use it. Lustre decorations were created by applying pigments made from silver or copper mixed with clay to an already fired and glazed surface in the form of an opaque white glaze. This was known as tin glaze because tin was the opacifing element in the glaze. Lustre is produced in the kiln by introducing material that burns quickly and takes oxygen out of the air (reduction) and it is this lack of oxygen that makes the metallic compound break down and form a thin metallic film on the glaze surface. The clay with which the silver or copper is initially mixed remains as a dark crust on the surface but this is rubbed off and the shiny lustre is revealed. Although this description of the lustre technique makes it sound simple, in practice it is a difficult technique and needs specialist input to obtain a successful outcome. Lustre was therefore only made at a few places. Initially it came from either Baghdad or Basra in Iraq in the ninth and tenth century, then from Fustat in Egypt in the tenth and

eleventh centuries. It spread from there to Raqqa in Syria and to Kashan in Iran in the late twelfth century and then to Malaga (from Egypt) and eventually to Valencia in Moorish Spain, which became famous for its lustre in the fourteenth and fifteenth centuries.

The expertise and skill necessary to make lustre ware were concentrated in certain families of potters. In a rare manuscript dating from 1301 compiled by Abu'l Qasim who belonged to a family of potters in Kashan in Iran, there is a technical description of how ceramic manufacture was carried out at that time, including the production of lustre ware. He refers to it as the 'enamel of two firings' which meant that lustre decorations were executed on an already once fired glaze before being fired again. He describes removing the residue of clay on the lustre after the pottery or tiles had been taken out of the kiln: 'rub them with damp earth so that the colour of gold comes out' and he describes the amazing effect of lustre as 'That which has been evenly fired reflects like red gold and shines like the light of the sun'. The metal sheen of lustre can be red or orange if copper has been used and yellow, amber or silver if it has been derived from silver. Lustre also changes constantly depending on the light

OPPOSITE [fig. 38] Lustre tiles decorating the *mihrab* of the Great Mosque at Qairouan near Tunis in Tunisia. Probably dating from the second half of the 9th century.

conditions in which it is seen, with iridescent rainbow effects of purple, blue or green, so it is easy to see why it became much sought after.

Early lustre tiles

Some of the earliest Islamic lustre tiles dating from the ninth century have been excavated in the town of Samarra in Iraq. Samarra was built by the ruling Abbasid dynasty as its new capital along the river Tigris north of Baghdad between AD 836 and 883. Lustre tiles were found on the site of the palace of Jawsaq al-Khaqani where they may have been part of the harem buildings (fig. 37). The tiles were decorated with wreath designs and bird motifs and executed in red and yellow lustre. Of an equally early date are the lustre tiles that still decorate the Great Mosque at Qairouan near Tunis in Tunisia (fig. 38). The *mihrab*, the prayer niche facing towards Mecca, has been decorated with square lustre tiles with abstract and schematized floral motifs which were probably installed during the second half of the ninth century when the mosque underwent reconstruction. Tradition has it that

the tiles came from Baghdad. The building serves as an important early example of how tiles were used in mosques as the *mihrab* is the holiest part of the mosque and therefore receives special attention when the interior is decorated.

During the late tenth and eleven centuries there were also important changes in the types of clay used for pottery and tiles, as developed by potters in Egypt, Syria and Iran. They created a new type of ceramic body now known as 'fritware' or 'stone paste' in which crushed quartz replaced clay as the major constituent of the ceramic body. Abu'l Qasim again tells us in his treatise of 1301 that the recipe consisted of ten parts ground quartz, one part ground glass and one part fine white clay. This white body was so different from the red or buff clay used previously and was so well suited to coloured glazes that by the end of the eleventh century the great majority of Islamic pottery and tiles in the Middle East were made of stone paste.

Kashan tiles

Kashan in Iran became one of the most well-known centres for the production of lustre tiles during the thirteenth and fourteenth centuries. The prominence of Kashan as a centre of ceramics and tile making is reflected in the fact that the Persian word for tile is *kashi*. The craft of potter was passed on from father to son and the names of some pottery families in Kashan are known, such as the Abu Tahir family who produced at least four generation of potters. A speciality of the Kashan workshops was lustre decorated star shapes and cruciform tiles which could be assembled together to form wall claddings for palaces, mosques and holy shrines (fig. 39). The tiles often took the form of eight-pointed stars decorated in lustre over an opacified glaze showing court scenes, animals, birds and foliage sprays with Arabic inscriptions as part of the border. Tiles that were decorated with humans and animals were most likely used in secular locations like palaces (fig. 40), while tiles with geometric shapes, plants and religious inscriptions were mainly destined for religious buildings where only non-figurative subjects were allowed. Despite the

ABOVE [fig. 39] Two star tiles, one with a flat base probably for the bottom row of a dado panel. The borders are decorated with a Qur'anic inscription in *nashki* surrounding central scenes showing birds and running deer. Stone paste. Kashan, Iran, *c*.1260. Diam. 31 cm. British Museum G.205 and G.206. Bequeathed by Miss Edith Godman.

OPPOSITE [fig. 40] Four eight-pointed star tiles made from stone paste, with opaque white glaze, under-glaze cobalt blue borders with on-glaze brown lustre decorations showing a human figure and animals (horse, ducks, hares) set against foliage and flowers. The crossover garment and plumed hat of the figure (top left) is typical of the Mongol garb depicted on Kashan lustre tiles. Kashan, Iran, 13th century. Average diam.: 21 cm. British Museum (clockwise from top left) G.229, G.212, G.219 and G.211. Bequeathed by Miss Edith Godman.

LEFT [fig. 41] Two rectangular tiles that were part of a tombstone and create the shape of a *mihrab* with pilasters in turquoise. Both tiles are decorated with *nashki* script picked out in under-glaze cobalt blue that included the name of the deceased Qadi Jalal al-Din 'Ali. Stone paste, opaque white glaze, on-glaze lustre. Kashan, Iran, first half of the 14th century. H. 131 cm. British Museum G.499. Bequeathed by Miss Edith Godman.

ABOVE [fig. 42] Finely painted *lajvardina* tile with a text from the Qu'ran that reads 'In the name of God'. The moulded inscription has been highlighted with gilding of which several traces remain. Stone paste. Kashan, Iran, late 13th century. 33 x 31.7 cm. British Museum G.189. Bequeathed by Miss Edith Godman.

upheavals brought about by the Mongol invasions of Iran which started in 1219, the potteries in Kashan kept up production except for some short intervals. By 1258 the Mongols had completed their conquest of Iran and Iraq and there was a new period of stability under the Il-khanids. The tiles of the Kashan potteries were again in great demand for the rebuilding of ruined towns.

There are two main types of Kashan tiles. The first were flat tiles with a white opaque glaze decorated with lustre, occasionally accentuated with under-glaze turquoise or cobalt blue. The other type had low-relief moulded decoration which combined under-glaze blue with on-glaze lustre (fig. 41). The latter technique is particularly effective for tiles with Qur'anic inscriptions as the moulded Arabic lettering stands out in blue against a flat background of finely painted foliage or branches with birds in lustre, creating tiles of rich splendour.

Other special techniques used by potters in Kashan were *minai* and *lajvardina*. In the minai technique, which was in use during the late twelfth and first half of the thirteenth century, various coloured pigments were applied on and under the glaze. Abu'l Qasim calls it *haft rang* which means 'seven-coloured', although the *minai* technique was used more for pottery than tiles. Tiles executed in the *lajvardina* (from the Persian for lapis lazuli or cobalt blue) technique, which was used during the second half of the thirteenth and the fourteenth centuries, had moulded decorations covered with cobalt blue or sometimes turquoise glaze on which decorations were executed in the form of on-glaze gilding (fig. 42), which was not the same as reduced lustre. Gilding was done with real gold which was fixed to the ceramic body in the form of gold leaf or gold powder that could be lightly fired onto the glaze with a flux of sodium silicate in an oxidized atmosphere in a muffle kiln. The gold decorations could be accentuated with red and white on-glaze enamels. This process was used during the second half of the thirteenth century for star-shaped and cruciform tiles but also for rectangular tiles for graves with the shape of a *mihrab* and appropriate texts from the Qu'ran as decorations. In all instances these tiles were expensive – special products which were only available to a privileged elite.

Although by the mid-fourteenth century the great period of Kashan lustre production was in decline, lustre pottery and tiles were still made intermittently, and there was a revival in the nineteenth century arising from nostalgia for the great age of Kashan lustre production (fig. 43).

Mosaic tiles

From the late twelfth century onwards, the production and architectural application of mosaic tiles played an important part in Islamic tile history. Mosaic was extensively used for the decoration of mosques, palaces, shrines and religious colleges known as *madrasahs* throughout the Islamic world, from Iran and India to Morocco and Spain. However the art of mosaic was not an Islamic invention but derived from earlier work by the Romans and Byzantines. They used small differently coloured cubes of stone and glass known as *tesserae* which were set in mortar or plaster to create pictorial images and decorative patterns on the floors and walls of prominent buildings. However, the use of tile mosaic in making installations of differently coloured and shaped pieces of ceramic was very much developed by Muslim potters.

There were two principal methods of making tile mosaic. One involved cutting tiles with a knife from a slab of 'leather hard' clay prior to firing. The templates used were slightly bigger than the final fired pieces as clay shrinks during the firing. After cutting and drying, the mosaic tiles were fired for the first time. They were then glazed with single monochrome coloured glazes and fired for a second time. Although cutting mosaic shapes prior to firing is relatively easy, the drawback is that during

ABOVE [fig. 43] Iranian revivalist lustre tile. The inscription in *nashki* reads 'the kingdom belongs to Allah the mighty, the just, the only one'. Stone paste, opaque white glaze, on-glaze lustre. 19th century. 19 x 33 cm. British Museum G.484. Bequeathed by Miss Edith Godman.

ABOVE LEFT [fig. 44] A Moroccan craftsman in Marrakesh laying out small mosaic pieces face down on the floor in a particular pattern, before plaster or mortar is run over the back fixing the pieces into place.

ABOVE RIGHT [fig. 45] Fragments of a mosaic star tile from the minarets of the Musalla of Gauhar Shad in Herat, Afghanistan, after they had been pulled down in 1885. The pieces have been cut from fired glazed slabs which allow them to be fitted very closely together. Stone paste. Afghanistan, early 15th century. 15 x 18 cm. British Museum 1907,1011.2.

firing the pieces do not always shrink at an equal rate so that when they are fitted together there will always be some gaps and spaces.

To overcome this a second method was devised where the pieces were cut from already fired and glazed coloured slabs. The shapes were marked with paint on the glazed surface using already fired mosaic pieces as templates. The shapes were then cut out by hand using a special brick axe, a two-sided hammer with razor sharp edges. The tile cutter tapped along the marked outlines and once the desired shape had been cut the edges of the tile body were bevelled to allow plaster or mortar to squeeze between them when the pieces were assembled. This method required great skill but if the pieces were cut exactly and precisely they allowed for a very tight fit without any gaps. Once the mosaic pieces were made, they were assembled face down on the floor and arranged into the required patterns and in this way manageable square or rectangular sections were created (fig. 44). Mortar or plaster was then poured over the back and when dry the panels were fixed to the wall to create large extended mosaic designs on the facades or in the interiors of buildings.

Tile mosaic shapes were often geometric but could also be curved and were assembled into a great many different repeat patterns and ornamental arabesque motifs. The taste for closely patterned and intricately embellished wall surfaces in the shape of geometrically interlocking tiles and ornate plasterwork is a tendency in the history of design known as *horror vacui* or fear of empty spaces. Since Islamic tradition frowns on representational art, Muslims often celebrate beauty through abstract decorative forms applied to all kinds of medium, not just tiles but also stucco work, pottery, textiles, metalwork and woodwork.

LEFT [fig. 46] Detail of the 17th-century polychrome tile mosaics on the facade of the Chini-Ka-Rauza Mausoleum in Agra, India, from *The Archaeological Survey of India*, 1901.

Iran and India

In Iran tile mosaic was popular for decorating the exterior of holy shrines. These were built after the death of important rulers or revered religious figures and usually took the form of round or square buildings crowned with a dome. The exterior brickwork was often ornamented with sections of blue, turquoise and white tile mosaic forming abstract repeat patterns and arabesques or with inscriptions from the Qu'ran. A fine example of this type of building and decoration is the Shrine of

RIGHT [fig. 47] Mosaic decorations on the *qibla* wall of the Great Mosque in Cordoba, Spain, late tenth century.

Jafar in Isfahan which dates from the Il-Khanid period (1256–1353) and was constructed during the first half of the fourteenth century. It is richly decorated with abstract ornament as well as Qur'anic inscriptions. The inscriptions below the dome are known as 'coupled' inscription. This means that the inscription is written in two rows using two kinds of different Arabic script, the upper row in Kufic and the lower in Thuluth script. The texts have two functions here, acting both as pious messages and as a beautiful ornament.

OPPOSITE [fig. 48] Detail of the tile mosaic decorating the walls in the 14th-century Court of the Myrtles in the Alhambra Palace, Granada, Spain. The overall design of squares and stars is topped with a border of black and white crested tiles.

If blue tile mosaic was much in vogue in fourteenth-century Iran, a much wider range of colours was used for Muslim shrines in India during the Mughal Period (1526–1858). These sometimes display a curious mixture of Hindu and Islamic design. The art of tile mosaic was probably introduced into India from Iran but once there it absorbed indigenous traditions and was given a characteristic local slant. In India abstract geometry was often replaced by stylized floral and foliage motifs of intricate complexity. Mosques and mausoleums were decorated with elaborately designed mosaic panels showing floral arrangements and flowering trees that symbolized paradise. A splendid example is the Chini-Ka-Rauza Mausoleum (fig. 46) in Agra in northern India built in 1635. It is the tomb of Mir Afzal Khan, a poet scholar who rose to be a minister in the court of Shah Jahan (ruler of the Mughal Empire from 1628 until 1658). It was once completely covered with a myriad of leaf and floral tile mosaics of many different colours, but time has taken its toll on the beautiful exterior. Polychrome tile mosaic panels with a wide variety of flowering trees are still in situ on the exterior of the Vezirhan Mosque in Lahore built in 1634 that show a range of vivid colours such as yellow, blue, purple, orange, green and white.

Spain and Morocco

Tile mosaic became particularly prominent in Islamic Spain and Morocco where it was a common method of decoration for Moorish architecture throughout the region. In Islamic Spain the use of mosaic decorations for mosques has a long history dating back to the tenth century. A prominent early example still extant is the Great Mosque of Cordoba which has a beautifully decorated *mihrab* covered with glass and stone mosaic of great intricacy (fig. 47). The mosque in Cordoba was extended during the second half of the tenth century under the rule of Caliph al Hakam II, and the *mihrab* was decorated with the assistance of Byzantine craftsmen from Constantinople (now Istanbul) between AD 965 and 971. They used floral motifs such as palmettes, lotus flowers, rosettes and trefoils to decorate upper sections of the *qibla wall* (facing in the direction of Mecca). Inscriptions from the Qu'ran executed in gold mosaic were set against a background of dark blue or red mosaic that frames the horseshoe arches of the *mihrab* and other sections of the *qibla* wall. Although the mosaic used was not actual ceramic tile mosaic it showed what splendid ornamentation could be achieved with the mosaic medium.

Simple tile mosaic as part of decorative brick decorations was first used in the twelfth century on the exterior of square minarets such as that of the Kutubiyya in Marrakesh, Morocco, probably built in around 1147, which has green glazed tiling at the top of the tower. The Kutubiyya minaret became the model for the Giralda tower in Seville, Spain, completed in 1197, which was the minaret of the Almohad Friday mosque. Although it has now lost its tile decorations, at the time it was one of the first instances of architectural glazed tile work in Spain.

These tentative beginnings reached their full glory in the Alhambra Palace (fig. 48)in Granada which was constructed by the Nasrid dynasty that ruled over the last Islamic sultanate in Spain from 1232 until it submitted to Christian forces in 1492. The building of the Alhambra on a rocky outcrop of the Sierra Nevada mountains overlooking Granada was started by the first Nasrid rulers, and was modified and embellished many times over the centuries. The whole complex is surrounded by a fortified wall strengthened by imposing towers. In addition to

LEFT [fig. 49] Detail of the tiled dado in the central courtyard of the 14th-century palace of Peter the Cruel in the Alcazar in Seville, Spain. The tile mosaic is characterized by the use of thin white glazed strips (interlace) that run between the coloured mosaic tiles creating interlacing designs and star patterns.

military and administrative sections there were palace quarters for the princely occupants lavishly decorated with colourful geometric tile work, ornamental plaster and richly carved wood, surrounded by luxurious gardens and ornamental ponds.

Much of the palatial quarters that are still extant today were constructed in the fourteenth century under the reigns of Yusuf I (1333–54) and Muhammad V (1354–91) whose building activities left their distinct marks on the Alhambra. It was during their reigns that the Mexuar, the Court of the Lions, the Court of the Myrtles, the Hall of the Kings, the Hall of the Two Sisters and the Salon of the Ambassadors were built. The tile mosaic decoration that lines many walls shows a great variety of different geometric designs ranging from simple chequerboard patterns to complex compositions with eighteen-pointed stars and interlacing white line work. The Nasrid motto 'There is no conqueror but God' is often found amongst the rich arabesque decoration of the plaster walls above the tiled dadoes. The glossy, flat and multicoloured tile mosaics create a striking contrast to the matt relief decorations of the plasterwork. The seemingly infinite tile patterns and plaster decorations have the effect of dematerializing the walls and imparting an ethereal quality to the interiors of the Alhambra Palace. Amongst the most important aspects of Islamic geometric design are repetition and variation and with only relatively few different shapes complex interlocking patterns were created which seem to stretch endlessly along the walls.

ABOVE [fig. 50] Muslim graves decorated with simple square mosaic patterns in the open air section at the Sa'dian Tombs in Marrakesh, Morocco, late 16th and 17th centuries.

The Alhambra had a great influence on the fourteenth-century palace built by the Catholic king Peter the Cruel (1333–69) in the Alcazar in Seville. Although Seville had been reconquered by Christian forces in 1248, admiration for Islamic culture and design had lingered and when Peter the Cruel built a new palace in 1362 (fig. 49) it was done with the aid of Moorish craftsmen from Granada. The palace has a central courtyard, the Court of the Maidens, surrounded by various rooms, such as the Salon of the Ambassadors and the Bedroom of the Moorish Kings, all decorated with ornate *mudejar* tile and plasterwork. The exquisite court style of the Nasrids was clearly much appreciated and copied by the Christian rulers of Spain.

Examples of tile mosaic can also be found in Morocco where it goes under the special name of *zillij* and was used in many religious as well as secular buildings. In Marrakesh is found the madrasah bin Yusuf that used to be a college of theology and jurisprudence dating back to the fourteenth century. The great interior courtyard not only has walls covered with abstract tile mosaic but such mosaic also covers the massive square columns that support part of the roof. Between the tiled dado and the ornate plasterwork runs a band of tiles that shows lettering in dense black Thuluth script set against a light ground.

Also in Marrakesh are the Sa'dian Tombs – a walled cemetery that was built in the sixteenth century on the site of an earlier graveyard. The first sultan of the Sa'dian dynasty was buried here in 1577. In the cemetery are ornately decorated covered sections where high born princes and their families are buried and where the walls

are covered with tile mosaic in the form of intricate star motifs and decorative plasterwork. Large sections of the cemetery are exposed to the open air and filled with numerous simple graves covered with plain chequerboard mosaic tiles set diagonally across the graves (fig. 50). Here death is symbolized with the simplest of all the mosaic forms, an alternating dark and light square mosaic arrangement, that stretches infinitely over countless graves as far as the eye can see.

Cuerda seca tiles

The making of tile mosaic was an arduous and time consuming process and similar effects could be achieved more quickly using the technique of *cuerda seca*, although it never completely replaced the manufacture and use of tile mosaic. *Cuerda seca* was probably first developed in the second half of the fourteenth century in Central Asia and Iran and became a popular form of tile decoration during the fifteenth century (fig. 51). The *cuerda seca* ('dry cord') technique consists of painting lines with a greasy medium (such as manganese oxide mixed with grease) on the surface of the tile and filling the areas in between with coloured glazes. The greasy lines keep the water-based glazes separated. When the tiles are fired the greasy lines burn away leaving a sunken dark outline around the glazed areas. In Islamic tiles, it was often used for designs which simulated interlacing mosaic patterns; when the tiles were fitted together over a large area they gave the impression of mosaic tile work. It was much quicker to draw tile mosaic patterns on a flat tile and fill the various spaces with glaze than to cut and reassemble all the various pieces separately. In addition to creating abstract patterns it could also be used to create stylized floral motifs (fig. 52) and various types of Arabic script as well as figurative scenes with animals and human figures.

ABOVE LEFT [fig. 51] Three *cuerda seca* star tiles with turquoise borders. Such tiles would have been set into brick facades. Stone paste. Central Asia, mid 15th century. Diam. 22 cm. British Museum 1908,0804.2.

ABOVE RIGHT [fig. 52] *Cuerda seca* tile with floral motifs set against a vivid yellow ground. Earthenware. Mughal, 17th century. 19.5 x 19.5 cm. British Museum 1856,1216.1.

ABOVE [fig. 53] Detail of the *cuerda seca* tiles on the facade of the throne room in the Topkapi Palace in Istanbul. *Cuerda seca* tiles remained an appreciated form of architectural decoration at the Ottoman court despite the ascendancy of underglaze painted tiles made in Iznik. Stone paste, first half of the 16th century.

Central Asia, Turkey, Iran and Spain

The earliest development of *cuerda seca* occurred in Central Asia during the rule of the Timurids (1370–1506). Based in Herat and Samarqand, the Timurids ruled an empire stretching to India and Iran. Typical tiles of this period are star-shaped stone paste tiles with geometric arabesque and floral ornaments that would have been used on brick buildings, but square tiles or convex tiles for use on columns were also produced. The Timurid style and technique of *cuerda seca* spread to Anatolia (now encompassing the Asian portion of modern-day Turkey) where it was used by the Ottoman Turks for decorating mosques and tombs.

The Ottoman Turks had established their first capital in Bursa in north-west Anatolia in 1326. The Yeşil Cami (Green Mosque) in Bursa, constructed in the latter years of the reign of Mehmed I (1413–21), has *cuerda seca* tiles in the *mihrab*, in a frieze of border inscriptions at the top of tiled wall dadoes and in the Sultan's lodge above the entrance. The Timurid influence on the tile work is explained by an inscription in the Sultan's lodge that states that the decorations were completed in 1424 by one Nakkas Ali, a native of Bursa who was one of the craftsmen taken to Samarqand after Timur had beaten the Turks at the battle of Ankara in 1402. When Nakkas Ali eventually returned to Bursa and supervised the decoration of the mosque and other buildings there he used what he had learnt from his exposure to the decorative and splendid Timurid tile work. The *cuerda seca* tiles in the mosque also carry inscriptions by the actual tile makers and one reads as 'made by the masters of Tabriz'. This city in northern Iran was a pottery centre so it seems that travelling bands of tile makers were plying their trade where there was a demand for their skills. Near the Yeşil Cami mosque is the tomb of Mehmed I where the cenotaph

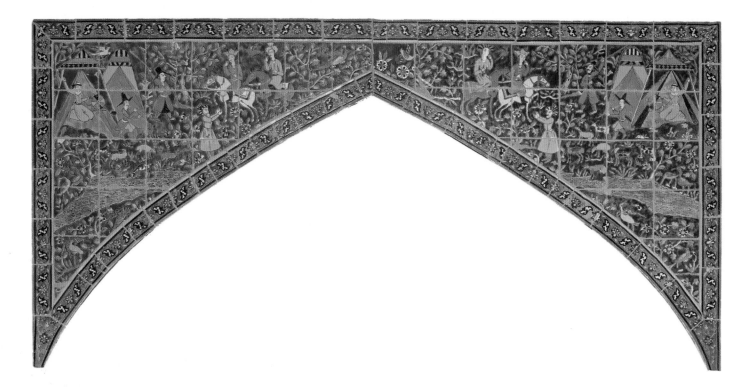

inside is also covered with finely executed *cuerda seca* tiles in various shades of blue and yellow-orange. A century later these tiles were still in vogue in Turkey as can be seen from the decor of the Topkapi Palace in Istanbul. *Cuerda seca* tile panels of the first half of the sixteenth century with floral arabesque motifs in green, yellow and different blues still grace the facade of the throne room (fig. 53). The fact that they were used in that location signifies that tiles in the *cuerda seca* technique were still admired despite the fact that much of the Topkapi palace was then being decorated with under-glaze painted tiles from Iznik.

Cuerda seca tiles were also used with stunning effect in Iran under the rule of the Safavids (1501–1722), in both religious and secular buildings. A splendid instance is the great mosque of Masjid-i-Shah in Isfahan built at the beginning of the seventeenth century. It was elaborately decorated with *cuerda seca* tiles with intricate floral arabesques executed in a colour range predominantly of different blues (turquoise and cobalt) accentuated with yellow. The Safavid period also saw the production of exquisite figurative *cuerda seca* tile panels for use in secular locations such as royal palaces (figs 54, 55). These depicted lavish court scenes reminiscent of the Arabian Nights, with elaborately dressed effete figures lounging in gardens holding flasks and cups, often against the strong yellow background which was a much used colour in seventeenth century Safavid tile work.

Cuerda seca tiles are also found in Spain where they began to be used as an alternative to tile mosaic. Moorish *cuerda seca* tiles were never figurative but had a repertoire of abstract geometric designs closely aligned to geometric tile mosaic so that when seen from a distance it is difficult to distinguish between these two techniques. Moorish *cuerda seca* tiles not only imitate tile mosaic patterns they also replicate the colours (blue, green, orange, brown, purple and white) which further masks the differences between them. There are some *cuerda seca* tiles in the Court of the Myrtles in the Alhambra but they are more commonly encountered in late

ABOVE [fig. 54] Architectural spandrel decorated with *cuerda seca* tiles. The outdoor scene shows Persian figures on horseback and figures outside tents. The men wearing wide-brimmed hats are probably Europeans. Stone paste. Isfahan, Iran, 17th century. 350.5 x 167.7 cm. British Museum 1937,1217.1. Donated by Charles Greenway, 1st Baron.

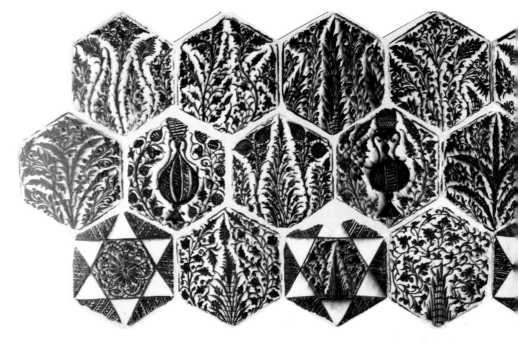

fifteenth and early sixteenth century Christian architecture where the ruling elite continued to use the Moorish building styles and decoration techniques. This can still be seen, for example, in the Casa de Pilatos in Seville where the walls in the chapel are ornately decorated with *cuerda seca* tiles imitating Moorish star patterns.

Tiles with under-glaze decorations

Tiles with under-glaze decorations form one of the most interesting and extensive categories in the history of Islamic tiles. Painting decorations and images under a transparent glaze, which allowed the tile painter more scope to draw and paint with various brushes, was first practised by Chinese potters, who inspired Islamic potters in the Middle East. During the first half of the fifteenth century potters in Egypt, Syria and Turkey were making blue-and-white under-glaze painted tiles with design motifs inspired by blue-and-white Chinese porcelain (fig. 56) and adding their own

repertoire of floral designs and patterns, figurative designs and lettering.

Because the raw materials for porcelain were not available in the Middle East Islamic potters could not make it, but by covering their stone paste pots and tiles with a white slip and by painting Chinese inspired designs under the glaze with blue pigment, they could approximate the look of blue-and-white porcelain. The allure of Chinese porcelain rested on its remarkable thin and semi-translucent white ceramic body as well as its fine painting executed in blue under the glaze. Porcelain is made of a mixture of pure white kaolin clay, white china stone and feldspar which is first biscuit fired to *c.* 1,000 Celsius. It is then decorated with cobalt blue oxide which is the only pigment that can withstand the great heat of the glaze firing, covered with a transparent glaze and fired at very high temperatures of up to 1,350–1,400 Celsius. The result is a much prized type of ceramic – strong, vitreous and translucent with vivid blue decorations. Its manufacture in China was based in Jingdezhen where the production of blue-and-white porcelain reached its height of technical excellence during the Ming period (1368–1644). During the Middle Ages porcelain came to the Middle East via the central Asian trade routes and by sea via the ports on the Persian Gulf. It was the luxury ware of the Indian Ocean trade and inspired many potters not only in the Middle East, but also in Europe.

Hexagonal blue-and-white tiles inspired by Chinese floral and foliage motifs were used in mosques such as the mosque and tomb of the dignitary Ghars al-Din Khalil al-Tawrizi in Damascus begun in 1423 and in the Murad II mosque in Edirne, Turkey, built in 1435–6, where hundreds of these tiles with a great variety of different designs decorate the *qibla* wall on either side of the *mihrab*. This type of under-glaze painted tile (fig. 57) can be regarded as the forerunner of the high quality tiles made later at Iznik and related workshops during the sixteenth and seventeenth centuries when the Ottoman Empire was at its height (fig. 58).

ABOVE [fig. 57] Two hexagonal tiles painted under the glaze in blue and turquoise. The arabesque motifs are typical of the repertoire of the international Timurid style and reflect the influence of tile mosaic patterns. Earthenware. Bijapur, Karnataka, India, 16th century. Average diam.: 16.5 cm. British Museum 1895,0603.152 and 1895,0603.154.

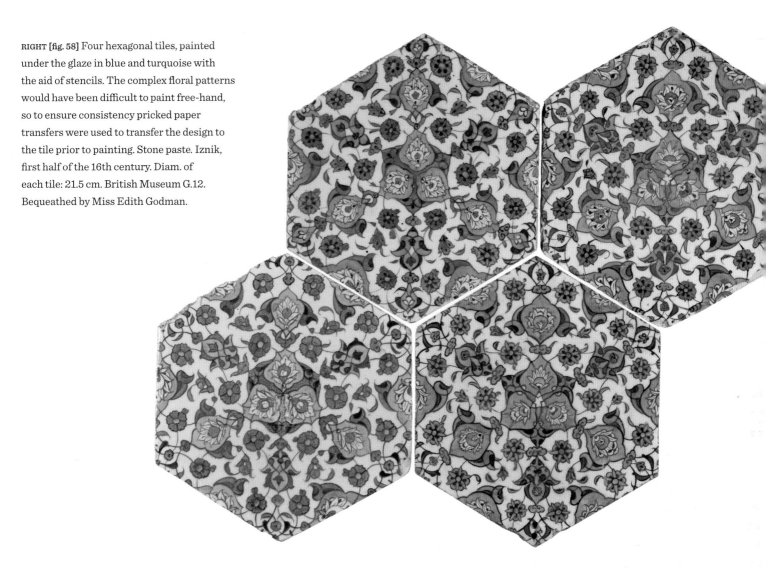

Iznik tiles

Sultan Mehmed II (1432–81) captured Constantinople in 1453 and brought an end to the Byzantine Empire. He renamed the city Istanbul and made it the capital of his Ottoman Empire with the Topkapi Palace, dating from 1467, as the royal and administrative centre. It was a huge sprawling complex occupying around 700,000 square metres and in its heyday up to four thousand people lived there. Over time there were many phases of construction and refurbishment that required a steady stream of tiles. In addition many mosques and tombs were built which were also decorated with tiles made in Iznik. The trade was controlled by imperial court orders (*firmas*) and under the supervision of the imperial *nakkashane* (court design atelier) in Istanbul.

Iznik itself is a small town (known as Nicaea in antiquity), situated about 100 kilometres south-east of Istanbul, where pottery was an established industry before the famous 'Iznik' ware began to be made there at the end of the fifteenth century. During the first half of the sixteenth century the main focus at Iznik was the production of under-glaze painted stone paste pottery and it was not until the second half of the sixteenth century that tiles were made in Iznik on a large scale.

The under-glaze painted tiles made in Iznik were of a very high technical quality. They had a fine stone paste body that mainly consisted of ground quartz with small additions of glass frit and white clay. No matter how careful the preparations there would always be impurities which gave the tile body a creamy off-white colour. In order to obtain a pure white ground to paint on, a thin layer of white slip was applied, its composition similar to the body of the tile but more carefully prepared and with all iron impurities removed. Painting was carried out with pigments derived from metal oxides and during the second half of the sixteenth century the potters in Iznik had developed an extensive colour palette that ranged from blue, turquoise, purple and black to grey, green and red (fig. 59). Red was a special colour and although it had been used before on a small scale in the thirteenth and fourteenth centuries, the bright tomato red made from Armenian bole used by the potters in Iznik was a novelty in the colour scheme of Iznik tiles and gave added vibrancy. Red was introduced *c.*1550 and saw its first extensive use on Iznik tiles made for the Süleymaniye mosque in Istanbul.

Iznik tile decorations were expertly painted with a range of different floral motifs. The Ottoman court liked flowers and there were special gardens in the Topkapi Palace where flowers like tulips and hyacinths were grown. The seventeenth-century Sultan Ibrahim even had his own chief florist, and flowers were also used to decorate illuminated manuscripts. Although flowers on tiles were decorative elements, they

ABOVE LEFT [fig. 59] Four under-glaze decorated tiles painted in blue, emerald green and red. The playful floral composition is made up of large split-leaf palmettes and overblown lotus blossoms. Stone paste. Iznik, 1550–1600. Each tile: 21 x 21 cm. British Museum G.77. Bequeathed by Miss Edith Godman.

ABOVE RIGHT [fig. 60] Detail of the Iznik tiles on the exterior of the mosque at Eyüp, Istanbul, painted in under-glaze blue and turquoise accentuated with red. 1550–1600.

ABOVE [fig. 61] A detail of the rich array of under-glaze painted Iznik tiles on the facade of the circumcision room at the Topkapi Palace in Istanbul, Turkey. 1550–1600.

were painted with enough naturalism to make them clearly recognizable. The most popular were tulips, roses, carnations, lilies, hyacinths and cherry blossom, which were often used in combination with more stylized floral motifs known as *hatayi* and *rumi*. The *hatayi* motif was based on Chinese lotus flowers, while the *rumi* was a kind of floral arabesque. The interplay of naturalistic flowers and semi-abstract floral patterns allowed the court designers tremendous scope. They probably created the patterns for the interior design of imperial buildings and it is therefore highly likely that the tile painters in Iznik were working according to designs made by the court artists in Istanbul.

The complex nature of some of the tile designs and the fact that they were used as repeat patterns meant that they were made using stencils. Stencils were pieces of stiff paper on which the outline of the design had been drawn and the lines pricked through with a needle. The stencil was placed on the tile and a substance like powdered charcoal 'dusted' through the perforated lines of the design. When the stencil was lifted from the tile there would be a faint outline of small charcoal dots which acted as a guide for the painter to trace the outlines of the design before filling it in with other ceramic colours. Despite the fact that stencils were used, painting on a surface of white slip was an extremely skilful craft. Corrections could not be made and it required a sure hand and deftness with the brush to paint floral patterns of consistent quality.

Iznik tiles can still be seen throughout the Topkapi Palace, decorating the private apartments of the sultan, the harem section and the throne room, as well as various pavilions, but the best and most unusual are found on the exterior wall of the Sünnet Odasi (circumcising room) (fig. 61). Two pairs of large blue-and-white panels of just over a metre high consisting of single ceramic slabs flank panels of Iznik tiles made up of multiple tiles. The latter have floral decorations consisting of blossom flowers accentuated with 'sealing wax red' indicating that they would have been made in Iznik sometime during the second half of the sixteenth century. The large single blue-and-white panels, however, have exquisitely painted Chinese style floral motifs and saz leaves, animals and birds painted in the style associated with blue-and-white pottery of the first half of the sixteenth century and may well have been made by potters at the Istanbul workshops in the 1520s rather than in Iznik. Court documents of the first half of the sixteenth century show that some potters working in Istanbul were employed directly by the court and that there were probably kilns in operation in Istanbul for special court commissions. The fact that these blue-and-white panels of an earlier date were reused in context with later Iznik tiles indicates that tiles were highly valued objects and were reused when possible.

Iznik tiles were also used throughout Istanbul in mosques and tombs, many of which were designed by the Ottoman imperial architect Mimar Sinan. One of his best tiled mosques is the Rüstem Pasha Mosque (1559–61) named after the Grand Vizier Rüstem Pasha, the son-in-law of Suleiman the Magnificent. Rüstem Pasha could not build a mosque that might rival that of his father-in-law, so instead of size and

ABOVE LEFT [fig. 62] Four under-glaze decorated tiles painted in blue, emerald green and red. The tulips, carnations and roses in the centre are painted on a white ground, but they are reversed against a brilliant red ground in the borders. Stone paste. Iznik, 1550–1600. 31 x 42.5 cm. British Museum G.71.a-d. Bequeathed by Miss Edith Godman.

ABOVE RIGHT [fig. 63] Square tile, under-glaze painted with Arabic script and carnations in blue, turquoise, red and yellow. In the top section is the word 'Allah' set against a yellow ground. Stone paste. Probably Tekfur Sarayi, Istanbul, Turkey, 1725–50. 25.7 x 25.5 cm. British Museum G.187. Bequeathed by Miss Edith Godman.

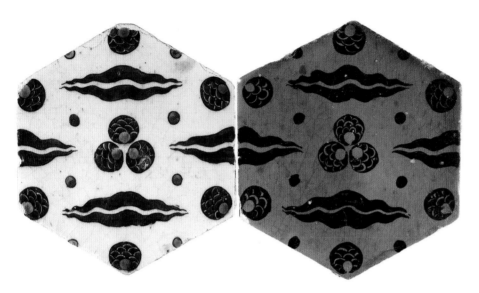

grandeur he sought the artistic refinement which the architect Sinan gave him. The Rüstem Pasha Mosque is a domed building covered inside and out with Iznik tiles with a large range of floral designs including tiles that have the much sought after 'sealing wax red'. On the exterior of the mosque there is also a single square tile showing the Ka'ba in Mecca dated 1659. The Rüstem Pasha Mosque is considered one of the finest tiled mosques in Istanbul.

The potteries in Iznik declined during the seventeenth century and were abandoned by the beginning of the eighteenth century. For a short period production was transferred from Iznik to Tekfur Sarayi in Istanbul where between c.1725 and 1751 under-glaze painted floral tiles and Ka'ba tiles (see p. 64) were made in the Iznik style for the Ottoman court and its ruling elite. The tiles made at Tekfur Sarayi had a wider colour range than those made at Iznik and included yellow in addition to blue, turquoise, green and red (fig. 63).

Tiles in the Iznik style were also made in Ottoman dominated Syria. The building of the Süleymaniye Mosque complex (1566–74) in Damascus as well as other mosques and tombs throughout Syria enhanced its status as an important Ottoman province. In the mid sixteenth century there was a revival in the Syrian ceramics industry probably initiated by tile workers from the Jerusalem workshops set up to refurbish the Dome of the Rock with new tiles on its exterior under orders of Suleiman the Magnificent. Tiles made in Syria echo Iznik patterns and designs but were more freely painted and usually have a colour palette of blues and green accentuated with dark purple but not including the colour red (figs 64, 65).

The sixteenth century was the heyday of Syrian tiles but they continued to be made until the nineteenth century.

Kubachi tiles

The name 'Kubachi' comes from Kubacha, a remote hill town of Daghestan in the Caucasus, where black-and-turquoise and blue-and-white under-glaze ware with Chinese inspired motifs dating back to the fifteenth century was discovered in the nineteenth century. This ware was not made in Kubacha but it revealed characteristics which linked it to pottery made in northern Iran, although the actual place of manufacture is still a matter of conjecture.

Two different types of polychrome Kubachi tiles were also made during the sixteenth and early seventeenth centuries. The first are square tiles with under-glaze painted busts of men and women set within hexagonal or eight-pointed star borders. The faces in three-quarter profile are sharply drawn with the brush and are reminiscent of the profiles found on late thirteenth-century lustre tiles made in Kashan (fig. 67). The black-purple outlines are washed in with blue, turquoise, and brown and yellow ochre. The second category is vertical or horizontal oblong tiles with languid full-length figures of men and women in Persian dress probably based on contemporary miniatures. Like the first tiles, the full-length figures have been outlined with a dark pigment and then painted in blues, yellows and browns (fig. 66). Although the painted figures are usually covered with a clear glaze, sometimes a semi-transparent turquoise glaze has been used.

ABOVE [fig. 66] A panel of three under-glazed painted Kubachi tiles. They are painted in polychrome colours under the glaze with figures in various poses, including a woman carrying a baby. Such tiles were made for palaces or pavilions built by the Safavid elite throughout Iran. Stone paste. Iran, 16th century. 26.5 x 46 cm. British Museum 1895,0603.123. Donated by Sir Augustus Wollaston Franks.

RIGHT [fig. 67] Under-glaze painted tile. It depicts a woman holding a flask and her tight curls follow contemporary female fashion of the time. Stone paste. Late Kubachi, possibly made in Tabriz, Iran, c.1600. British Museum 1913,1223.1.

RIGHT [fig. 68] Tiles on one of the interior walls of Hagia Sophia in Istanbul, Turkey. The tiles are under-glaze painted with representations of the holy cities of Mecca and Medina. The tile here showing Medina features the pulpit (*minbar*) of Muhammad and the garden of Fatima; the daughter of Muhammad, which is indicated by a palm tree. Stone paste. Probably Iznik, probably dating to the second half of the 17th century.

LEFT [fig. 69] Tile painted in under-glaze colours. The tile represents a stylized and schematic view of the Ka'ba at Mecca and marks the positions of the four schools of Islamic law. The *nashki* inscription shows that the tile was made for Shebab al Din Efendi. Stone paste. Iznik or Kütahya, Turkey, 17th or 18th century. *c.* 18 x 25 cm. British Museum 2009,6039.1.

Ka'ba tiles

Under-glaze painted Ka'ba tiles were made in Turkey in the seventeenth and eighteenth centuries in places like Iznik, Kütahya and Tekfur Sarayi, for use in mosques or as mementos for Muslims who had undertaken the pilgrimage (Hajj) to Mecca. They form a special category of tiles as they have an overtly religious subject matter. The images on Ka'ba tiles were established by convention and similar representations can be found in Islamic manuscripts, and on textiles and carpets. The Ka'ba in Mecca stands at the centre of the al-Haram Mosque that was built in the seventh century, but it was used as a religious shrine long before Prophet Muhammad's time, and Muslims believe that it was originally built by Adam. It is a cubic stone structure measuring 12 by 13 metres and 15 metres high, with a doorway set into the eastern wall about 2 metres above ground. On the corner of the south-east wall is the Black Stone which according to tradition was put there by Abraham and the whole structure of the Ka'ba is normally bedecked with a black cloth called the *Kiswa*.

Other important religious locations are situated around the Ka'ba such as the Zamzam Well and the Maqam Ibrahim and these are usually also shown on Ka'ba tiles, although in a simplified way. This schematic way of representing the Ka'ba can

ABOVE [fig. 70] Under-glaze painted panel of stone-paste tiles in the Hekimoğlu Ali Pasha Mosque in Istanbul, Turkey, built in 1732–5. It shows the Ka'ba in Mecca seen from a perspective that reveals the influence of Western European painting. Yellow forms part of the colour scheme that was a special feature of the Tekfur Sarayi potteries in Istanbul that were active during the second quarter of the 18th century.

be seen on seventeenth century Ka'ba tiles that were either made as single tiles or in the form of tile panels. They were part of the decoration of mosques and some of them are still in situ on the exterior of the Rüstem Pasha Mosque and in the mosque of the Black Eunuchs in the Topkapi Palace in Istanbul. Western pictorial conventions began to influence the design and composition of Ka'ba tiles in the eighteenth century, and the Ka'ba was then depicted from a single view point which gave the scene a more natural look. A good example of this new way of depicting the Ka'ba can be found on a panel probably made by the potteries at Tekfur Sarayi in Istanbul and now part of the Hekimoğlu Ali Pasha Mosque in Istanbul built in 1732–5 (fig. 70). Tiles with images of the holy city of Medina are also known which feature the tomb and pulpit (*minbar*) of Muhammad, and the garden of Fatima, the daughter of Muhammad, indicated by one or two palm trees. Tiles depicting Medina also accompany Ka'ba tiles as in the Hagia Sophia in Istanbul where they are placed together on a wall behind the pulpit (fig. 68). Arabic inscriptions are often part of the pictorial Ka'ba images giving the date the pilgrimage was undertaken and who commissioned the tile (fig. 69).

OPPOSITE [fig. 71] Rectangular tile depicting Armenian Church fathers translating the Holy Scriptures under the divine guidance of angels and the Holy Ghost in the guise of a dove at the top of the tile. The Armenian inscriptions at the bottom describe the various personages in the picture. Stone paste painted in under-glaze polychrome colours. Kütahya, Turkey, 18th century. 26 x 19 cm. British Museum 1932,0615.2. Donated by Oscar Charles Raphael.

ABOVE [fig. 72] This tile, decorated with angels and crosses, is similar in design to those found on ceramic eggs placed above oil lamps in the Armenian Cathedral of St James in Jerusalem. Stone paste painted in under-glaze colours .Kütahya, Turkey, 18th century. 11.5 x 23.5 cm. British Museum 1885,0609.2.

Armenian tiles with Christian subject matter

A very unusual group of tiles are Armenian tiles with a religious subject matter. They are unusual because they depict saints, church fathers, angels and sometimes even the Madonna and Child in apparent contravention of the strict Islamic rules on depicting such things (figs 71–3). Although Armenians were Christians, they were allowed to live and work in the Ottoman Empire because Muslims considered them as People of the Book (which included Christians and Jews) and they were respected if not full members of Ottoman society. They were known as *dhimma* which refers to non-Muslims living in a Muslim state who in return for paying a special tax were guaranteed their religious autonomy. Christian Armenian potters were very active in Kütahya, a pottery centre 120 kilometres south of Iznik, where they made pottery and tiles for Islamic customers but also for Armenian churches.

Although pottery was made at Kütahya from the sixteenth century at least, the workshops initially operated in the shadow of their more famous counterparts in Iznik, but with the decline of Iznik potteries in the late seventeenth century they began to flourish. Armenian potters made decorative tiles with abstract floral motifs which were used in both mosques and churches. Occasionally they also made pictorial tiles with Christian subject matter. A well-documented case is the tiles originally commissioned in 1718–19 for the planned redecoration of the Church of the Holy Sepulchre in Jerusalem but which ended up on the walls of the Cathedral of St James in Jerusalem. The majority consist of patterned tiles of various designs executed in blue and white or in polychrome, but the most fascinating tiles are those showing biblical scenes, saints and angels. These pictorial tiles also carry Armenian inscriptions identifying scenes or historical personages. The clothing of the figures and the way some of the saints and church fathers are depicted show that these tiles were made in the pictorial tradition of the Eastern Orthodox Church.

Persian tiles of the Qajar period

The Qajars who ruled Iran between 1795 and 1925 revived Persian tile making of the thirteenth and fourteenth centuries and the later Safavid periods by encouraging the use of tiles in nineteenth-century Persian revivalist architecture, such as the Gulistan Palace in Tehran built between 1867 and 1892. *Cuerda seca* tiles as well as under-glaze painted tiles were used in palaces and monuments in the cities of Shiraz and Tehran which actively celebrated Persia's great cultural past. This tile revival also meant that individual tile makers came to the fore, such as Muhammad Isfahani who worked in Isfahan and Tehran during the second half of the nineteenth century. He wrote a treatise on ceramic production called *On the Manufacture of Modern Kashi Earthenware Tiles and Vases*, published in 1888, following the example of the medieval Persian Abu'l Qasim who had written a treatise on ceramics in 1301.

During the Qajar period interesting and unusual square tiles with moulded figurative decorations were made and painted in a wide range of under-glaze colours. The moulded figures were first outlined in black and various details added, after which the delineated areas were filled in with blue, brown, yellow, pink and green under-glaze colours. The tiles decorated in this way show court and hunting scenes reminiscent of the pictorial tiles of the seventeenth-century Safavid period, but also scenes from pre-Islamic Persian history such as Achaemenid rulers sitting on thrones guarded by spear-bearing Persian soldiers (fig. 74). These tiles represent an unexpected late flowering of Islamic tile culture.

OPPOSITE [fig. 73] Panel of two tiles depicting the Virgin and Child and two adoring angels. The rather mature looking baby Jesus reflects traditional representations of the Christ child in icon paintings of the Eastern Orthodox Church. Stone paste painted in under-glaze colours. Kütahya, Turkey, 18th–19th century. Each tile: 10.5 x 13.7 cm. British Museum 1928,1017.1.

ABOVE [fig. 74] Rectangular tile with moulded decoration painted under the glaze in a range of different colours. The scene depicts an Achaemenid ruler on a throne surrounded by his bodyguards and an attendant holding a flywhisk. Below the ruler's throne are the Arabic words 'King Jamshid'. Stone-paste. Shiraz or Tehran, third quarter of the 19th century. 30 x 31 cm. British Museum 1981,0604.2. Bequeathed by Woodward.

MEDIEVAL MAGNIFICENCE

Do we not revere at least the images of the Saints, which swarm even in the inlaid pavement whereon we tread?

St Bernard of Clairvaux

*Apologia, c.*1125

OPPOSITE [fig. 75] Mosaic floor tiles in situ at Byland Abbey, North Yorkshire, England. Earthenware, lead-glazed, 13th century.

From the early thirteenth century onwards magnificent ceramic tiled floors were laid first in the Gothic churches of monastic orders, then in the palaces of kings and later also in the homes of wealthy merchants and important citizens. Being able to afford ceramic tiles was a clear outward sign of wealth, prestige and power as the labour and skill required for the manufacture and installation of these tiles made them a luxury item that could only be afforded by the ruling elite. Tiled floors were prized for their functional and decorative properties as they made the interior more comfortable and hygienic, provided a level base for wooden furniture and added an extra aesthetic element. In particular, it was the variety of designs and images depicted on these floors, ranging from simple geometric patterns to complex figurative schemes, that made medieval churches, palaces and the homes of the well-to-do so resplendent.

Mosaic, marble and stone floors

With the fall of the Roman Empire the use of tiles and bricks in architecture had declined over most of northern Europe. A return to less sophisticated building construction techniques meant that most structures consisted of timber frames with walls of wattle and daub and thatch for roofs, while floors were often made of beaten earth covered with rushes. It was not until the tenth century that stone buildings, particularly churches, began to be built again. These required more durable floors, and before ceramic floor tiles were introduced in churches other decorative flooring material, such as mosaic, marble and stone, was used.

Mosaic floors were a legacy from the Roman building traditions when palaces, important public buildings and the villas of the well-to-do had floors created out of small cubes of stone and marble. These tesserae were fitted closely together to create

both purely ornamental and figurative designs on the floor. Mosaic floors had continued to be installed in southern Europe where Roman building traditions had been kept alive during the early Middle Ages. A case in point is the tenth century church of Pau del Camp in Barcelona that still has a section of its original black-and-white mosaic floor in place.

The technique of laying decorative marble floors using larger specially cut pieces (*opus sectile*) had also survived, particularly in the eastern Roman Empire centred on Constantinople. We learn, for example, from Leo of Ostia's *The Chronicle of Monte Cassino* (1090) that Abbot Desiderius hired craftsmen from Constantinople to decorate his church and part of their task was that of laying a decorative marble pavement. Ornamental marble floors became something of an Italian specialty in the twelfth and thirteenth centuries when a specific decorative technique was developed for intricate floor construction using marble and semi-precious stone known as *cosmati*, a name derived from the Cosmati family who became the European experts in this kind of work. The Baptistery in Florence still has a mosaic marble pavement in

ABOVE [fig. 76] Inlaid tiles with the Latin words 'AVE MARIA' (hail Mary) repeated four times to form a circular inscription around a central rosette, from Meaux Abbey, East Yorkshire, England. Four tiles are needed to complete the whole design. Earthenware, lead-glazed, late 15th century. Each tile *c*.12.4 x 12.4 cm.

ABOVE [fig. 77] Mosaic floor tiles in the Baptistery of Florence, Italy. The design of the marble mosaic corresponds closely with 13th century ceramic mosaic floor tiles at Byland Abbey in North Yorkshire, England (fig. 75). Marble, 13th century.

place which dates back to 1209 and is made up of different coloured marbles (fig. 77). The geometric patterns in the Baptistery floor are varied and correlate in their layout and design with the ceramic mosaic floors laid in Cistercian abbeys in Yorkshire, England during the first half of the thirteenth century.

In addition to mosaics and marble, ornamental stone tiles were used for the floors of churches. In Pas-de-Calais in northern France, a type of white limestone was found which when polished resembled alabaster. Because it was relatively soft, designs were easily cut into it and the indentations were filled with a kind of red or black bitumous material (mastic) creating a two-coloured design. Some fine thirteenth-century slabs of this kind have survived in the Cathedral of Notre Dame in Saint-Omer (fig. 78), particularly in the less-used side chapels. They show a great variety of all kinds of medieval floral and figurative designs. Tiles of this type have also survived in the Trinity Chapel at the east end of Canterbury Cathedral in Kent, England. Here there are magnificent stone roundels with black inlay showing images of the signs of the zodiac, the labours of the months and the cardinal sins.

These inlaid stone tiles are sometimes seen as precursors of the true medieval inlaid ceramic tiles.

The emergence of floors covered with ceramic tiles as an alternative to floors made from mosaic, marble and stone probably came about on economic grounds. Marble in particular was very expensive and often had to be imported whereas clay was usually locally available and could be worked by any potters with the necessary know-how and skill. It is now generally accepted that, with the exception of Anglo-Saxon tiles (see p. 81), the earliest developments in the making of ceramic floor tiles occurred in Britain, France and Germany towards the end of the twelfth century and from there spread swiftly to other parts of northern Europe where tile makers quickly became adept in the production of various types of ceramic floor tiles.

Tile makers and their workshops

Despite their simple materials, tools and kiln equipment, medieval tile makers proved to be very skilful in the manufacture of all kinds of floor tiles. These ranged from differently shaped plain tiles which were assembled into mosaic style floors, to moulded tiles with relief patterns and eventually to two-coloured inlaid tiles decorated with a wealth of different designs.

Major changes and developments affected the medieval tile industry between the late twelfth and the early sixteenth century, but all medieval workshops that

ABOVE [fig. 78] Floor with inlaid decorations at Saint-Omer Cathedral, Pas-de-Calais, France. Stone, 13th century.

ABOVE (LEFT) [fig. 79] A tile mould for roof tiles and a template for a ridge tile crest to make replicas of medieval roof tiles. The tools date to 1990.

ABOVE (RIGHT) [fig. 80] Tilers' tools that date to the 19th and early 20th centuries but which are probably only a little different from those used by medieval tilers. *Left* A bow and tile mould. *Right* A draw knife and a wooden strike.

successfully made and installed tiled floors had to meet certain conditions relating to production methods, forms of transportation, market demands, and use of skilled and unskilled labour in order to function effectively. Tile workshops could only operate if sufficient supplies of clay, sand and water were available in the immediate vicinity, as well as access to wood to fire the kilns and lime deposits for making mortar to lay the tiles. Although the various processes of tile decoration differed from each other, the basic production processes such as preparing clay, shaping the tiles, glazing and firing them in a kiln were common to them all.

Tile making was a seasonal business. Clay was dug locally and allowed to 'weather' in heaps during the winter months. The making and firing of tiles took place during the spring and summer when the weather was relatively dry. Tiles were usually formed out of malleable clay hand pressed in wooden moulds without a base. The moulds rested on a sanded board which prevented the clay from sticking (fig. 79). Once the clay was pressed into the mould, surplus from the top was levelled off with a wire bow and the tile was smoothed down with a wet flat piece of wood called a 'strike' (fig. 80). The tile was then tipped out and sometimes stabs or scoop marks were made on the back to help it stick to the mortar when it was installed. When this process was finished, the tiles were allowed to dry. An allowance of about ten per cent was made for shrinkage during the drying and firing stages. When small square or triangular tiles were required the tile maker would first make a tile in the normal way

and would then score the surface deeply before it was fired, so that after firing it could
be broken along the score lines to create smaller units. This avoided the cutting of
very small tiles at the start which would hinder the production process since they
are labour intensive to handle and are awkward to stack in the kiln for firing.

Transparent lead glaze was the basic material available to medieval tile makers to
glaze their products. Despite the limitations this imposed, tile makers proved to be
inventive in developing a range of different colours. The standard glazing method was
to apply a clear lead glaze over the surface of the tile that would make the red clay
body look brown. If, however, they first coated the tile with white slip (slip is clay
mixed with water to form a liquid of smooth pouring consistency) and then applied a
transparent lead glaze, the tile would look yellow. By adding a small amount of copper
oxide to the lead glaze they could make a green translucent glaze which would appear
as light green on a tile covered with white slip and dark green when applied straight
to the red body of the tile. A near black was achieved by coating the red tile with a
copper-saturated lead glaze. It was customary to apply the glaze directly to the
unfired tile so the tile was fired and glazed in one operation as this also helped
keep down the cost and the hours of labour involved in the process.

Medieval tile kilns were rather basic (fig. 81). They usually consisted of two or
more rectangular furnace chambers built below ground level with stoke holes at the
entrances. They were strengthened by brick arches to allow the construction of a

ABOVE [fig. 82] Section of paving made up of relief tiles found on the site of a Leper Hospital in Leicestershire, England. These tiles are 'seconds' as the tilers failed to reach a sufficient temperature to melt and fuse the glaze. It also shows how difficult it was for medieval tilers to obtain consistent results with primitive kilns. Earthenware, lead-glazed. Burton Lazars, Leicestershire, England, late 15th or early 16th century. Each tile: *c.* 11 x 11 cm. British Museum 1947,0505.4660. Purchased with contribution from The Art Fund.

rectangular chamber on top where the tiles were stacked and fired. These kilns were mainly built of waste tiles and bricks held together by clay. They had no roof but were given a temporary covering of waste tiles to help contain the heat in the kiln during the firing. The kilns were usually fired with brushwood, and it was important to get the temperature to around 1,000 Celsius to ensure the proper firing of the clay body and fusing of the lead glaze, but medieval tile makers had none of the temperature measuring devices that are now available. Successful firings depended entirely on the experience of the craftsmen involved. This is perhaps why medieval tiles can vary so greatly. No two batches turned out exactly alike, but to the modern eye the diversity of their appearance can be an attractive visual element (fig. 82). The whole cycle of loading the kiln, firing, cooling down and unloading took about six days. Waste tiles found during excavations of medieval kiln sites at various locations in Britain such as at Meaux Abbey in East Yorkshire, Clarendon Palace near Salisbury, Norton Priory in Cheshire and the commercial kiln sites at Danbury, near Chelmsford in Essex, have increased understanding of how the various types of tile were produced.

At the beginning of the thirteenth century when monastic establishments were the most important customers for floor tiles, it is likely that tile makers travelled from site to site. When working at prestigious locations for monastic or royal clients, they were usually paid a daily wage and records of this remain. They were normally called

ABOVE [fig. 83] Stamped relief tiles.
The tiles show a wide selection of bold
patterns consisting of leaf motifs,
animals, inscriptions, heraldic shields, and
geometrical designs. Earthenware, lead-
glazed. Bawsey, Norfolk, England, latter half
of the 14th century. Each tile: 10 cm square.
British Museum 1947,0505.7074. Purchased
with contribution from The Art Fund.

in when building work at abbeys neared completion as the floor tiles were usually
laid towards the end of building operations. Tiles were heavy and could not be
transported over great distances so making tiles 'in house' on site when the job
was big enough would make sense. Abbeys were usually located close to rivers and
suitable clay was likely to be found in the vicinity. The areas of flooring covered in
some abbey churches were quite immense. At Fountains, where the floor was laid
under the rule of Abbot John of Kent (1220–47) an area of 2,695 square metres
was tiled, while at Byland a pavement covering an area of 2,325 square metres was
constructed. It is likely that with these large tiling operations, lay brothers assisted
the professional tile makers in some of their tasks. These lay brothers would not have
been paid for what they did, as they would have worked for the greater glory of God,
but without their free labour such vast tiling schemes would probably not have been
feasible given the manpower and economic costs involved. The tiles of this period are
often thick and heavy and complex in their shapes and designs, and were therefore
labour intensive to produce. The itinerant craftsmen may well have passed on their

ABOVE [fig. 84] The wooden tile stamp (centre), the only one known to survive, was used by craftsmen to decorate the tile on the left. The stamp was found at North Walk Pottery in Devon, Barnstaple, England in 1906 and was then used there to make the glazed relief tile on the right. 17th–18th century. British Museum 1906,1222.1. Donated by J. Charbonnier.

skills to local potters who could then continue the craft. It was not unknown for kilns to remain in operation after the initial job was finished and to continue making not only floor tiles for other clients in the area but also ceramic roof tiles for which there was always a demand.

From the second half of the thirteenth century onwards production became more commercial. Tiles were then made in standard formats which could range from about 10.5 to 14 centimetres square with an average thickness of about 2 centimetres. Such tiles could be produced more quickly in greater quantities and they were easier to install. Tile making was now more often carried out in fixed production centres serving a range of religious and secular clients in the region. Piecework was the norm and tilers were usually paid per thousand tiles produced. There were limits to how far tiles could be transported overland given the state of the roads, but they could be delivered fairly easily and over greater distances where navigable waterways were accessible to the tileries.

A good example of a fixed production centre was Penn in Buckinghamshire, England. A study of the fourteenth-century tile industry at Penn has revealed one of the most remarkable English commercial tile enterprises. Situated near the main London-Oxford road and less than 10 kilometres from the river Thames, the producers could supply customers with floor and roof tiles by road as well as by river transport. They were only 21 kilometres from their royal patron in Windsor and within easy distance of London using the Thames. They supplied customers not only in Buckinghamshire where they were located, but also in neighbouring counties like Oxfordshire, Hertfordshire, Berkshire and Essex. Apart from their royal patron at Windsor they found a market among abbeys, cathedral and parish churches, and manor houses. From tax accounts it seems that tilers in Penn kept tiles in stock, which indicates that apart from direct commissions they also catered for an open market. Recent excavations at Penn have brought to light a number of kilns giving further support to its role as a major tile production centre.

Fixed production centres also became common on the Continent, particularly in the later Middle Ages. Tileries in the Low Countries were often located on the

ABOVE [fig. 86] Relief tile with a monochrome glaze found during excavations at St Albans Abbey, Hertfordshire, England. Earthenware, lead-glazed, late 12th century. 21 x 21 cm. British Museum 1982,1001.1. Donated by St Albans Archaeological Research Committee.

outskirts of major towns as excavations in Utrecht and s'Hertogenbosch have shown. They were part of the urban economy and supplied floor and roof tiles as well as bricks for the buildings of wealthy religious patrons and rich citizens. The town's authorities actively encouraged the use of roof tiles to replace thatched roofs and the replacement of wooden houses with brick ones in order to reduce the risk of fire. It is therefore not suprising that there was a steady demand for these products, perhaps more so than for floor tiles. Much of the floor tile production consisted of plain glazed tiles which were used in local churches, religious institutions and the houses of private citizens. A study of excavated medieval houses in s'Hertogenbosch has shown that plain floor tiles could be afforded by even the moderately well-to-do and that the use of tiled floors in Holland was therefore more widespread among the middle-class population than was previously thought.

We know little about the medieval craftsmen who made floor tiles and hardly any medieval tile makers have emerged by name. In Britain names occasionally appear on tiles, such as those found at St Mary's Priory, Hurley, Berkshire with the inscription 'Ricard me fecit' ('Richard made me'). Sometimes a name can be found in written records, such as that of William Tyelere of Otterbourne who is mentioned in late fourteenth-century Winchester College accounts rolls. However, most tile makers have remained anonymous which is indicative of the medieval attitude towards craft production, whereby the end product made for the greater glory of God or prominent earthly clients was more important than the humble workman who made it.

ABOVE LEFT [fig. 85] Inlaid tiles with elaborate floral motifs. They have distinctive nail holes in two corners which are traces of the production process. Earthenware, lead-glazed. Probably made in the Lisieux area of France, 16th century. Each tile: *c*. 13 x 13 cm. Nederlands Tegelmuseum, Otterlo, The Netherlands.

ABOVE [fig. 87] Line-impressed tile with a vine leaf decoration. Earthenware, lead-glazed. England, 14th century. *c.* 10.5 x 10.5 cm. Private collection.

ABOVE RIGHT [fig. 88] Anglo-Saxon tiles recovered during excavations at All Saints Church pavement, in York, England in 1963. They are the earliest medieval tiles recorded in Britain. The decorations consist of geometric raised lines. Earthenware, coloured lead-glaze. Late 10th or early 11th century. Each tile: *c.* 9.5 x 9.5 cm. British Museum.

Types of medieval tiles

The major types of medieval tiles – relief, line-impressed, mosaic, inlaid and tin-glazed – developed at different times from the twelfth century onwards but by the beginning of the fourteenth century the main tile decoration techniques were all in production. Chronologically speaking relief tiles were made first, followed by mosaic tiles, then two-coloured tiles, with tin-glazed tiles being the last in line. Ceramic roof tiles were used from the twelfth century onwards and were produced in increasing numbers throughout the Middle Ages.

Relief and line-impressed tiles

The earliest medieval ceramic relief tiles date from the late tenth or early eleventh century when the Anglo Saxons made tiles that show figurative or geometric relief patterns decorated with coloured lead glazes. Excavations carried out in such places as York, St Albans, Peterborough and Winchester have confirmed that they were used in churches, as at this time stone churches were replacing wooden ones and Anglo-Saxon relief tiles were used in the sanctuary. Some tiles have flanges on the back which suggests that they were used as risers in steps or on the wall, but those without flanges show irregular stab marks on the back which would aid adhesion to mortar: these were probably used on the floor. However, Anglo-Saxon tiles were rare occurrences and no sustained tradition developed from them.

From the second half of the twelfth century relief tiles were made throughout northern Europe, but they were particularly popular in Germany and Switzerland. The way in which relief tiles were produced changed over time. Relief tiles could be decorated by impressing small separate stamps into the clay before firing, as can be seen in the thirteenth century tiles from St Urban Abbey near Zofingen in Switzerland, or the whole surface of the tile could be decorated by using a single wooden stamp (fig. 84). Many relief tiles, particularly those in Germany, were left unglazed and therefore depended for their colour on the tint of the clay.

Relief tiles fall into three broad categories: high-relief, counter-relief and line-impressed. Some very early glazed high-relief tiles of the second half of the twelfth century have survived from the chapter house of St Albans Abbey, Hertfordshire, England (fig. 86). They have the design raised on the surface and the background forms sunken areas around the design. They show patterns like Gothic stiff leaf designs set within a quatrefoil. In counter-relief tiles things are the other way around with the design sunk into the tile and the background (the surface of the tile) standing up around it. A tilery producing counter-relief tiles was located at Bawsey in Norfolk during the second half of the fourteenth century. Line-impressed tiles have a design of thin lines impressed into the tile surface (fig. 87). They can still be found at several sites in Britain such as Prior Crauden's Chapel in Ely, Strata Florida Abbey, Wales, and village churches in Hughley and Acton Burnell in Shropshire. In some instances lines were scored into the soft clay by hand, producing a kind of engraved drawing. Such tiles showing birds have been excavated at Norton Priory, Runcorn in Cheshire.

What all relief, counter-relief and line-impressed tiles have in common is that they were produced by making stamped impressions in the clay. The indentations were made with a wooden stamp, which had the design either in relief or counter relief

ABOVE [fig. 89] Section of a circular mosaic pavement from Byland Abbey, North Yorkshire, England, reassembled from loose tiles found on site following examples still in situ. The various mosaic tiles have a rich variety of different geometrical shapes and the main colour contrast relies on juxtaposing yellow and green glazed tiles. Where the glaze has worn off it reveals either the white slip with which some tiles are covered or in the instances of extreme wear the red clay colour of the tile body. Earthenware, lead-glazed. 13th century. British Museum 1947,0505.6645. Purchased with aid from The Art Fund.

RIGHT [fig. 90] Reconstruction drawing of one of the circular mosaic pavements at Meaux Abbey, East Yorkshire, England, installed between 1249 and 1269. The alternating brown-red and yellow mosaic tiles have been arranged in a series of concentric circular bands.

depending on the final result required. It is also possible that line-impressed tiles were created by metal stamps with raised lines fixed to a wooden backing which would be more durable than if such stamps had been made entirely out of wood. After the tiles were stamped and had dried sufficiently, they were covered with a lead glaze. Light coloured tiles were made by applying a lead glaze to tiles which had first been covered with a thin layer of white slip. Darker coloured tiles were obtained by coating the tile directly with a lead glaze. The light and dark tiles could then be alternated when laid on the floor to create striking visual effects. But whatever the final result, the decoration of this type of tile ultimately relied on the effect of light and shade to set off the impressed or raised relief designs on its surface.

Mosaic tiles

The second main type of tile is the mosaic tile, which probably evolved from marble mosaic floors in southern Europe. Some of the earliest ceramic mosaic floors were made in France at the end of the twelfth century and laid in abbey churches like St Denis in Paris. Mosaic tiles were also used in large numbers in the churches of the Cistercian monks during the first half of the thirteenth century in both France and England. Mosaic tiles consisted of pieces of clay cut into various shapes and then assembled to form geometric patterns (fig. 89). Different tile shapes were cut out of processed clay with the aid of templates and allowed to dry. Tiles were cut at a slight

angle, so that the surfaces tapered inwards. When the tiles were laid, the top surfaces would touch, but the tapered sides allowed the mortar to squeeze in between for greater adhesion to the floor. With the use of white slip and lead glazes a range of light and dark colours could be made and patterns were created by alternating light and dark coloured mosaics tiles.

The most basic form of tile mosaic consisted of plain square tiles with light or dark glazed surfaces that could be laid in a variety of different chequer patterns, which looked stunning over an extended area. This evolved into the production of more complex geometric shapes (fig. 91), which could be laid in different patterns alternating light and dark tiles. The most complex forms of tile mosaic were large circular pavements (fig. 90). Their making and installation required considerable skill and experience. A circular pavement necessarily meant that the pieces converged toward the centre, so each individual piece had to be cut to an exact size to fit in an exact position in the overall design and great care needed to be taken to lay every piece in its rightful place. This could be one of the main reasons why these complicated circular pavements were abandoned later in the thirteenth century.

An unusual and elaborate form of tile mosaic known as *opus sectile* has survived in situ in Prior Crauden's Chapel at Ely Cathedral, Cambridgeshire, England. In around

ABOVE [fig. 91] Panel assembled from loose mosaic tiles from Rievaulx Abbey, North Yorkshire, England. It shows sections with different tile mosaic arrangements that medieval tile makers had used at Rievaulx when they paved the floors of the abbey. Earthenware, lead-glazed. 13th century. British Museum.

RIGHT [fig. 92] Detail of an *opus sectile* panel still in situ in front of the altar in Prior Crauden's Chapel at Ely Cathedral, Cambridgeshire, England. It shows the figure of Eve who gives the apple taken from the Tree of Knowledge in Paradise to Adam. Some of the lines in the face and body have been incised by hand. Earthenware, lead-glazed. *c.*1324.

1324 the whole chapel was paved with mosaic tiles, and in front of the high altar an unusual panel of *opus sectile* tiles was laid with figurative designs depicting Adam and Eve eating the forbidden fruit from the Tree of Knowledge (fig. 92). There are also several panels with the figures of lions executed in *opus sectile*. The tilers cut shapes following the outlines of the human and animal forms, similar to the way that was used to produce shapes in stained glass. These tiles were made to look yellow by coating them with white slip and lead glaze and then set against a background of dark coloured tiles. Details of the faces of Adam and Eve and the lions have been accentuated with incised lines. Prior Crauden's Chapel is of further interest because a number of tiles in the mosaic pavement have been decorated with line-impressed rosette decorations. There are also tiles which have had straight lines scored into them creating diamond-shaped patterns across their surface, giving these tiles the appearance of mosaic although they are in effect a kind of 'pseudo mosaic'.

Two-colour tiles

The most important type of medieval tile is the two-colour tile. The term 'two-colour' usually denotes tiles that have a yellow design set against a red-brown background (sometimes it can be the other way around and have red set against yellow). The exact origins of two-colour tiles are not clear but they were probably first made in France at the beginning of the thirteenth century and the technique was passed on by itinerant French tile makers. It quickly became a much used type in Britain and Ireland and also spread to the Low Countries. The earliest two-colour tiles for which there is documentary and archaeological evidence are the tiles made for Clarendon Palace built for Henry III between 1240 and 1244.

Two-colour or inlaid tiles, as they are also known, were made as follows. Prepared clay was pushed into a wooden mould and the excess scraped off to create a flat level surface. Before the tile was removed from the mould a wooden stamp with a design in relief was placed on the tile and struck a blow with a hammer to create an indented impression in the clay. Wooden stamps were specially cut and were valuable tools of the trade. After making the impression with the stamp the tile was removed from the mould (fig. 93), its edges trimmed, and it was allowed to dry to a leather-hard stage. White clay, with a consistency that could range from thick paste to liquid slip, was trowelled or poured into the indented areas and allowed to dry. Excess white clay was then scraped off to reveal the white design sharply and clearly against the contrasting body of the tile (fig. 94). The tile was then coated with a transparent lead glaze and fired in a kiln. Once fired, the transparent glaze made the tile body appear brown and the white inlaid clay yellow. Another possible process of manufacturing inlaid tiles was 'stamp on slip'. This is a method whereby the tile was first covered with a coat of

ABOVE LEFT [fig. 93] The tile maker Diana Hall is seen lifting a wooden stamp with a fleur-de-lis design from a tile, which is the first stage of inlaid tile production. The impressed design is filled with white clay and after drying scraped level, glazed and fired.

ABOVE RIGHT [fig. 94] Tile fragment showing the structure and make-up of a medieval inlaid tile. The tile body in its unbroken state would have measured 16.5 cm square and 3.5 cm thick. The deep impression the wooden stamp made can be seen where the white inlaid clay has dropped out. Where the glaze has worn the white inlaid clay can be seen; it becomes a honey-coloured yellow where it is still covered by the glaze. Earthenware, lead-glazed. Rievaulx Abbey, North Yorkshire, England, 13th century.

RIGHT [fig. 95] Panel of inlaid tiles from the site of Ulverscroft Priory, Leicestershire, England. The designs vary from emblematic birds, fleur-de-lis and a sign of the zodiac (Aries) to a fantastic creature and a heraldic device. Earthenware, lead-glazed. England, second quarter of the 14th century. Each tile: approx. 12 x 12 cm. British Museum.

white slip. Once it was leather hard, a wooden stamp was used to force the white slip into the tile body. The surplus slip would then be scraped from the top revealing the red body of the tile and after further drying the tile would be glazed.

Two-colour tiles allowed for richer ornamentation of the surface by the use of patterned and figurative designs that could be confined to one tile or stretch over several tiles. The patterned tiles often had a single motif like a fleur-de-lis, or a floral design or geometric motif which, when fitted together, created a stunning overall design. A tile can also show just part of a design, with a group of tiles needed to show the whole design layout. Such design layouts can stretch over groups of four, nine or sometimes sixteen tiles.

In Britain some of the finest inlaid figurative tiles were produced in the thirteenth century. Particularly good examples were found at Chertsey Abbey in Surrey, which are dated to the period 1250–60 (fig. 96). They came to light at various times throughout the nineteenth century either by accident when building work was carried out or during excavations. The Chertsey tiles have become famous because of their high quality craftsmanship and their intriguing range of subject matter including scenes from the romance of Tristan and Isolde and combats between Richard I and the Muslim warrior Saladin. The tiles also have unusual shapes. The inlaid pictorial scenes are depicted on round tiles, which are fitted into a complex set of decorative border tiles with intricate inlaid patterns.

In France inlaid tiles were also used widely in cathedrals, abbey churches and secular residences from the thirteenth to the sixteenth centuries. The best workshops were at first located in or near Paris because that is where the most prestigious commissions were to be found. But from the fourteenth century onwards tileries in other areas like Normandy or the regions of Troyes and Epernay were active and were able to transport their tiles along the rivers Seine and Marne to where they were needed. Some interesting tiles were made as late as the early sixteenth century showing figures like hunters and falconers where the figures are shown as dark against a light ground (fig. 97).

The device of using a dark design against a light ground was also utilized by tile makers in the Low Countries. They employed this on tiles with inscriptions and moralizing mottos which once they were laid on the floor exhorted the owner of the tiles to reflect on the fugitive qualities of life and do well while they were still alive. Mottos like 'Die tijt is cort, die doot is snel, wacht u van sonde, soe doedi wel' ('Time is

ABOVE [fig. 96] Two circular inlaid tiles set in an elaborate two-colour background from the site of Chertsey Abbey, Surrey, England. They show the battle between King Richard I and Saladin leader of the Saracens during the third crusade in the Holy Land. However in reality they never met and the scene where Richard drives his lance through Saladin is purely fictional. Earthenware, lead-glazed. c.1250–60. Diam. of each round tile: 26 cm. British Museum 1885,1113.9065–9070.

OPPOSITE (TOP LEFT) [fig. 97] Inlaid tile carried out in the reversing technique (to create a dark design against a light ground) depicting a gentleman with a falcon. Earthenware, lead-glazed. France, late 15th or early 16th century. 12.8 x 12.6 cm. British Museum 1947,0505.1401. Purchased with contribution from The Art Fund.

ABOVE (TOP RIGHT) [fig. 98] Inlaid tile carried out in the reversing technique (dark design against a light ground) showing a stag. Earthenware, lead-glazed. France, late 15th or early 16th century. 11.8 x 11.8 cm. British Museum 1947,0505.7647. Purchased with contribution from The Art Fund.

ABOVE (BOTTOM LEFT) [fig. 99] Inlaid floor tile. The motto on the tile reads 'ALLE DINC HEEFT SIJNEN TIJT' ('For everything there is a season'). In the centre is the emblem of the Dukes of Burgundy. Earthenware, lead-glazed. The Netherlands, 1525–75. 13.8 x 13.8 cm. Nederlands Tegelmuseum, Otterlo, The Netherlands.

ABOVE (BOTTOM RIGHT) [fig. 100] Inlaid tile with a six-petalled flower set within a circular band. Earthenware, lead-glazed. France, late 15th or early 16th century. 12.2 x 12.2 cm. British Museum 1924,0414.51.CR. Donated by Dr Walter Leo Hildburgh.

short, death is swift, avoid sin, so do you well') were popular. These tiles were not used only in the houses of Dutch or Flemish clients but were also exported to England where they have been found in Kent, East Sussex and London.

Although inlaid tiles had established themselves as the dominant type in the thirteenth century, the two-colour effect could also be achieved in other ways. An unusual method to achieve this, called *sgraffito*, was sometimes used during the first half of the fourteenth century. It involved coating the tile with white slip and incising the design in it. After this the white slip was cut or scraped away around the design revealing the contrasting colour of the tile body. After glazing, the designs appeared yellow against a red-brown background. Some fine tiles executed in this technique, dating from the early fourteenth century, were discovered at Tring Church in Hertfordshire. They show scenes from the Apocryphal Gospels depicting stories from the childhood of Jesus (fig. 101). The iconography of the scenes is intriguing and shows various miracles enacted by the young Jesus such as straightening the broken beams of a plough and turning water into wine at the wedding in Cana.

Tin-glazed tiles

An unusual development, albeit on a relatively small scale, was the production of tin-glazed tiles in northern Europe during the fourteenth century. In the south of France tin-glazed floor tiles were used in the early fourteenth century in the papal palace in Avignon but this can be partly explained by its proximity to Spain where the tin-glazed technique was commonly used by Hispano-Moresque potters in pottery centres like Manises and Paterna near Valencia. Much rarer are the tin-glazed tiles found as part of medieval tile production further north in, for example,

ABOVE [fig. 101] An unusual group of *sgraffito* tiles from Tring Church, Hertfordshire, England, showing scenes from the Apocryphal Gospels about the childhood and schooling of Jesus. They represent stories such as a father who locks his boy in a tower to stop him playing with Jesus after which Jesus miraculously pulls him through the lock so that they can play (see bottom left tile). Earthenware, lead-glazed, early 14th century. Each tile: 16.1 x 32.5 cm. British Museum 1922,0412.4.CR. Purchase funded by The Art Fund.

ABOVE LEFT [fig. 102] Tile excavated on the site of Abbey of the Dunes near Koksijde, Belgium. It shows the deftly painted face of a man executed in manganese oxide on a tin glaze. 1300–1325. 10.5 x 10.8 cm. Abdijmuseum Ten Duinen, Koksijde, Belgium.

ABOVE RIGHT [fig. 103] *The Virgin with Canon Joris van der Paele* painted by Jan van Eyck. The accuracy of the picture is so good that it shows the exact design of blue-and-white painted Spanish floor tiles on either side of the carpet on which the Virgin and Child sit enthroned. The blue-and-white tiles point to Valencia as the place of manufacture and they are part of a 'mixed floor' where they alternate with plain brown tiles. The rarity and expense of tin-glazed tiles in Flanders at that time made their use as insets into floors of sacred spaces in religious pictures entirely credible. The tiles depicted are lead-glazed and tin-glazed. Oil on wood panel, Flanders, *c.*1434–6. 122 x 157 cm. Groeninge Museum, Bruges, Belgium.

the Suscinio Palace of the Duke of Brittany in Morbihan, the Abbey of the Dunes in Flanders or the house of a prominent church official in Utrecht in the Netherlands. Such tiles found during excavations at production sites were painted in green and purple-brown and show fantastic beasts but also human figures (fig. 102). They were mainly used as occasional insets in a type of floor that consisted of a mixture of tin-glazed tiles, inlaid tiles and plain tiles. For the fourteenth-century potter who normally made inlaid tiles or relief tiles this would have been a technically difficult and expensive process. Tin oxide which is needed to make tin glaze was then rare and therefore tended to be an expensive material particularly in areas where this technique was not normally used. Making the actual glaze requires expertise and involves dexterity in handling a paint brush but above all tin-glazed tiles usually need two separate firings , one for the tile body and one for the glaze, and this of course added extra time and cost to the process.

When Count Jean the Duc de Berry in Poitier wanted tin-glazed tiles with lustre decoration bearing his coat of arms for the Palais de Justice in Dijon in 1384 he brought craftsmen from Spain to carry out the commission. Documents relating to this commission make mention of a Moorish tile maker called 'le Sarrazin' who probably came from Valencia and was practised in the art of making tin-glazed tiles embellished with cobalt blue and lustre. He was provided with all the materials he needed, a place to work and local potters to help him, and he was paid well for his endeavours.

There is further evidence of the use of medieval tin-glazed tiles in northern Europe. Because they were so rare and colourful and therefore highly prized, they were sometimes depicted in religious paintings by fifteenth century Flemish artists like Jan van Eyck. Van Eyck painted with such incredible accuracy that individual tile patterns on floors can clearly be seen. A case in point is his oil painting *The Virgin with Canon Joris van der Paele* (fig. 103) made in *c.*1434–6 and now in the Groeninge

Museum in Bruges. The painting shows the virgin and child sitting on an elaborately carved wood throne below which is an intricate woven carpet draped across a tiled floor. The floor has plain brown and blue-and-white Spanish tiles with an interlacing Moorish motif, depicted in a way that is so true to life that the painted tiles can be matched to real Spanish tiles of that time.

Roof tiles and fireplace bricks

As had happened with floor tiles, ceramic roof tiles had also fallen out of use after the breakup of the Roman Empire, and thatch or sometimes wooden shingles were then normal roofing materials until the twelfth century. From then on ceramic roof tiles (as well as stone tiles and slates) began to be used for prestigious buildings like abbeys and royal palaces (fig. 104) and later in the Middle Ages their use was also encouraged in medieval towns to counter the risk of fire posed by houses with thatched roofs. As with the production of floor tiles, the makers of roof tiles produced simple rectangular flat tiles on a sanded table by rolling out prepared clay and cutting the required shapes around a template or with the aid of a wooden four-sided frame. Holes were made at the top of the tile through which wooden or iron nails could be pushed to hang the tiles from the battens on the roof. Sometimes a small projecting flange was created at the back of the tiles at the top and they could then be hung by hooking the flange over the roof battens.

More complex roofs needed special tiles like 'hips' and 'valleys' to cover joints

ABOVE [fig. 104] Roof and ridge tiles from Britain, 13th century. *Left* Pieces of glazed roof tile from the site of Clarendon Palace, Wiltshire. *Centre top* Crested ridge tile from Eresby Manor, Lincolnshire. *Centre below* Cut out ridge tile from the kiln site at Haverholme Priory, Lincolnshire. *Right* Roof tiles and glazed ridge tile from the site of Clarendon Palace, Wiltshire. Earthenware. British Museum.

ABOVE [fig. 105] Brick with the head of a crowned ruler between two grotesque motifs. It probably depicts Emperor Charles V. Earthenware. Flanders, 16th century. 14.9 x 10.5 x 14.9 cm. British Museum 1887,0211.29. Donated by Sir Augustus Wollaston Franks.

and angles. Ridge tiles were needed to seal the gap between the sloping roofs and these were sometimes decorated by running an extra strip of clay along the top which could be cut into ornamental crests, adding decoration to medieval roof tops. The ridge tiles at the end of the roof were at times made with very ornate decorations known as 'finials', somewhat reminiscent of the ornamental terracotta roof ornaments of the Greco-Roman world.

Within the house, ornamental fireplace bricks were a special feature of the open hearths in Holland and Flanders from the late Middle Ages until the seventeenth century. Towns like Antwerp and Utrecht had fire regulations and to make hearths safer they were required to be constructed of solid brick and stone. During the sixteenth century it became quite common to build up the back of the hearth with high-fired bricks that had an average size of 14 by 10 centimetres with a thickness of 5 to 7 centimetres. An average hearth would be seven courses of brick high at the back. The first three brick courses at the bottom were often seven bricks wide but then became progressively narrower towards the top and the uppermost course would be three bricks wide and often capped with a large single semi-circular brick.

Although fireplace bricks were made in the first instance for utility and safety, they were ornamented with relief decorations pressed into the front at the time of manufacture in special brick moulds. Ordinary brick moulds are open at the bottom but moulds for fireplace bricks had a special panel at the bottom with a design in reverse. Clay was pushed into the bottom of the mould first and the bulk of the

remaining space was then filled up. The bricks were then left to dry and fired to a higher temperature than normal because if the brick was too soft, it could not withstand the constant heat of the fires in the hearth. Hearths with moulded fireplace bricks were common in the homes of well-to-do burghers and in addition to their obvious safety function they added a decorative feature to the room as a whole.

The decorations pressed onto the surface of these bricks have become objects of study because of their interesting range of figurative imagery. Biblical scenes were common, such as Adam and Eve, the Nativity and the story of Susanna and the Elders, but there are also bricks that show kings and queens and heraldic devices like the 'Plus Ultra' motif of Charles V and the heraldic lions which are symbols of the Netherlands and Flanders (figs 105, 106). Most scenes are set within borders which make the images look like framed pictures. There are also bricks that are borderless but have an overall diamond-shaped lattice framework with images and decorative devices within each diamond shape so that, when the bricks are put together, a continuous overall design is created on the back wall of the hearth.

Some fireplace bricks are dated which makes them even more interesting as they can be placed more accurately within the cultural context of the time. Others have scenes that relate to the history of a specific town. The coat of arms of the Dutch town of Utrecht is half red and half white symbolizing St Martin's cloak which he cut in two so he could give half of it to a beggar, and fireplace bricks with images of this event were popular for hearths in town houses in Utrecht.

ABOVE [fig. 106] Brick depicting the story of the Nativity showing Mary and Joseph kneeling on either side of baby Jesus with the crib, and the ox and the ass in the background. Earthenware. Flanders, 16th century. 10.4 x 14.7 cm. British Museum 1887,0211.23. Donated by: Sir Augustus Wollaston Franks.

ABOVE [fig. 107] Circular mosaic pavement in situ in the north chapel of the south transept at Byland Abbey, North Yorkshire, England. The pavement is flanked on three sides by different sections of geometric tiles. Earthenware, lead-glazed, 13th century.

The layout and design of medieval floors

The floors in abbey churches, but also in royal palaces and the houses of wealthy merchants, were representative of certain traditions in floor layout and design, but what a floor finally looked like also depended on the type of tile that was used and the specific preferences of the patrons for whom the pavements were laid. Since so many of the medieval tiles that have been left to us have been taken from their original context and are now individual items in public or private collections, it is difficult to form an idea of how they were used and what they must have looked like as part of bigger tile arrangements on the floors of medieval buildings. The layout of medieval floors can only be studied when pavements or sections of pavements have been left in their original locations or where careful recordings were made before tiles were lifted. When we look at what is now left in northern Europe the instances of original tile pavements in situ are few and far between. It is only in England and Wales that tiles in situ have survived in any numbers and then mainly only at monastic sites.

Floors in ecclesiastical buildings

By the end of the twelfth century there were more than three hundred and fifty Cistercian monastries throughout northern Europe. The Cistercian monks adhered to the rule of St Benedict and strove for simplicity, austerity and spiritual reflection. Their churches shunned excessive decoration as recommended by St Bernard of

ABOVE [fig. 108] Figurative inlaid tiles on the floor of Westminster Abbey Chapter House, London, England, showing medieval musicians and a tile with King Edward the Confessor giving his ring to a pilgrim. Earthenware, lead-glazed, *c.*1250.

Clairvaux in his *Apologia* of 1125 and this influenced the kind of tiled floors that were laid initially in their monastic churches. The abstract designs of these floors show a simplicity which matched the ideals of the religious lifestyle of the Cistercian monks. They believed in a life of prayer, quiet contemplation and simple manual work, and although the churches they built were there to glorify God, no unnecessary distractions like figurative images or superfluous decoration should draw their attention away from their devotions.

From the very beginning therefore Cistercians favoured floors made of plain geometric mosaic tiles or line-impressed tiles with very simple patterns. Early evidence of the latter has been found at the Cistercian abbey church at Sorø in Denmark and at the abbey of Fontenay in France, where tiles stamped with simple floral motifs and circular designs have been found dating from the late twelfth century. Line-impressed tiles were also used frequently in Cistercian monasteries in Germany as can still be seen at the former abbey at Bebenhausen. The fashion for tiles must have spread quickly amongst the Cistercians throughout Europe, including Britain, with abbots travelling between monasteries for church meetings or paying visits to their daughter houses.

The ruins of the Cistercian abbeys of Fountains, Byland and Rievaulx in North Yorkshire, England have significant remnants of thirteenth-century mosaic tiles in situ which are of international importance. Byland in particular is rich in large areas

of surviving mosaic pavements in the areas that used to be the presbytery and south transept. Dark and light coloured square tiles were laid alternately in a chequerboard fashion but it was also possible to create more intricate arrangements like zigzags or interlacing bands. There are also areas with more complex arrangements of tiles cut in shapes like triangles, circles, lozenges and oblongs which have, like square tiles, been fitted together on a light versus dark basis but arranged as more complicated designs. There are also impressive circular mosaic pavements. One circular pavement surviving in the south transept consists of a large circle set within a square with four small satellite circles in the corners (fig. 107). Similar round pavements made from cut marble were installed at the abbey of Monte Casino (c.1070) and at Westminster Abbey in front of the high altar where in 1268 a magnificent *cosmati* pavement was installed which is still in situ. There was a convention as to how these pavements were laid out. The large circle and four small subsidiary circles arrangement may have had symbolic meanings denoting the divine order of the cosmos, or the severe geometric layout could have signified creating order out of chaos and allude to the creation. There is no doubt that these pavements had underlying meanings for those who were educated enough to read the signs.

Tiled floors were not only installed in abbey churches but also in other parts of monastic buildings such as the chapter houses where monks met for daily business. An impressive tile pavement can still be seen in Westminster Abbey Chapter House

in London. This octagonal chapter house was built under the patronage of Henry III, and the floor was laid by 1258. The square and rectangular two-colour inlaid tiles cover the whole chapter house floor and are seen in juxtaposition with wall paintings, elaborately carved sculpture, fine architectural detailing and colourful stained glass windows. The whole makes clear how medieval pavements were an integral part of richly ornamented Gothic church interiors. The beautiful interior of Westminster Abbey Chapter House was recognized in its own day and the contemporary chronicler Mathew Paris (c.1200–59) described it as 'a chapterhouse beyond compare'.

The Westminster Abbey Chapter House floor consists of various groups of floral designs and figurative motifs that run in panels from east to west separated by strips of rectangular tiles. The range of subject matter and design motifs is extensive. Often four tiles are placed together to show a particular design. There are for example groups of four tiles which make up circular rose window patterns as well as four-tile arrangements creating quatrefoils enclosing scenes with a cock and a fox from Aesop's Fables. Particularly impressive are the panels of four tiles showing the royal coat of arms of Henry III. Some of the most interesting scenes can be found on single square tiles depicting figures of a seated king, a queen, a bishop, minstrels playing music and figures engaged in hunting, but the most interesting tile in the whole floor depicts King Edward the Confessor giving a ring to a pilgrim (fig. 108).

Images on medieval tiles can be based on popular stories and the tile showing Edward the Confessor is a good example (fig. 109). Historical sources tell us that Edward the Confessor, the last Saxon king of England, built the first Abbey of Westminster on the site of an Anglo-Saxon church. He was buried there in 1066 and canonized in 1161. One of the legends associated with him is that as he was riding by a church in Havering in Essex, an old man (variously described as a beggar or a pilgrim) asked the king for alms. As the king had no money he drew off his ring and gave it to the old man. A few years later two pilgrims travelling in the Holy Land became stranded and an old man helped them. When he learned that they came from England, he told them he was St John the Evangelist and asked them to return a ring

OPPOSITE [fig. 110] Part of a panel of late medieval inlaid wall tiles from Great Malvern Priory church, Worcestershire, England. The decorations include the Royal Coat of Arms and the sacred IHS monogram (an abbreviation for the Greek word of Jesus) set within architectural canopies. Earthenware, lead-glazed, 1457–8. Each tile: *c.* 22 x 16 cm. British Museum 1947,0505.1333. Purchased with contribution from The Art Fund.

Edward had given him and to tell the king that in six months he would be in heaven.

In the light of this story we can identify the figure of the king both by his crown and his large ring, and the old man in his bare feet as St John the Evangelist in disguise. The ring became Edward the Confessor's emblem and can be found elsewhere in paintings, illuminated manuscripts, stone carvings and stained glass windows. There is therefore no doubt about what has been represented on the tile in question, but there is still more to it. The fact that this tile is found on the floor of the chapter house built on the orders of Henry III also links him to the story. It was Henry III who completely rebuilt the Confessor's earlier abbey in the Gothic style. Because he held Edward the Confessor in great veneration he erected a costly shrine in the new abbey and translated the Confessor's body to this in 1269 where it became a famous place of pilgrimage for the sick. With this wider context it becomes clear that the medieval tile showing Edward the Confessor giving his ring to the pilgrim was not part of the chapter house floor by mere chance, but is there because this tile refers to the many connections between past history and the patronage of Westminster Abbey.

Another large floor with late thirteenth-century inlaid tiles has been preserved in situ at Cleeve Abbey in Somerset in an area where the old refectory (monks' dining room) used to be. The floor is therefore no longer inside the original refectory but its great size still conveys something of the majestic qualities of large areas of inlaid tiles. The tiles are particularly rich in heraldic designs showing the arms of King Henry III's brother Richard Earl of Cornwall as well as the arms of England, Clare and Poitou.

Great Malvern Priory is unusual because instead of all the tiles having been laid on the floor, the inside wall of the reredos behind the altar is covered with tiles with dates of 1453, 1456 and 1458 (fig. 110). Because they have always been on the wall, the glaze has not worn as much and these tiles now provide a rare glimpse of what medieval tiles must have looked like when their glazed surfaces were still mainly intact. Tiles were also used on the floor at Great Malvern Priory but after the nineteenth-century refurbishment they were put on the back wall of the reredos

where they can still be seen today. The tiles at Great Malvern were made on site and not only used in the priory church itself but also sold further afield. For example, tiles made at Great Malvern were used in Gloucester Cathedral where the pavement made for Abbot Thomas Sebrok, dated 1455, is still in place in front of the high altar. It is important to see such floors in situ as they provide us with the experience of seeing medieval tiles as part of an overall floor design and not only as loose specimens in museum showcases.

Floors in secular buildings

In Britain royal palaces were the first non-ecclesiastical buildings to have ceramic tiles made for them. A good example is Clarendon Palace in Wiltshire (built between 1240 and 1244) where impressive tile pavements made of two-colour inlaid tiles were found during a series of archaeological digs which also unearthed the kiln where the tiles were made. Excavated sections of these royal floors are now on show in the British Museum. The most impressive tiles found were in a circular pavement for Henry III's chapel consisting of concentric circles of segmented inlaid tiles separated by plain green tiles (fig. 112). The outer circle contained an inscription and is a very early instance of letter tiles. Other sections of floor tiles were discovered in what used to be the ground floor chamber of Queen Philippa's apartment installed in 1250–2 (fig. 111). They are square tiles featuring lion and griffin designs and tiles based on Gothic leaf motifs and geometric patterns laid in a series of different arrangements

ABOVE [fig. 112] Section of a round pavement
from the first floor chapel at Clarendon
Palace, Wiltshire, England. The chapel
was built for Henry III by Elias of Dyrham
between 1240–44 and is one of the first
recorded examples of inlaid tiles in Britain.
This section was assembled from loose tiles
recovered from the site during archaeological
excavations. Earthenware, lead-glazed.
British Museum 1957,1006.54.c. Donated
by Maj. S. V. Christie-Miller.

as single tiles, blocks of four or larger continuous areas separated from each other by plain tiles. Some sections were set parallel with the walls while others were laid down diagonally creating a lively and rich floor layout. The conspicuous show of these sumptuous furnishings in the royal apartments, of which luxury tile pavements were an integral part, was a conscious effort to impress and help to maintain and enhance the status of the king and his queen.

Over time as tiles were made in larger quantities at fixed production centres and therefore became cheaper, they found a wider market. Archaeological excavations of houses of richer citizens in London have revealed tiled floors like those at Seal House in Upper Thames Street dating from either the late thirteenth or early fourteenth century. Occasionally complete tiled floors have been found in situ like the early fourteenth-century tiled floor in the solar at Clifton House, a merchant's dwelling in King's Lynn and the late fifteenth or early sixteenth-century Canynges pavement found in a private house in Redcliffe Street in Bristol which is now in the British

ABOVE [fig. 113] A section of the pavement from Canynges House, Redcliffe Street, Bristol, England. The decorations on some of the tiles include the monogram of Robert Eliot on a shield. This is a rare survival of a complete late medieval tile pavement. Earthenware, lead-glazed, 1481–1515. British Museum 1957,0505.5039. Purchased with contribution from The Art Fund.

Museum (fig. 113). The latter is rare as it is a complete floor consisting of panels of four and sixteen decorative tiles set diagonally separated by dark glazed tiles. The whole is framed by a double row of tiles which were used to edge the walls.

Generally speaking most medieval floor tile production came to an end in the first half of the sixteenth century. In Britain this was partly due to the Dissolution of the Monasteries in 1537 as they had been one of the main sources of demand for medieval inlaid and relief tiles. On the continent the Reformation doomed many religious houses to extinction. The greatest blow, however, came with the emergence of painted tin-glazed tiles. They were introduced to northern Europe from Italy and Spain and the limited colours and decorative techniques of medieval tiles could not compete with these brightly painted products with their luscious colours such as blue, orange, yellow and purple, and their infinite variety of subject matter and design.

Gen. 19. v. 21. 26..

Gen. 7. v. 17. 24..

Gen. 22. v. 12. 13

Gen. 2. v. 22..

Gen. 4. v. 8..

Gen. 28.. v. 12..

Exod. 20. v. 2..

Exod. 32. v. 1. 6..

Richt. 14. v. 5. 6.

RENAISSANCE AND BAROQUE SPLENDOUR

The fireplace was an old one, built by some Dutch merchant long ago, and paved all round with quaint Dutch tiles, designed to illustrate the Scriptures.

Charles Dickens

A Christmas Carol, 1843

OPPOSITE [fig. 114] Detail of a Dutch tiled fireplace with a wide range of images from the Old Testament. Below each picture is a reference to the Old Testament book, chapter and verse. See pp. 150–1 for full view and caption. Nederlands Tegelmuseum, Otterlo, The Netherlands.

The Renaissance and Baroque periods in tile making fall broadly between 1400 and 1750, and have proved to contain some of the most diverse and splendid episodes in the history of tiles. This was due in the first instance to the introduction and development of the techniques involved in the production of tin-glazed tiles, but more importantly this 'Golden Age' was brought about by the ingenious use of tin glazing by potters and tile makers across Europe. Tin-glazed ceramics changed their name according to their place of manufacture: in Italy they were called 'maiolica', in France 'faience' and in Holland and England they became known as 'delftware'.

Tin glazing involved potters and tile makers covering their products with a white glaze made of lead oxide to which tin oxide had been added. The tin acted as an opacifier which turned the original transparent lead glaze into an opaque white covering over the yellow or red colour of the clay. Furthermore it produced a brilliant white surface which could be painted with colourful ceramic pigments. Artisans could now treat their pots or tiles as white canvases on which they could paint whatever they or their clients wanted.

In the case of tiles it led to an explosion of practical applications, artistic creations and stylistic developments, and the countries where the technique became established all made their own unique contributions to this period of rapid change. Painting with colour on white tin glaze can produce visual effects of startling vividness and this was used to create striking designs for single tiles as well as large panels to provide grand tiling schemes for palaces, churches and bourgeois homes throughout Europe.

Southern Europe

Some of the earliest developments of tin-glazed tile production in Europe took place in Spain where in the fourteenth century tiles were painted with a blue pigment made from cobalt oxide. This technique of using tin glaze had already been used by the Moorish potters who worked in Islamic Spain and they had passed it down to the potters who stayed on after the Christian reconquest. They not only became adept in the making of painted tin-glazed tiles but also developed the technique of lustre painting, and it was Spanish potters who transmitted these techniques in the fifteenth century to the Italian potters who developed it into what is now known as 'maiolica'. They transformed the initial blue-and-white tin-glaze technique from Spain into a truly Italian process with a much expanded palette of colours which, in addition to the original blue, also included orange, yellow, green and purple. It was Italian potters who then in turn introduced their maiolica technique to Spain during the first half of the sixteenth century. It spread from there to Portugal where it became recognized as a truly national art form.

Hispano-Moresque tiles in Spain

The Christian reconquest of Moorish Spain was slow and piecemeal. Valencia was recaptured in 1238 and ten years later in 1248 Seville fell to Christian forces, but Granada, the last city to be conquered, remained under Muslim control until 1492. Moorish potters who decided to stay on and work under Christian rule became known as *moriscos* (Moors) and those who converted to Christianity as *conversos* (converts) or *christianos nuevos* (new Christians). Many continued to ply their trade successfully for the new markets emerging not only in Spain but also in Italy. The merging of the Islamic and the Christian cultures in Spain resulted in a hybrid style which became known as *mudéjar* and is seen in the plaster work, embroidery, metal

ABOVE [fig. 115] Border tiles showing a boldly painted design of two cherubs holding a draped cloth between them. Tin-glazed earthenware. Valencia, Spain, 1550–1600. Each tile: 13.7 x 13.7 cm. Museo del Azulejo, Onda, Spain.

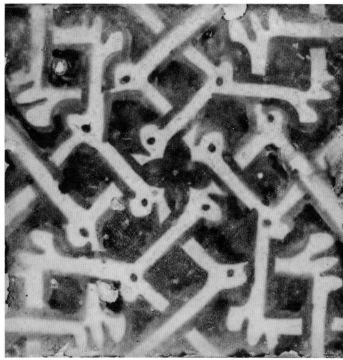

ABOVE LEFT [fig. 116] Floor tile depicting two iron manacles with a Gothic inscription in old Castilian that reads *'me faze bevir penado ta libre captivat'* ('your free captivity makes me live in sorrow'). It is probably a motto dictated by a lover to a lady who has chosen to pursue the religious life as a nun. Tin-glazed earthenware. Manises, Spain, 1450–1500. 13.4 x 13.4 cm. Nederlands Tegelmuseum, Otterlo, The Netherlands.

ABOVE RIGHT [fig. 117] Floor tile with a pattern based on tibia (shin) bones. Tin-glazed earthenware. Manises, Spain, 1450–1550. 14 x 14.2 cm. Museo del Azulejo, Onda, Spain.

work, pottery and architecture of the time. In the history of ceramics the products by Moorish potters working under Christian rule are also referred to as 'Hispano-Moresque'. This label applies in particular to the tin-glazed pottery, ceramics with lustre decorations and tiles made at this time in and around Valencia, but it is also used with reference to the *cuerda seca* ('dry cord') and *arista* ('ridged') tiles made in Seville and Toledo during the fifteenth and early sixteenth centuries.

The trade in fifteenth-century Spanish tin-glazed tiles was centred on Valencia, and production was concentrated in the two small towns of Paterna and Manises on the outskirts of the city where many Moorish potters had established their workshops. The blue-and-white tin-glazed ware they made was not produced in the way that is normally associated with tin-glaze painting, which is painting on top of the unfired white glaze. The potters of Paterna and Manises painted their blue decorations directly on the unfired clay (fig. 116). The tiles were then fired and only afterwards coated with a layer of white tin glaze before being fired for a second time. During the second firing the cobalt blue decoration would work its way through the tin glaze from below and become clearly visible on the surface of the tile. This was the old Islamic method which had been in use in Spain for hundreds of years. Sometimes lustre decorations were painted on to the already fired tin glaze and this would require a special third firing which made lustre tiles an expensive commodity.

Hispano-Moresque tin-glazed tiles were mainly used on floors as occasional insets among terracotta tiles. The latter were laid in such a way that there were square spaces left over and these were then filled with small square blue-and-white tin-glazed tiles. This method created striking floors because the red-orange terracotta tiles contrasted sharply with the blue in the tin-glazed tiles since orange and blue are complementary colours. The strong decorative effect of these floors was not lost on Spanish painters of the fifteenth century who would often depict

ABOVE LEFT [fig. 118] Ceiling tile painted with cobalt blue. It shows a heraldic device and such tiles were made exclusively for the castles and houses of the Spanish elite. Tin-glazed earthenware. Manises, Spain, 1400–1450. 43.7 x 35.8 cm. British Museum G.618. Bequeathed by Miss Edith Godman.

ABOVE RIGHT [fig. 119] Ceiling tile, body covered with white slip and painted with manganese oxide (dark colour) and iron oxide (red colour). Unlike twice-fired tin-glazed ceiling tiles, once-fired so-called *socarrats* were cheaper and quicker to produce. Fired earthenware. Paterna, Spain, 1450–1500. 43.1 x 35.2 cm. Museo del Azulejo, Onda, Spain.

such floors in their religious paintings – a good example of how one artistic medium can influence another.

The decorations on blue-and-white Hispano-Moresque tiles are varied. They can consist of simple floral and leaf motifs, and one pattern featuring a large central Gothic rose is now an iconic design of this genre, but designs can also have geometric interlacing motifs reminiscent of the Islamic tile mosaics which were such a strong feature of medieval Moorish architecture in Spain. Emblematic devices were common, showing the shields or heraldic symbols of wealthy Spanish families, religious institutions or organized guilds. These tiles could sometimes be embellished with a second colour like manganese purple or in some instances with copper lustre. There was also a type of tile which carried mottos or inscriptions. Some of these could be in Arabic acknowledging the Islamic past, but they were mostly in an ornamental type of Gothic script. Valencian tiles of the fifteenth century can therefore show a curious mixture of Islamic and Christian motifs.

Valencian tin-glazed tiles were also used for ceilings and such tiles were made in a much bigger format than that of the floor tiles (fig. 118). They were laid on the rafter beams to create permanent and highly ornamental ceilings. Examples of such tin-glazed ceiling tiles that have survived mainly date from the first half of the fifteenth century and are often decorated with coats of arms. They must have been an expensive luxury. A cheaper kind of ceiling tile known as *socarrats* came into fashion during the second half of the fifteenth century. These were large rectangular tiles shaped in moulds and when dry covered in white slip and painted with simple designs of floral patterns, birds or animals (fig. 119). The images were usually outlined in black and filled in with a reddish pigment and were then given a single firing which made them much cheaper to produce than the twice fired tin-glazed tiles.

Cuerda seca tiles with white interlace creating a Moorish twelve-pointed star. Seville, Spain, 1450–1550. Each tile: *c*. 13.9 x 13.6 cm. Nederlands Tegelmuseum, Otterlo, The Netherlands.

In addition to tin-glazed tiles, potters also manufactured other kinds of tiles such as *cuerda seca* and *arista* tiles which are technically very different from tin-glazed tiles. The *cuerda seca* or 'dry cord' technique was already a commonplace method employed by Islamic potters throughout the Middle East and tile makers in Valencia and Seville were continuing an established tradition. The *cuerda seca* technique consisted of painting lines with an oily medium (such as iron oxide mixed with grease) on the surface of the tile and filling the areas in between with coloured glazes. The greasy lines kept the water-based glazes separate. When the tiles were fired the greasy lines would burn away leaving a sunken dark outline around the glazed areas. The technique was often used for designs which simulated the Moorish interlacing mosaic patterns (fig. 120) and when the tiles were fitted together over a large area they gave the impression of mosaic tile work.

Another way to achieve this 'pseudo mosaic' effect was to use a stamp with lines incised into the surface. When the mould was pressed into the soft surface of the tile, it created raised ridges and tiles of this type were called *arista* ('ridged') tiles. After firing, the areas between the ridges were filled with coloured glazes and then the tiles were assembled on the wall to create geometric mosaic designs. In addition to these mosaic patterns, there were tiles with floral patterns, animals, classical designs and heraldic devices. They were particularly in vogue during the first half of the sixteenth century and Seville and Toledo became important production centres that also

exported *arista* tiles abroad and executed special orders for foreign clients. *Arista* tiles were mainly used as wall tiles, but rectangular ceiling tiles are also known with the rims on the short side left unglazed where they would rest on the ceiling beams (figs 122–4).

One of the best architectural examples of a building with *arista* tiles still in situ is the Casa de Pilatos in Seville (fig. 121). It was built by the Marquis of Tarifa in 1519 after he had been on a pilgrimage to the Holy Land and was given its present form between 1520 and 1539. Tiles are usually the last thing to be installed in a new building and in 1538 the tile maker Juan Polido was commissioned to make the thousands of *arista* tiles necessary to cover all the walls. The layout of the house is supposed to be based on that of Pontius Pilate in Jerusalem, and it became one of the most magnificent domestic residences in Seville with a large courtyard and many rooms. Stylistically it is a curious blend of Moorish, Byzantine, Gothic and Renaissance architecture. The walls of the courtyard, the rooms on the ground floor and the grand staircase are covered in *arista* tiles featuring many different designs and patterns, some of them decorated with gold lustre. The tiled walls of the great courtyard create a spectacular display of form and colour as well as providing a cool refuge during the summer heat.

ABOVE [fig. 121] *Arista* tiles on the wall in the courtyard of Casa de Pilatos. The interlacing patterns simulate 14th century Moorish tile mosaic. Glazed earthenware. Seville, Spain, *c.*1538.

ABOVE [fig. 123] A very rare *arista* tile with a strap-work design incorporating a diamond ring, attributed to the workshop of Niculoso Francisco. The diamond ring is a Medici family symbol and is linked to the Medici Pope Leo X (1513–21). An *arista* biscuit tile with a similar diamond ring device was excavated at Calle Pureza in Triana, Seville, where Niculoso Francisco's workshop was located. Glazed earthenware. Seville, Spain, 1518–21. 13 x 13 cm. British Museum 1865,0508.58. Donated by Sir Augustus Wollaston Franks.

ABOVE [fig. 124] Tiles with eight-pointed stars moulded in the *arista* technique and embellished with lustre. They are probably ceiling tiles designed to create a starry vault and each tile has three kiln-support marks on the upper surface. Glazed earthenware. Seville, Spain, 1500–25. Each tile *c.* 13 x 13 cm. British Museum G.519.a-d. Bequeathed by Miss Edith Godman.

ABOVE [fig. 122] Hexagonal floor tiles. *Top* Islamic tile from the Alhambra Palace painted in blue and lustre. The shield in the centre bears the heraldic device of the Sultans of Granada, Spain with an Arabic inscription ('There is no Conqueror but God'). Tin-glazed earthenware. Granada, late 14th century. *Below* A Spanish copy of the Alhambra tile executed in the *arista* technique. Seville, 1542–1550. Diam. of each: *c.* 16 cm. British Museum 1802,0508.1.d. Donated by: Hon Mrs Anne Seymour Damer.

Italian maiolica tiles

The tin-glaze techniques developed by Islamic potters had reached southern Italy by the thirteenth century, if not earlier, and a prototype of thirteenth-century Italian tin-glazed pottery was made in Orvieto. This was painted in a limited range of colours consisting mainly of copper green and manganese purple. In the fifteenth century a more sophisticated type of Spanish tin-glazed pottery painted in blue and white and sometimes embellished with lustre was exported to Italy. Made in Valencia, it was brought to Italy via the island of Majorca which became an important stopover for ceramics traders. It may be that the origin of the word 'maiolica' comes from Majorca, but there are also theories that it derived from the Spanish term *obra de Mallequa* (Malaga ware) or from Majolo the name of a Genoese merchant family who traded in pottery. Italian potters first copied and then made their own version of the Spanish-imported tin-glazed ware, adding many new touches, and Italian maiolica pottery and tiles were to become one of the important chapters in the history of European ceramics.

Much of what we know about the technique of Italian maiolica comes from the *Three Books of the Potter's Art* by Piccolpasso first published in 1557. It covers such matters as the preparation of the clay, the making of vases, and various pottery tools and kilns. It also deals with the composition of glazes, ceramic pigments and lustre. It is the use of coloured pigments and lustre, combined with a new style of painting, which made Italian maiolica stand out. Having seen and studied the Valencian pottery, Italian potters began to use cobalt blue (sometimes with the addition of purple) and at the beginning of the fifteenth century this new style began to supersede the archaic green and purple combination of Orvieto ware. Orange and yellow were introduced later in the century enabling stunning colour combinations to be created.

The painting was carried out directly on unfired white tin glaze (known as *bianco*) which differed from Spanish techniques of the fourteenth and fifteenth centuries where the pigment was usually painted on the clay before firing and glazing.

ABOVE LEFT [fig. 125] Floor tile with a boldly painted foliate motif set in a solid border from the pavement in the Cappella Caracciolo del Sole in San Giovanni a Carbonara. Tin-glazed earthenware. Naples, Italy, 1441–67. 10.1 x 10.1 cm. British Museum 1887,0611.5. Donated by Charles Drury Edward Fortnum.

ABOVE RIGHT [fig. 126] Floor tile from the pavement in the Cappella Caracciolo del Sole in San Giovanni a Carbonara. The oblong hexagonal tile shows an animal running bordered by oak leaves. The latter was a much used decorative design on 15th-century maiolica pottery. Tin-glazed earthenware. Naples, Italy, 1441–67. 10.4 x 19.5 cm. British Museum 1897,0511.13.

ABOVE LEFT [fig. 127] Floor tile from the pavement of the Mazzatosta Chapel in the church of Santa Maria della Verità, with a vigorously painted quatrefoil motif. Tin-glazed earthenware. Viterbo, Italy, c.1470. 10.6 x 10.6 cm. British Museum 1895,1023.6.

ABOVE RIGHT [fig. 128] Floor tile from the pavement of the Mazzatosta Chapel in the church of Santa Maria della Verità painted with the profile of a young man. Profile portraits were fashionable in Renaissance painting during the second half of the 15th century and this also found its reflection in tile decoration. Tin-glazed earthenware. Viterbo, Italy, c.1470. 10.9 x 10.9 cm. British Museum 1895,1023.5.

The pigments used by Italian potters were derived from metal oxides: blue from cobalt, purple from manganese, green from copper, yellow from antimony and orange from a combination of antinomy and iron. Black could be obtained by mixing metallic oxides of copper, manganese and cobalt. Red was only occasionally used as it was always a difficult colour to manufacture and apply. It could be made by grinding Armenian bole in red vinegar but the results were often unpredictable and it was never a mainstream colour in Italian maiolica.

The painter outlined the design first and then filled in the required colours and shades. Painting on unfired tin glaze is like painting on blotting paper as the pigment is almost immediately absorbed and mistakes cannot be rectified, so great sureness of touch is required. After painting, the tile was fired for a second time causing the tin glaze to turn into a white glassy coat. The colours sank into it, fusing permanently with it and the technique is therefore known as 'in-glaze' decoration. In Italy it was customary to add a transparent glaze (known as *coperta*) over the tin glaze to achieve extra brilliance. Certain Italian towns became closely associated with the production of maiolica and Siena, Urbino, Gubbio, Castel Durante and Faenza became well known for their tin-glazed ware.

During the fifteenth and sixteenth centuries Italian maiolica tiles were mainly used to cover floors and were produced in various shapes. A common layout consisted of a square tile surrounded by four elongated hexagonal tiles; this became one of the standard floor arrangements for tin-glazed tiles not only in Italy but also later in other European countries. Other shapes came into fashion such as evenly sided hexagonal tiles which could be laid as a continuous pavement without the need of 'filler' tiles. Round, triangular and cruciform tiles were made as part of more complex floor arrangements which often complemented other interior features such as marble altar pieces, frescoes and painted ceiling decorations.

Important tiled floors dating from the second quarter of the fifteenth century have been preserved in the British Museum (figs 125, 126). One floor dated 1440–45 came from the Cappella Caracciolo del Sole in San Giovanni a Carbonara in Naples.

ABOVE [fig. 129] Roundel with two putti flanking a coat-of arms, attributed to the Della Robbia workshop. Tin-glazed earthenware. Florence, Italy, 1500–1520. Diam. 52.3 cm. British Museum 1891,1018.1.

It is arranged in the conventional manner of a square tile flanked by four hexagonal tiles creating an octagonal floor unit, and the tiles are painted in a bold manner in blue and white decorated with floral designs, animal motifs, heraldic devices and interlacing ornaments which have been influenced strongly by Spanish tiles made in Valencia. However, a tiled floor of a similar date from the Cappella Brancacci in Sant' Angelo a Nilo in Naples consists of square tiles with armorial devices surrounded by hexagonal tiles featuring male and female portraits in profile, alongside hexagonal tiles with bird and fruit motifs. All these tiles were painted strongly in a glorious range of dark blue, pale blue, orange and yellow showing a more uniquely Italian identity.

Much can be learned from tiles that are still in situ like the tiled pavement of the Mazzatosta Chapel in the Church of Santa Maria della Verità in Viterbo. These floor tiles are part of an authentic interior with a sculptured altar and frescoes adorning the walls dated to 1469 which gives a clue as to the date of the tiles. The tiles that are left on the floor (some have been lifted and dispersed to museum collections) are laid out in the standard square tile flanked by four hexagonal tiles arrangement. Many of the square tiles show profile busts of young men but there are also animals and motifs of swirling Gothic foliage (figs 127, 128) predominantly painted in blue and black-blue relieved by touches of green and orange-brown. The tiles were painted robustly in the

RIGHT [fig. 130] Custom-made floor tiles from the *studiolo* (study) of Isabella d'Este at her palace. Isabella was Marchesa of Mantua and one of the leading women of the Italian Renaissance – a major cultural and political figure. The octagonal tile bears the abbreviated inscription ISAB[ELLA] ESTE [NISS] MAR[CHIONESSA] MAN[TUA]. Tin-glazed earthenware. Mantua, Italy, *c.*1525. International Ceramics Museum, Faenza, Italy.

simple and direct style that was so typical of maiolica pottery of that time.

One of the greatest fifteenth-century maiolica floors still completely in situ can be found in the Cappella di San Sebastiano in the church of San Petronio in Bologna. Most of the tiles have an evenly sided hexagonal shape that interlocks in a uniform way to create a continuous pavement. This is probably one of the first Italian floors to which the name of an individual tile maker can be assigned. In 1478 Pietro Andrea da Faenza, commissioned by the Vaselli family, made approximately a thousand tiles for the floor of the chapel. Each tile is an independent unit in terms of its design and together they show an extraordinary repertoire of ornamental, floral and figurative designs linked to a complex underlying iconography. The floor is a cornucopia of different subject matter showing coats of arms, masks, musical instruments, weapons, sacred emblems, portraits and fabulous beasts. The pictures shown on the tiles are also symbolic of important ideas and concepts of the time. For example, a tile with a unicorn denotes chastity and purity, a boar is a symbol of strength, a snail means patience, a deer signifies prudence and a blindfolded cupid exemplifies illicit love. There are also tiles with busts of men and women in not only the customary profile view so common on many Italian tiles, but shown in three-quarter view or seen full face, revealing the influence of the naturalism of Early Renaissance

painting. The most remarkable tile is one that shows a tile painter at work sitting on a chair decorating a hexagonal tile: on a board hanging from a column next to him is the name Petrus Andrea de Favecia. This tile could be a self-portrait and is clear evidence that tile artists were emerging as known individuals and were shedding the anonymity of the craftsmen of the Middle Ages.

Italian maiolica decorations for churches were not only in the shape of tiled pavements but also in the form of glazed relief sculptures. This was a new and specialized craft and was the preserve of certain families, such as the Della Robbias who ran a well-known workshop in Florence. The founder of the Della Robbia workshop was Luca (1400–82), a trained sculptor. He worked not only in marble and bronze but also in glazed maiolica and is often credited with the invention of the tin-glazed relief sculpture. One of his commissions was the maiolica medallions that decorate the ceiling of the Pazzi Chapel in the church of Santa Croce in Florence which are noted for their vigorous and earthy quality. He was succeeded by his nephew and pupil Andrea della Robbia (1435–1525) who worked exclusively in the maiolica medium and expanded it to include sculpture in the round (fig. 129). He is best remembered for the roundels that still decorate the facade of the Foundling Hospital in Florence with charming foundlings wrapped in swaddling clothes. Andrea's sons followed in his footsteps: Giovanni (1469–1529) is the most well known and he assumed control of the workshop when his father died. One of his early works was the tiled lavabo in the sacristy of Santa Maria Novella, Florence made in 1497. He created sumptuous altarpieces often with the Madonna and Child as the

ABOVE LEFT [fig. 131] Plaque with raised ridge near the rim painted with the Madonna and Child in front of a curtain; the border is decorated with an egg and dart pattern. Tin-glazed earthenware. Veneto, Italy, 1493. 26 x 26 cm. British Museum 1884,0726.1. Donated by Sir John Charles Robinson.

ABOVE RIGHT [fig. 132] Group of rectangular floor tiles finely painted with deer set against 'grotesque' ornament. The painting shows great deftness and control of the brush. Tin-glazed earthenware. Italy, c.1513. Average size: 16 x 22 cm. British Museum 1904,0706.6–8.

ABOVE LEFT [fig. 133] Floor tile from the
Petrucci Palace. The 'grotesque' designs
with dolphins, urns, masks and cornucopias
set against a black ground show the fashion
for this type of decoration which was
sweeping Italian art and design at the
beginning of the 16th century. Tin-glazed
earthenware. Siena, Italy, c.1509–13.
19.8 x 13.5 cm. British Museum 1854,1102.2.

ABOVE RIGHT [fig. 134] Plaque showing the
Virgin Mary with baby Jesus on her lap and
baby St John at a her feet, watched over by
Joseph. Attributed to Nicola da Urbino. The
composition of the figures, the architectural
setting and landscape in the background
show the influence of Renaissance painting.
Tin-glazed earthenware. Urbino, Italy, c.1530.
28 x 22.2 cm. British Museum 1885,0508.28.
Donated by Sir Augustus Wollaston Franks.

main subject. His work showed greater elements of naturalism, which was one of the
chief characteristics of High Renaissance art. His most ambitious work is a frieze
with representations of the Works of Mercy on the Ospedale del Ceppo at Pistoia
(1525–9), in which he was assisted by his pupils Benedetto Buglioni and Santi
Buglioni who became noted maiolica sculptors in their own right.

If maiolica tiles had initially found many applications in churches and chapels
they became increasingly used in the palaces and villas of the Italian aristocracy
towards the end of the fifteenth century. The political map of Italy was one of
independent city states ruled by wealthy and powerful families like the Medici in
Florence and the Gonzaga in Mantua. The famous patroness of the arts, Isabella
d'Este, wife of the Duke of Gonzaga, extended her patronage to tile makers in 1494
when she ordered tiles bearing emblematic devices of the Gonzaga family for the
ducal palace in Mantua. Around 1525 she ordered tiles again but this time for her
own private *studiolo* (study) and the tiles carried abbreviated inscriptions with her
own name and title (fig. 130).

From the late fifteenth century onwards a new type of decoration appeared on
Italian maiolica pottery known as *istoriato* (story painting). Maiolica plates, vases
and plaques were painted with naturalistic figurative scenes running across the
entire surface which was literally used as a canvas. The stories depicted were based
on Greek and Roman mythology as well as biblical tales taken from the Old and
New Testaments. The intricate figurative images painted on square or rectangular
maiolica plaques were not used for floors but were display items or were used as

devotional images. The figures in *istoriato* scenes were often composed within architectural or landscape settings and showed the use of perspective that was such a characteristic feature of Renaissance painting. Scenes were not painted freehand but were usually copied from prints by engravers like Marcantonio Raimondi whose copies of the work of well-known Renaissance artists found a receptive audience amongst well-to-do and educated Italians. The fact that maiolica painters copied drawn or printed images is confirmed by Piccolpasso who in his *Three Books of the Potter's Art* shows an illustration of painters sitting on chairs with vases and plates on their knees while on the wall behind them are what look like a selection of drawings or prints.

Faenza, Urbino and Castel Durante became important centres for *istoriato* painting with pieces that were sometimes signed by the artist. A very early *istoriato* plaque in the British Museum showing a Madonna and Child (fig. 131) has a date of 1493 on the back, but most plaques are from the sixteenth century. One of the most noted *istoriato* painters was Nicola da Urbino who from about 1520 onwards painted (and sometimes signed) some very fine dishes and plaques using a figurative style heavily indebted to Raphael (fig. 134). Some beautifully designed *istoriato* plaques with biblical scenes were also made in Faenza, some of which are attributed to the Bergantini family workshop active in 1502–58. *Istoriato* plaques represent some of the best of maiolica tile painting in terms of draughtsmanship, design and colouring.

Fashions and changes in interior decoration also affected tile design. An example of this was the craze for decorations with elaborate ornamental grotesques (figs 132, 133) which became a 'must have' for the rich seigniorial families. This latest fashion was sparked by the discoveries of ancient Roman architecture and design which took

ABOVE [fig. 135] Floor tiles probably from the Palazzo Marsili. The 'grotesque' decorations incorporate birds, animals and part-human figures and one tile bears the arms of Bandini of Siena. Tin-glazed earthenware. Siena, Italy, c.1600–20. Square tiles: 10.6 cm square. Hexagonal tiles: 18.5 cm long. British Museum 1885,0508.83–89. Donated by Sir Augustus Wollaston Franks.

ABOVE [fig. 136] Detail from the tiled floor in the Santuario di Santa Caterina at the Oratorio della Cucina showing grotesque motifs with cherubs, birds, griffins, cornucopias and strap work. The floor was restored in 1972. Tin-glazed earthenware. Siena, Italy, early 16th century.

place at the end of the fifteenth century. One of the most intriguing discoveries was Nero's Golden House in Rome with its elaborate wall decorations known as 'grotesques'. Nero's house was found under a great mass of accumulated earth and could only be reached by descending into it like a cave or grotto. This is where the Italian name *grotteschi* used for the ornate Roman decorations found in Nero's house comes from. Artists copied the Roman designs and they also found their way into engravings. Raphael (1483–1520) used grotesque ornament in his frescoes when he was painting rooms in the Vatican and this was much admired and imitated and also influenced tile design. The painted lines on tiles became more delicate, the ornamentation richer and more refined and the designs were sometimes set against either a black or yellow background. Floor tiles of this type were installed in the Petrucci Palace in Siena around 1509 (fig. 133) and were carefully chosen to blend in with the interior decorations of the rooms as a whole. Later sixteenth-century tiles showed delicate and spidery grotesque figures set against a predominantly white ground (fig. 135). This style was paralleled in the decoration of maiolica pottery.

One of the main characteristics of Italian maiolica tiles was keeping the design to a single tile or plaque. Each tile or plaque was an independent unit and although they were arranged over large areas on the floor creating a coherent overall layout, the basic elements were grounded in the shapes and patterns on each tile. With the exception of maiolica compositions of the Della Robbia workshop, what was not found on Italian maiolica tiles were large figurative compositions running across multiple tiles such as were undertaken in Spain by Niculoso Francisco, an Italian tile maker who had moved to Seville in Spain and who gave maiolica tile painting a whole new direction.

Spanish tin-glazed tiles

Dated works and documents record the Italian potter Niculoso Francisco's presence in Seville between 1503 and 1529 where he ran a workshop in the pottery district of Triana, but it is likely that he had settled there by the end of the fifteenth century. In Seville he was known as Niculoso Francisco Italiano or Niculoso Francisco Pisano. His original Italian name was probably Niculoso di Francisco and he received the names 'Pisano' and 'Italiano' as nicknames in Spain. He brought with him not only the new techniques and palette of Italian maiolica painting, but also the new Italian fashion for grotesques and the ability to paint naturalistic figure compositions. Although the tin-glaze technique was already known in Spain, it had until that time been confined to the use of the colour blue (sometimes with purple) that was used under the tin glaze as practised at the workshops in Valencia. The technique of painting on the unfired white tin glaze with a range of colourful pigments was something new in Spain and Niculoso soon found patrons for his new style and technique.

His earliest surviving commission was a tiled tomb for Inigo López in the church of Santa Ana in Triana showing an effigy of a full length recumbent figure which is now set against one of the lower walls at the back of the church (fig. 137). It is signed 'Niculoso Francisco Italiano me fecit' ('Niculoso Francisco Italiano made me') and the image is dated 1503. Here again is an instance of a tile painter elevating himself as an individual artist and original creator by putting his name on his work. His fame soon spread and in 1504 he was commissioned to make two painted tiled altars with figurative compositions for the private oratory of Isabella the Catholic, wife of Ferdinand V, in the Alcazar in Seville. He was also patronized by the church and in 1504 he carried out tile work for the convent church of Santa Paula in Seville. The Santa Paula commission involved the creation of a tiled archway over the entrance door to the church. He did this in cooperation with another Italian

immigrant potter Pedro Millán who created Della Robbia style maiolica roundels for the archway which were set against a background of tiles made by Niculoso showing Italian style grotesque decorations. He received commissions from other parts of Spain such as the tiles for the Palace of El Real in Valencia in 1511. The palace no longer exists but some tiles that reputedly came from it bear the name Pisano and are decorated with an Italianate cherub's head and grotesques in Niculoso's trademark style.

After Niculoso's death in 1529 there seems to have been no direct successor to carry on the maiolica tile side of his business, but the manufacture of *arista* tiles which had been carried on alongside the making of the maiolica tiles continued strongly. It was probably the arrival in Seville of another immigrant potter Frans Andries, whose father Guido di Savino had emigrated from Italy to Flanders at the end of the fifteenth century, which acted as a catalyst for the revival of maiolica tile making. Frans Andries brought with him skills in painting Antwerp-inspired mannerist designs and entered into partnership with the Sevillian tile maker Roque Hernández in 1561. When in 1577 the enormous Salón de Carlos V in the Alcazar in Seville needed to be tiled with maiolica wainscoting, it was Hernández's son-in-law, Christobal de Augusta, who got the job. The designs with their deep yellow backgrounds show the influence of both Italian and Flemish tile design and are also an example of how tile designs and techniques made their way across Europe through the men who produced them (fig. 138). Valencia and Seville are now accepted as the centres of the early developments and initial flowering of tin-glazed tile production during the fifteenth and first half of the sixteenth century, but during the second half of the sixteenth century Talavera de la Reina became a prominent producer of tin-glazed tiles.

The rise of Talavera de la Reina began in 1563 when King Philip II appointed the Flemish tile maker Jan Floris as his 'servant and tile maker' and gave him the task of providing royal buildings with tiles. Jan Floris, or Juan Flores as he became known, had done his potter's training in Antwerp, Flanders and like the Italian Niculoso Francisco he had come to Spain to ply his trade as a maiolica specialist. Tiles were already being produced in Talavera de la Reina but production was restricted to *cuerda seca* and *arista* tiles. The king's direct interest in maiolica pottery and tiles did not stop at the appointment of Jan Floris as he also ordered the Sevillian potter Jeronimo Montero to Talavera in 1566 with the express purpose of conducting experiments in producing tin-glazed ware.

The tin-glaze technique must have become established quite quickly as the master potter Juan Fernández was commissioned in 1570 to make blue-and-white wall tiles decorated with acanthus leaf patterns for the royal monastery at El Escorial. Churches in Talavera de la Reina were also richly furnished with painted tile panels. One such was Nuestra Señora del Prado which still has late sixteenth and seventeenth-century tile panels in situ that decorate the interior and the exterior of the church. One of the most impressive polychrome panels depicts St Anthony with his pet pig at his feet (fig. 139). An inscription at the bottom of the panel reads 'This Church was rebuilt with the aid of God and of the townsmen in the years of the Lord 1569 and 70, Pius V being Pope and Philip II King of Spain'. Royal interest in the Talavera potteries not only ensured a market for their pottery and tiles in the highest circles but was also an endorsement which created demand for Talavera pottery

throughout Spain and abroad. Talavera did not only export its ceramics, it also exported its knowledge of tile and pottery making to Spain's colonies in South America and in particular to Mexico.

A thriving local pottery industry had already been in existence when the Spaniards conquered Mexico at the beginning of the sixteenth century and from about 1550 onwards Spanish potters from Talavera de la Reina went to Mexico. Here they introduced the potter's wheel and tin-glazing techniques. Puebla became a major pottery centre where these new Spanish methods were combined with indigenous designs. Added to this was the influence of the blue-and-white Chinese porcelain that had begun to reach Mexico during the second half of the sixteenth century. A very distinctive style developed in Puebla that became known as Talavera Poblana. A curious mixture of Spanish, Italian, Islamic and Chinese design motifs, it was used for the decoration of all kinds of ceramic ware and tiles. The latter were in great demand in the seventeenth and eighteenth centuries for the decoration of churches and monasteries. Tiles were usually made of red firing clay covered with a thick white glaze and then painted in blue and white (fig. 140). The tile bodies of Puebla tiles are often slightly convex which adds an interesting visual characteristic when they are used over large wall areas. The figurative subjects on the single tiles can range from saints and angels to animals and hunting scenes, painted in naive but spirited style. Blue-and-white ornamental motifs based on floral designs were also popular: this type of tile can still be seen on the stunning eighteenth-century tiled facade of the baroque church of San Francisco, Acatepec, just outside Puebla.

Meanwhile, back in Spain, Barcelona, the capital of Catalonia, developed tile production much later than Valencia, Seville and Talavera. Although tiles had been made there since the sixteenth century, it was not until the second half of the seventeenth century that a local demand for tiles and pottery led to the growth of a

ABOVE [fig. 140] Tiles depicting a hunting scene. Tin-glazed earthenware. Puebla, Mexico, 18th century. Each tile: *c.* 14 x 14 cm. Private collection.

ABOVE [fig. 141] Panels of tiles in the Casa Convalescència at the former Santa Cruz Hospital, Barcelona, depicting scenes from the life of St Paul, painted by Lorenzo Passoles. Tin-glazed earthenware. Barcelona, Spain, 1550–1600.

sizable ceramics industry. The most notable seventeenth-century tile painter in Barcelona was Lorenzo Passoles who specialized in large religious tile pictures. A fine example of his work is still extant at the Casa Convalescència at Santa Cruz, in Barcelona (fig. 141). This was built with money bequeathed in 1649 by Pau Ferran, a wealthy merchant whose coat of arms can be found in the magnificent tile panels depicting scenes from the life of St Paul lining the walls of the hospital entrance. The panels display a vigorous naturalism and are painted in strong blues, yellows and greens, set in tiled borders decorated with rich baroque ornament.

Tiles with decorative floral motifs that stretched over four tiles were also popular. These were initially painted in blue but were later produced in the full range of maiolica colours. A particular Catalonian type of tile that was first developed during the second half of the seventeenth century but remained very popular during the eighteenth and nineteenth centuries is known as *rajoles d'oficis* (tiles showing trades). They were mostly executed in polychrome and the scenes painted on single tiles show an intriguing range of figures engaged in various trades and occupations like carpentry, tailoring, shoe making and basket weaving (fig. 143). In this respect they show affinity with seventeenth and eighteenth-century Dutch delftware tiles that have a large range of different trades and occupations painted on single tiles. The range of subject matter on the *rajoles d'oficis* is greater than just the depiction of trades and occupations. There are also scenes showing hunters, musicians, and birds

and animals. Most of these tiles have a narrow yellow border accentuated with a purple line with the subject painted in a dark outline and then coloured in with vibrant yellow, orange-brown, green and blue. Because of their naive charm and small size many of these tiles were collected and have survived in many public and private collections.

Portuguese tin-glazed tiles

Portuguese tiles, or *azulejos* as they are commonly known, are a remarkable feature of the history of Portuguese architecture and design and are still used with exuberance and on a scale that is matched nowhere else in Europe. Initially Portuguese culture absorbed ideas from Spain and this is seen in the use of tiles. The Royal Palace at Sintra, built between 1497 and 1530 during the reign of King Manuel I, benefited from the wealth of Portugal's colonial expansion. It was conceived in a distinctive Gothic-Renaissance style called Manueline, but it also shows a revival of Islamic architectural influence in the choice of tiles as the preferred medium for wall decoration. The tiles used to decorate the palace were made in Seville and consisted of *arista* and *cuerda seca* tiles which were common and popular in Spain at that time.

Spanish tin-glazed tiles came into vogue during the second half of the sixteenth century as can be seen in the Jesuit church of São Roque in Lisbon where so-called 'diamond point' pattern tiles still adorn the walls. But São Roque is also the site of one of the first manifestations of native Portuguese tile making which had begun in earnest during the third quarter of the sixteenth century. The chapel of São Roque has panels of tiles on the walls executed in a naturalistic style showing scenes from the life of St Roque painted by Francisco Matos in 1584 and set within decorative tiled borders of Flemish mannerist ornament.

Home-produced tiles were also used in Portuguese domestic architecture. Away from Lisbon are a number of country houses and palaces with beautiful gardens

ABOVE LEFT [fig. 142] Panel of tiles showing a hunting scene set within as rococo border. Tin-glazed earthenware. Valencia, Spain, *c*.1775. 105 x 105 cm. Museo del Azulejo, Onda, Spain.

ABOVE RIGHT [fig. 143] Tile depicting a basket maker at work. This type of painted tiles with images of occupations is known as *rajoles d'oficis* (tiles showing trades). Tin-glazed earthenware. Catalonia, Spain, 18th century. 13.5 x 13.5 cm. Private collection.

RIGHT [fig. 144] Central detail from a tile panel in a tiled room at the country estate of Quinta da Bacalhôa near Azeitão, Portugal. It shows the biblical story of Susanna and the Elders executed in an assured naturalistic style reminiscent of Italian Renaissance painting. Tin-glazed earthenware. Portugal, 1565.

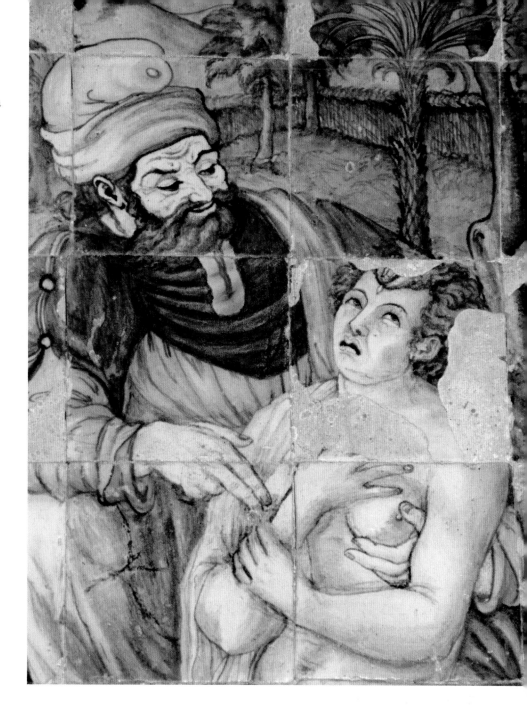

featuring important tile installations. Gardens with water features play a major part in Portuguese landscape architecture and have their roots in Moorish culture. One of the oldest and most distinguished country houses is Quinta da Bacalhôa near Azeitão which has Portuguese tiles dating from the second half of the sixteenth century, making it one of the most important surviving sites of early Portuguese tiles.

The house has a large veranda overlooking the extensive gardens and lake; this is decorated with a tiled dado showing personifications of major European rivers painted in a Flemish mannerist style. The sources of the rivers are shown as reclining male classical figures, pouring water out of large jars. Away from the house in the gardens are tiled benches, some of which date back to the sixteenth century. One bench in particular shows a mythological scene of the Greek god Zeus in the guise of a bull abducting Europa and is a rare survivor of the period. Near the lake are some

LEFT [fig. 145] Detail of a panel of tiles showing a masked lady in the gardens of Fronteira Palace near Lisbon. Tin-glazed earthenware. Portugal, *c.*1670.

tiled rooms (Casa do Tanque) overlooking the water, with all their interiors completely covered in Portuguese tile work. One of the surviving tile panels in those rooms is dated 1565 and shows the biblical story of Susanna and the Elders executed in an assured naturalistic style reminiscent of Italian Renaissance painting (fig. 144).

An astounding example of seventeenth-century garden architecture can be found at the Fronteira Palace not far from Lisbon. Garden walls and steps are covered in pictorial tiles showing the leisure activities of the Portuguese aristocracy, the liberal arts, the signs of the zodiac, and classical gods and goddesses (fig. 145). However, all these are overshadowed by a large water feature known as the Gallery of the Kings. This is a stepped terrace built around 1670 overlooking a narrow strip of water. At the upper level is a balustraded walkway where busts of kings are displayed in niches tiled with unusual tin-glazed tiles with embossed decorations painted in blue

ABOVE [fig. 146] Dado of tiles in the cloisters of the Monastery of São Vicente de Fora in Lisbon showing a landscape set in an elaborate baroque decorative border. The scenes are based on prints from Jean Lepautre (1618–82). Tin-glazed earthenware. Portugal, 1730–35.

and copper lustre. On the lower level just above the water line are tiled arches depicting the ancestors of the Mascarenhas family on horseback.

Portuguese-made tiles were also used on a large scale in Baroque churches and monasteries throughout the country, and were, by this time, often blue and white. This change from the earlier polychrome schemes popular in the late sixteenth and seventeenth centuries may well have been the Portuguese answer to the competition they faced from Dutch tile makers, who at the end of the seventeenth century began to make inroads into the Portuguese tile market. The influence of Dutch blue-and-white tiles was one reason why Portuguese tile painters began to adopt this colour scheme. The strength of the Dutch challenge can clearly be seen in the Church of Madre-de-Deus in Lisbon (now part of the National Tile Museum, in Lisbon) where the walls are completely covered with enormous blue-and-white tile panels showing religious scenes. The panels were made by Jan van Oort in Amsterdam and then shipped to Lisbon where they were installed in 1698.

Fine examples of Portuguese blue-and-white tiles can still be appreciated in the Monastery of São Vicente de Fora in Lisbon (fig. 146). The entrances to the

monastery have panels depicting the Portuguese kings painted by Manual dos Santos around 1710. Even more impressive are the large cloisters which are lined with countless blue-and-white tile panels showing hunting scenes and scenes with fables based on stories by La Fontaine. These are all set within elaborate baroque style borders. Blue and white tiles were used for an even more extravagant venture in the grounds of the royal palace at Queluz where a section of the local river was converted into a tiled canal in 1755 for boating expeditions by the royal family. The tiles that line the entire length of the canal show landscapes and views of towns painted in a fully developed baroque style.

Colour came back later in the eighteenth century but by then it was usually a matter of placing blue-and-white figurative scenes within ornate polychrome rococo borders. This is a feature of the tiled gardens which proliferated in the eighteenth century as a 'must have' for Portuguese palaces. A fine example still extant is the infirmary garden of the Colégio Militar near Lisbon which used to be the palace of the Counts of Mesquitela. The garden has walls on three sides covered with a plethora of tile panels showing classical figures and representations of the visual, musical and liberal arts all executed in polychrome in an exuberant rococo style (fig. 149). The panels are not square but follow the outlines of the figures or ornamental features such as vases and scrolled borders. This kind of cut-out technique is a characteristic of many eighteenth-century Portuguese tile panels.

The great earthquake that destroyed a large part of Lisbon in 1755 led to an even greater use of tiles in all kinds of buildings. The reconstruction of Lisbon was directed by Marquês de Pombal, the prime minister to the king, who set up new industries to aid the recovery. These included the founding of a royal ceramics factory – the Real Fábrica de Louça do Rato – in Lisbon in 1767. The factory also made tiles and this was regarded as a kind of royal endorsement for the continuing practical and decorative use of tiles in Portugal.

ABOVE LEFT [fig. 147] Portuguese tile with a section of a boldly painted face that originally formed part of a larger panel. Tin-glazed earthenware. Portugal, 1750–1800. 13.5 x 12.5 cm. Private collection.

ABOVE RIGHT [fig. 148] Portuguese tile with a painted polychrome floral design. Tin-glazed earthenware. Portugal, 1750–1800. 13.7 x 13.7 cm. Private collection.

OPPOSITE [fig. 149] Panel of tin-glazed tiles in the gardens of the Colégio Militar (formerly the Palácio of the Counts of Mesquitela) near Lisbon, showing the muse of drawing and design. The panel is attributed to the tile painter Francisco Jorge da Costa. Tin-glazed earthenware. Portugal, c.1780.

O Desanho

Northern Europe

At the beginning of the sixteenth century the maiolica technique for making pottery and tiles spread from Italy to northern Europe, first to Flanders and France and then to other countries like Holland and England, following in the wake of the new Renaissance style which had developed in Italy during the fifteenth century and had then swept north. This was characterized by a more naturalistic style in painting and sculpture, using classical forms derived from ancient Roman architecture. In tile making it manifested itself in the replacement of medieval brown and yellow inlaid floor tiles by colourful Italian style maiolica tiles. It also affected the design of the stove tiles which had been a typical northern European phenomenon that had developed during the later Middle Ages, particularly in Germany and Switzerland, and that were also sporadically produced in Britain.

German and Swiss stove tiles

Free-standing wood-burning closed stoves made of special ceramic tiles were a common way of heating rooms in central Europe from the late thirteenth century onwards, springing from the need to have a secure and sustained source of heat during the long winters. Tiled stoves are a very efficient form of heating as they warm rooms more effectively and cleanly than open fires. The heat does not escape up the chimney, and it is safer and easier to keep them going overnight. A good ceramic stove needs to satisfy three basic criteria. It has to produce temperatures high enough to burn wood completely (482 Celsius), and because the hot combustion gasses are circulated through a series of flues in the stove before exiting the chimney, the tiles have to enable the stove to both absorb the heat and to release it gradually and evenly over a long period of time into the room. The tiles which make up these stoves are therefore usually hollow and quite thick in order to retain the heat and are very different from floor and wall tiles. The early medieval stove tiles were often just hollow conically shaped ceramic tiles set into mortar or stone. The hollow design of the tiles increased their surface area and therefore the potential heat radiation. From the fifteenth century onwards stoves were usually made from glazed rectangular relief tiles with deep flanges on all four sides to ensure the stove would be stable when it was built. A typical ceramic stove consisted of a square or rectangular firebox topped by an upper round or rectangular tower-like structure which could be up to 2.5 metres high. Stoves were usually placed in the corner of the room against a wall through which a hole had been cut. The firebox was connected to the wall so it could be stoked from the adjacent room and the fumes extracted there. This meant that there would be no smoke or soot in the room where the stove stood. It was not until the eighteenth century that stoves that could be directly stoked from the front became more common.

The main production centres for stove tiles were in Germany and Switzerland but they were also made in Austria, Hungary, Russia and Sweden. The making of stove tiles and the building of stoves was regarded as a specialist craft in Germany and this is emphasized by the distinction made in the German language between stove tiles and other kinds of tiles. Stove tiles are known as *kacheln* while tiles used on walls and floors are called *fliesen*. In the sixteenth century German stove tiles were being manufactured in large towns like Cologne and Nuremburg. They were usually rectangular or square tiles with relief decorations covered with a monochrome

OPPOSITE [fig. 150] Stove tile with moulded decorations. It shows the figure of Rhetoric, one of the Seven Liberal Arts, beneath a Renaissance arch based on an engraving of 1539 by Hans Sebald Behan. Polychrome lead-glazed earthenware. Germany, 1561. 33.4 x 23.5 cm. British Museum 1853,0423.3. Donated by Sir Augustus Wollaston Franks.

translucent green or brown-black glaze. However, expensive types of stove tile were often more colourful and might be decorated with yellow ochre and blue accentuated with touches of green and brown and elaborate relief designs. These tiles exhibited a wide range of subject matter that conformed to certain conventions in the way the figures are shown. Square stove tiles can have busts of ancient Roman emperors or portraits of contemporary German rulers set within a circular medallion with ornamental corner motifs. Rectangular stove tiles tend to have figures, depicting saints or scenes from the Bible, set beneath archways with columns in the Renaissance style. Another popular theme was figures personifying the seven liberal arts including grammar, logic and rhetoric: these were often based on engravings by German printmakers. Water, earth, fire and air – the four elements – were also a frequent subject matter. Some tiles were dated indicating when a particular stove was built (fig. 150).

In contrast stove tiles made in Switzerland in the seventeenth century were usually flat and coated with white tin glaze painted with cobalt blue and manganese purple. The painted scenes could be elaborate and sometimes had long inscriptions in German Gothic script. The Pfau family, who worked in Winterthur not far from Zurich, specialized in making this kind of stove tile, examples of which are now regarded as minor works of art (fig. 152). Some of the most notable potters of the Pfau dynasty were Hans Heinrich II (1598–1673) and David II Pfau (1644–1702). Pfau tiles were painted with stories from the Old and the New Testaments as well as from the lives of the saints, clearly reflecting the particular interests of the educated clientele for whom they were made. People obviously spent time sitting near warm stoves and would therefore have had time to reflect on the images and inscriptions in front of them.

ABOVE LEFT [fig. 151] Stove tile with moulded decorations. It depicts the king of Bohemia holding a double cup (as Butler of the Empire). Polychrome lead-glazed earthenware. Germany or Bohemia, 1525–50. 16.9 x 14.8 cm. British Museum 1858,0827.6. Donated by Sir Augustus Wollaston Franks.

ABOVE RIGHT [fig. 152] Stove tile probably made in the Pfau family workshop in Winterthur, Switzerland. It shows a scene with a town on the edge of a lake and the sun with a face reflected in the water. The German biblical inscription at the bottom reads 'Selig sind die einens reinen Herzens sind dann sie werden Gott anschauwen' ('Blessed are the pure in heart: for they shall see God'). Tin-glazed earthenware, c.1680. 41 x 27 cm. British Museum OA.7475.

RIGHT [fig. 153] Stove tile with moulded decorations. The elaborate Royal Coat of Arms include the initials I R (Iacobus Rex) for James I. Stove tiles like this were made by potters on the Surrey/Hampshire border in England, between the early 16th and early 17th centuries. Lead-glazed earthenware. England, 1603–25. 34.5 x 25 cm. British Museum 1981,0306.1.

In Britain stove tiles were produced in very small numbers in the sixteenth and early seventeenth century in the south of England and were probably made as special commissions as only the very wealthy could afford such stoves. There is evidence that there were tiled stoves in Henry VIII's Whitehall Palace in the period 1540–45. Like their continental counterparts they were made of elaborately decorated relief tiles coated with a single translucent green lead glaze. Some fine later examples of English stove tiles have survived that show the royal Stuart coat of arms (fig. 153). The use of wood-burning stoves never really caught on because by the end of the sixteenth century coal became popular for burning in stoves, but it could not be used in ceramic wood-burning stoves. Coal was preferable because it was a more suitable fuel for the smaller fireplaces which were being introduced at this stage,

particularly in the upper stories in buildings. Coal was more convenient to carry up the stairs compared with large bundles of wood. This change also coincides with the increasing use of brick for the construction of fireplaces in timber-framed buildings to reduce the risk of fire.

French and Flemish tin-glazed tiles

The influence of Italian maiolica also extended to France and at the beginning of the sixteenth century a number of potteries showed evidence of contact with Italian methods and design. There were workshops in Lyon, Nevers and Rouen, and one of the most busy and prominent belonged to Masséot Abaquesne, a potter and tile maker active in Rouen between 1525 and 1564. He specialized in tile pavements, but also made drug pots and other tin-glazed ware. He used the Italian maiolica technique, painting on white tin glaze with bright colours, and his choice of ceramic decorations was influenced by the style created by the Italian painters like Rosso Fiorentino, who had been invited by François I to come to France and decorate his Château de Fontainebleau. Fontainebleau gave its name to a French-Italian mannerist style based on Renaissance decorative motifs such as grotesques, strap work and putti, sometimes spiced up with a certain degree of mild eroticism, but it also exposed Masséot Abaquesne to the complex figurative compositions favoured by the Italian mannerist painters, and this is evident from the tiled floors which he produced.

Some of Abaquesne's important commissions were carried out for the Constable of France, Anne de Montmorency (1493–1567), at the Château d'Ecouen near Paris. A most impressive floor using tiles decorated with the arms and emblems of de Montmorency was installed in the Salle d'Honneur and is still there today. Two tile panels made for the sacristy of the chapel at Ecouen (now in Musée Condé, Chantilly) are painted in an Italian mannerist style and show two Roman heroes.

ABOVE [fig. 154] Floor tiles from the workshop of Masséot Abaquesne. The left-hand tile depicts an Italian style 'grotesque' motif in the form of a winged harpy. Tin-glazed earthenware. Rouen, France, *c*.1551. Each tile: 10.8 x 10.8 cm. British Museum 1853,0401.70–71. Donated by Sir Augustus Wollaston Franks.

ABOVE [fig.155] Tiles from the workshop of Masséot Abaquesne. The one on the left shows the face of a man dressed like a jester. Tin-glazed earthenware. Rouen, France, c.1551. 11 x 11 cm. British Museum 1853,0401.68–69. Donated by Sir Augustus Wollaston Franks.

One is Mucius Scaevola plunging his arms into burning coals; the other depicts Marcus Curtius leaping on horseback into the chasm opened by an earthquake in the Forum of Rome. This panel also incorporates a banner with the inscription 'A Rouen 1542'. Other tile commissions carried out by Abaquesne's workshop were for Château de la Batie d'Urfe (now in the Louvre) and depict Faith and Justice with various grotesque designs that include a harpy, naked to the waist down, with the lower part of her body terminating in ringlets of ribbons. These tiles based on classical mythology and Roman history plainly show the influence of the Italian Renaissance (fig. 154).

If Abaquesne is an example of a French potter influenced by Italian techniques and artistic notions, there are also instances where the technique of making tin-glazed pottery and tiles was directly introduced by immigrant Italians. A celebrated case in point was Guido di Savino, a native of Castel Durante who had moved to Antwerp in Flanders (now part of Belgium) at the end of the fifteenth century. Antwerp at that time was an important harbour city with a flourishing business and cultural life and was an ideal place to manufacture and sell a new kind of pottery. By 1510 Guido di Savino was, according to local records, well established. He had married a local woman and changed his name to the more Flemish sounding Andries. Piccolpasso, who was himself a native of Castel Durante, later referred to Guido in his *Three Books of the Potter's Art*. He wrote 'In Flanders quarried clay is used. I mean at Antwerp, where this art was introduced some time ago by one Guido di Savino of this place [Castel Durante] and is still carried on at the present day by his sons'. Guido Andries manufactured pottery and tiles by covering already fired clay pots, plates and tiles with white tin glaze and painting decorations on them in blue, yellow, orange and green in the Italian manner. This strikingly colourful maiolica pottery soon became very popular and tiles made by this technique were used as floor tiles as was the fashion in Italy and France.

LEFT [fig. 156] Border tile with a strap-work pattern. Tin-glazed earthenware. France, 1553. International Ceramics Museum, Faenza, Italy.

ABOVE [fig. 157] Flemish tiles from Antwerp on the floor of the Vyne Chapel, Basingstoke, Hampshire, England, early 16th century. The profile and three-quarter portraits show the influence of Italian maiolica tiles. Tin-glazed earthenware. National Trust.

Maiolica tiles made in Antwerp were also exported to England since there is a remarkable early example at the Vyne, Sherborne St John, near Basingstoke. The Vyne is a redbrick Tudor house built between 1500 and 1520 for William Sandys, Lord Chamberlain under Henry VIII. The chapel in the house has a floor (re-laid at a later date) covered with maiolica tiles, many of which are surviving Antwerp products (fig. 157). They are painted and laid in the Italian manner and though several of the figurative tiles show portraits of men clean shaven with long hair cut level at the back of the neck and wearing caps and clothes in true early sixteenth-century style, there are also classical busts of men and women wearing laurel wreaths which show a strong link to Italian maiolica tiles. The Flemish connection and therefore a possible link with the workshop of Guido Andries have been established by examining the inscriptions on some of the tiles which depict busts of men and women. Names like Lisebeth (Elizabeth), Iasper (Jasper) and Iannet (Jannet) are Flemish ways of spelling these names. One tile in particular showing a jester is labelled *Sotge* which is the Flemish word for fool. An excellent case for this argument was made by the ceramic historian Bernard Rackham in his ground breaking book *Early Netherlands Maiolica* (1926).

Another important floor of Antwerp manufacture (now in the Royal Museum of Art and History in Brussels) was made for the Abbey of Herckenrode in Flanders, and

a document dated 5 May 1532 ordering the floor issued by Abbess Mathilda de Lexhy has survived. The tiles were delivered in 1533 and were laid in the Italian fashion of square tiles flanked by elongated hexagonal tiles (fig. 158). Like those at the Vyne Chapel, the square tiles carry portrait busts and images of animals so this floor may also have been a product of the workshop of Guido Andries.

Guido's workshop was an important concern. He married twice and had a large family who were all involved in the pottery business. Potteries were kept within families and skills passed from father to son. After his death his second wife Anna van Dueren married François Frans, a local potter, in 1543, and in 1562 she passed the business to her son Lucas Andries who was active until at least 1572. However the fortunes of Antwerp were changing. At that time Spain ruled the Low Countries, but when the Dutch demanded independence, war broke out between Spain and the Netherlands. Antwerp was at the centre of the hostilities and was sacked a number of times. Merchants, artists and craftsmen left the city for safer places in the north or moved to England. The maiolica potters also left Antwerp, amongst them Guido Andries' sons. Frans Andries moved to Seville, Spain in 1561, Joris Andries settled in Middelburg, Zeeland, The Netherlands in 1564, and Jasper Andries and Jacob Jansen came to England and settled in Norwich in 1567. This is how the technique of making maiolica pottery and tiles spread to Holland and England where it became the progenitor of the famous Dutch and English delftware industries.

ABOVE [fig. 158] A section of floor tiles from the Flemish Abbey of Herckenrode. The tiles are laid out in the Italian fashion: square tiles are surrounded by elongated hexagonal tiles. The square tiles are painted with half-length portraits, animals and rosettes. The blue-and-white hexagonal tiles show Islamic inspired palmettes/arabesque motifs and the polychrome hexagonal tiles feature Italianate floral pattern. Tin-glazed earthenware. Attributed to the workshop of Guido Andries, Antwerp, Flanders, 1533. Royal Museum of Art and History, Brussels.

RIGHT [fig. 159] Dutch tiles with a cross motif in the centre filled with arabesque motifs and large arabesque corner motifs reversed in white against blue, 1580–1600. When this design is extended over sixteen tiles it shows cross-shaped motifs alternating with eight pointed stars revealing a pattern influenced by Islamic tiles. Tin-glazed earthenware. The Netherlands, 1580–1600. Each tile: *c.* 13.4 x 13.4 cm. Nederlands Tegelmuseum, Otterlo, The Netherlands.

Dutch delftware tiles

Since the Middle Ages floor tiles had been made in Holland from red firing clay covered with a thin coat of transparent lead glaze. Sometimes patterns of white clay were laid into the red tile body. During the second half of the sixteenth century these tiles were superseded by the newly introduced painted maiolica tiles made by immigrant potters from Antwerp. Despite the attractive qualities of maiolica tiles, they were not very suitable for walking on as the painted decorations wore off quickly if subjected to heavy wear. This may not have mattered for rich Italian or French nobility who could replace worn floor tiles when needed, but in the context of Dutch middle-class homes this was not a realistic option. It was therefore not long before the thrifty Dutch began to use these tiles on walls where they would last longer.

At the beginning of the seventeenth century Holland had emerged as an independent nation free of Spanish domination and its ports and worldwide sea trade brought considerable prosperity. Towns expanded and many new houses were built. The absence in Holland of an absolute monarchy, a powerful landowning aristocracy and a centralized church meant that there was more power in the hands of *burghers* living in semi-independent towns which pledged allegiance to a ruler known as a *Stadtholder*. Holland was a mercantile society and during the economic boom of the seventeenth century a large multi-layered middle class was created who all shared

to a greater or lesser extent in the national wealth. So many householders could afford tiles to make their homes more hygienic, comfortable and attractive. In Holland canals intersected many towns and the high water table meant that many town houses stood with their foundations in water, resulting in constant problems with damp. Tiles were therefore used in cellars, but also in kitchens, in fireplaces and as wall skirting, closing the gap between the floor and the wall, and in all these locations they proved effective against damp and dirt. Paintings by seventeenth-century artists like Jan Vermeer and Pieter de Hoogh confirm how tiles were used in Dutch domestic interiors. Even in the seventeenth century Dutch housewives were noted for the high standards of cleanliness in their homes and tiles helped them to achieve this. The glass-like surfaces of tiles were easily cleaned, and their patterns and pictures introduced a decorative element, so millions of tiles were produced to keep pace with increased demand.

The design evolution of Dutch tiles shows they were subject to changing fashions. The tiles produced at the end of the sixteenth century were not very different from the sixteenth-century Flemish tin-glazed tiles with their Italianate designs. Square pieces of pink firing clay were covered with white tin glaze and painted with polychrome decorations that ran over more than one tile. At the beginning of the seventeenth century when the Dutch wall tile became an important functional and decorative wall cladding, different designs were introduced. Animals, flowerpots, and designs with grapes and pomegranates (fig. 160) were used on single tiles as

ABOVE LEFT [fig. 160] Panel of Dutch tiles with a design based on pomegranates, carrots and grapes. Only four tiles are needed to show the complete pattern. Polychrome tin-glazed earthenware. The Netherlands, 1580–1620. This type of tile was also made in London at the beginning of the 17th century. Each tile: *c.* 13.2 x 13.2 cm. British Museum 1853,0401.47. Donated by Sir Augustus Wollaston Franks.

ABOVE RIGHT [fig. 161] A rare set of Dutch tiles with a picture of a naturalistically painted tulip stretching over two tiles. Tulips were carefully cultivated and were much prized and expensive flowers in The Netherlands in the 17th century. Tin-glazed earthenware. Probably made in Hoorn, The Netherlands, 1620–40. Each tile: *c.* 13.2 x 13.2 cm. Nederlands Tegelmuseum, Otterlo, The Netherlands.

ABOVE [fig. 162] Dutch tiles with blue-and-white designs copied from Chinese porcelain. Imported blue-and-white Chinese porcelain had an enormous influence on the decoration and design of Dutch delftware pottery and to a lesser extent on the decoration of tiles. Tin-glazed earthenware. The Netherlands, 1620–40. Each tile: *c.* 13.2 x 13.2 cm. Nederlands Tegelmuseum, Otterlo, The Netherlands.

central motifs within a diamond-shaped or circular border. The corners of each tile were filled with stylized leaf motifs executed in the so-called 'reversing technique' where the background around the pattern is painted in blue leaving the actual design standing out in white. When put together on the wall the corner motifs met and formed large decorative units almost equal in size to the central figurative designs.

A decisive change in the decoration of early seventeenth-century Dutch tiles occurred when the United Dutch East India Company, founded in 1602, began to import blue-and-white Chinese porcelain. The craze for Ming porcelain that followed had an adverse effect on the local manufacturers of maiolica pottery, although tiles were not directly affected as no tiles were imported from China. To maintain their hold on the market, Dutch potters began to imitate Chinese porcelain. Although they could not make actual porcelain, by preparing their clay more carefully, making their earthenware thinner and painting blue-and-white Chinese motifs on the white tin glaze, they produced a type of pottery which at a first glance was almost indistinguishable from real porcelain (fig. 162). The term 'delftware' often used to describe it comes from the town of Delft where so much high quality tin-glazed pottery was made. Tiles followed the fashions and around 1620 Dutch tiles with blue-and-white Chinese designs appeared on the market. A popular scene on tiles was the so-called 'Chinese garden', which usually consisted of a variety of plants, flowers and birds copied from Chinese porcelain set within a decorative border with Chinese meander motifs in the four corners.

LEFT [fig. 163] Dutch tile showing an artist behind his easel and ox-head corner motifs. Scenes from everyday life in 17th-century Holland were a special feature of Dutch tiles at that time. Tin-glazed earthenware. The Netherlands, 1640–60. 13.2 x 13.2 cm. Nederlands Tegelmuseum, Otterlo, The Netherlands.

The fashion for Chinese designs on tiles did not last long and by 1650 the interest of the Dutch tile painter had turned to other more domestic subjects. Pictures of men and women in Dutch costumes, of trades and occupations, of soldiers, cupids and animals began to appear on tiles, mostly painted in blue and embellished with all kinds of different corner motifs (figs 163, 164). By the end of the seventeenth century the range of subject matter had been extended with sea creatures, soldiers on horseback, landscapes, ships, biblical scenes and mythological subjects all becoming popular. Engravings often served as examples for tile decorations. Around the same time, the corner motifs became smaller and were sometimes omitted altogether.

A peculiarly Dutch theme on many tiles was the depiction of children's games. This was part of a wider Dutch artistic tradition which had its roots in sixteenth-century Flemish painting as can be seen in *Children's Games* by Pieter Bruegel (*c.*1525–69) in the Kunsthistorisches Museum in Vienna. Bruegel showed over ninety different games and it was this aspect of children's everyday activities that inspired Dutch tile painters (fig. 165). They depicted games like walking on stilts, skipping, shuttle cock, leapfrog, playing with hoops or on a swing, archery, blowing soap bubbles, flying kites and pole jumping. These images also carried underlying meanings with moral messages. Children blowing soap bubbles could indicate the notion of *homo bulla* ('man is like bubble'), a symbol of the fugitive and transitory

OPPOSITE [fig. 164] Dutch tiles showing a variety of animals with ox-head corner motifs. Tin-glazed earthenware. The Netherlands, 1650–75. Each tile: 13.2 x 13.2 cm. Nederlands Tegelmuseum, Otterlo, The Netherlands.

nature of life, since soap bubbles are beautiful but short-lived things. Walking on stilts could signify pretentiousness or getting above your status and this kind of symbolism appealed to Dutch Calvinist notions of morality.

The many images painted on tiles were not executed freehand even if the artist could copy them from a print or picture. The best way of producing an image was to use a specially made piece of paper (*spons*) which had the design pricked through with a pin. This was placed on the unfired white tin glaze and charcoal was 'dusted' through the little holes which left a faint imprint on the tile once it was lifted away. The dotted lines on the tile acted as a guide to the painter who would usually trace the outlines first before adding other tints and shades. The only things that were sometimes painted freehand were the little corner motifs, which may well have been one of the tasks given to apprentices.

Delft had more than thirty pottery factories in operation by the end of the seventeenth century, and although not many tiles were actually made in Delft, the ones that were, were often of outstanding quality. The domination of the Delft factories in terms of their numbers, output and quality led to tin-glazed pottery and tiles made in Delft to be known as 'delftware'. Potters in Delft had become very successful in imitating various forms of Chinese porcelain and in some instances this expertise was transferred to tiles. Some exquisite tile panels have been attributed to De Roos (The Rose) factory in Delft which combine in-glaze pigments such as blue

ABOVE [fig. 166] Plaque depicting Daniel in the Lion's Den. A high quality piece of delftware painting based on an engraving after a painting by Peter Paul Rubens (1577–1640). Tin-glazed earthenware. Delft, The Netherlands, 1670–90. 28.6 x 32.5 cm. British Museum 1888,1110.30. Donated by Sir Augustus Wollaston Franks.

and purple with on-glaze enamels like red, yellow and gold. The Grieksche A (Greek A) factory in Delft was awarded prestigious commissions by King William III of England and his wife Queen Mary II. When Hampton Court, near London, was refurbished between 1689 and 1694 the Grieksche A was asked to make tiles and pottery for Queen Mary's dairy based on designs by the famous French immigrant designer Daniel Marot.

A feature of Dutch tile production was the development of specialist tile factories. The very early workshops set up in the second half of the sixteenth century, like those in Haarlem, would have had a mixed output of pottery and tiles. During the course of the seventeenth century, when the demand for tiles rose, more specialization took place and tile 'factories' emerged that were capable of a large output. Rotterdam became a huge tile production centre with up to nineteen factories in operation during the seventeenth and eighteenth centuries, of which De Bloempot and the Delftsevaart factories were the most notable. De Bloempot factory was set up in 1675, and came into the ownership of the Aalmis family in 1692. Under the family's direction it grew into a prominent concern that not only supplied tiles to the local area but also found an export market in Germany where its tiles were taken by river transport. Around 1730 De Bloempot factory supplied thousands of tiles for the Jagdschloss Falkenlust at Brühl near Cologne built for the Elector Clemens August where the grand staircase is still decorated with specially designed tiles showing hunting scenes with falcons made in Rotterdam.

The Delftsevaart, founded c.1640, became well known because of the high quality

LEFT [fig. 167] Dutch tile panel showing an Italianate scene of travellers resting near a fountain. Tin-glazed earthenware. Attributed to the Aalmis factory in Rotterdam, The Netherlands, 1720–40. Each tile: *c.* 12.5 x 12.5 cm. British Museum OA.4581. Donated by Sir Augustus Wollaston Franks.

ABOVE [fig. 168] Dutch tile with an elaborate purple border design and a central scene painted in blue showing a hunter returning home. Tin-glazed earthenware. The Netherlands, *c.*1750. 13 x 13 cm. Private collection.

output of the tile painter Cornelis Boumeester who worked there between 1676 and 1732. He became a renowned specialist in painting tile panels with harbour scenes, seascapes and sea battles, all executed in fine tones of blue and often signed with his initials. His work was in great demand and his panels were exported abroad and used in such prestigious locations as Château de Rambouillet near Paris, built for the Comte de Toulouse about 1730.

The focus on specialist tile production also meant technical improvements in the way tiles were made. The concentration of factories in big production centres like Delft and Rotterdam made economies of scale possible. Support industries were established to supply pigments and glazes which were ground at windmills adapted for this purpose, and clay preparation plants situated on the city outskirts prepared and cleaned both the local and imported clays. Wood was cut and transported to the factories to fire the kilns. All these raw materials were moved by boat along the extensive canal system which was an efficient means of transportation, and once the tiles were made they were sent by boat to domestic and overseas markets. These better prepared Dutch clays meant that tile manufacturers could make their products thinner and therefore not only save on the cost of clay but also fire more tiles in one kiln session. This had an impact on prices. Lighter tiles were also easier for the tradesmen fixing them to handle.

Factory output, given the production methods of the day, was staggering and

OPPOSITE [fig. 169] Dutch fireplace decorated with tiles. This type of fireplace is called a *smuiger* and has been decorated with painted tiles showing scenes from the Old and the New Testaments. Originally from a house in Wormer near Zaandam. The tiles in their original context had five functions: they were fireproof, easily cleaned, reflected heat into the room, added colour and decoration to the interior, and with their scenes from the Bible aided the religious life of those sitting around the fireplace. Tin-glazed earthenware, 1800–1850. Nederlands Tegelmuseum, Otterlo, The Netherlands.

the survival of written records, such as the oven books at the Tichelaar factory in Makkum in Friesland (the factory still exists today) have made it possible to estimate the number of tiles made since the late seventeenth century. It has been calculated that some 125 million tiles were made in this one factory alone. If this figure is extrapolated to all the other factories in Holland it is easy to see how dominant and productive the Dutch tile industry was and how it was able to outstrip foreign competition. Not only could the Dutch tile makers satisfy a strong domestic market and export tiles abroad to places where few tiles were made, but they were also able to export tiles to countries like Spain and Portugal where there was already a strong indigenous tile industry.

If at the end of the seventeenth century and the beginning of the eighteenth the export market for Dutch tiles had been extended with high profile commissions from abroad, the home market had undergone changes which affected the production of tiles. Towards the end of the seventeenth century the demand for tiles in urban areas declined. Changes in fireplace design influenced by French fashions were one cause as fireplaces became smaller and fewer tiles were used. At the same time the demand for decorative tiles in rural areas increased. Well-to-do farmers installed large fireplaces decorated with tiles and occasionally whole rooms were lined with them. In the Zaandam region north of Amsterdam where houses were often built of wood rather than brick, large fireplaces were particularly in vogue because a special type called *smuigers* was developed in this area for use in the principal living room to make fireplaces safer for wooden houses. *Smuigers* stretched from floor to ceiling with a canopy that curved outwards at the top. They could be used for open fires but it was also possible to place a cast-iron stove below the canopy. Up to 300 tiles might be needed to tile one *smuiger* and these would often be decorated with landscapes or biblical scenes. The latter were particularly in demand as they appealed to the taste of strict Protestant farming communities (fig. 169).

During the eighteenth century there was also an increased use of tiles with purely decorative patterns mostly painted in blue or purple. Purple became an increasingly popular colour at that time and it was not uncommon then to see tiles with purple borders surrounding a blue painted scene in the centre. The influence of French decorative design is noticeable on many tiles with rococo scrolls or the elaborate borders that were used for landscape tiles. Tile panels with ships, bird cages, views of towns or portraits of Dutch royalty were also in demand.

The late eighteenth century was a difficult time for the Dutch tile industry. The rising fashion for wallpaper was damaging to the industry and so was Napoleon's conquest of The Netherlands which had an adverse effect on Dutch trade and exports. The increasing output of Staffordshire tableware was also felt by the whole Dutch tin-glazed earthenware industry. Many factories had to close and tiles were manufactured in only a few places of which Rotterdam, Utrecht, Makkum and Harlingen were the main centres, managing to survive into the nineteenth century.

English delftware tiles

The technique of making tin-glazed ceramic ware was brought to Britain by Flemish and Dutch potters like Jasper Andries and Jacob Jansen who had settled in Norwich in 1567. In 1570 they both went to London to petition Queen Elizabeth for permission to set up a pottery business for the production of 'Galley Pavinge Tiles and Vessels

for Apothecaries'. The petition was not successful and Andries moved to Colchester in 1571, but Jansen stayed in London where in 1571 he is recorded with fellow Flemish potters as a 'painter of pots' in Aldgate. In Aldgate they made tin-glazed floor tiles alongside tin-glazed pottery, and Flemish potters may well have been responsible for some of the sixteenth-century polychrome floor tiles showing animals within a border of concentric circles (fig. 170).

Dutch potters also moved to London in the seventeenth century. A Dutch potter by the name of Christian Wilhelm was active in Pickleherring, Southwark, and established a pothouse there in c.1618, while in 1676 the Dutch potter Jan Ariens van Hamme moved from Delft to Lambeth in London for 'making Tiles and Porcelain and other earthen wares after the way practiced in Holland'. His workshop has been credited with the production of the 'Popish Plot' tiles based on engraved scenes found on playing cards made in 1679 depicting the supposed plot hatched in 1678 by so-called papists to assassinate Charles II (figs 171, 172). Compared to production in Holland at that time, however, the output of delftware tiles in London was small.

Not only was the output small, the London delftware industry had to compete with imported Dutch tiles. The use of tiles had changed and the fashion in Holland, where tiles were no longer applied to flooring but were used in fireplaces or as skirting to close the gap between the wall and the floor, was also catching on in London. Tiles made in London were usually 12 to 15 millimetres thick while the Dutch imported tiles were thinner and at the middle of the seventeenth century had a thickness of 10 to 12 millimetres. By c.1670–80 Dutch tiles could be as thin as 8 millimetres, which made them lighter and easier to handle. The thicker London tiles were fine for floors but less suitable for walls. Although London tile makers could copy the blue-and-white scenes on Dutch tiles, they could not make their tiles thinner as they did not have the superior clay preparation methods developed by the Dutch at that time. This

ABOVE [fig, 170] Tiles featuring a lion and a cow within a border of concentric circles. Polychrome tin-glazed earthenware. Probably originating from Aldgate, London, England, 1590–1620. Similar tiles were also made in The Netherlands. Average size: 13.5 x 13.5 cm. British Museum 1839,1029.106.

ABOVE LEFT [fig. 171] Tile attributed to the workshop of Jan Ariens van Hamme. The painted scene depicts the execution of the five Jesuits and is one of a series of tiles showing images from the Popish Plot of 1678, based on printed playing cards that were in circulation at that time. Tin-glazed earthenware. Lambeth, London, England, c.1680. 12.3 x 12.3 cm. British Museum 1987,1204.1.

ABOVE RIGHT [fig. 172] Tile painted in purple with a scene from the Popish Plot series. The scene shows Titus Oates disclosing the plot to King Charles II and his Council; although the supposed plot was hatched in 1678, the design of the tile without border and corner motifs suggest a later date for its manufacture. Tin-glazed earthenware. London, England, 1700–50. 13 x 13 cm. British Museum 2009,8015.4. Purchased with contribution from the Newmarch Fund.

is perhaps one reason why the manufacture of delftware tiles in London declined in the middle of the seventeenth century and why an import ban was imposed on Dutch tiles in 1672. It was not until the eighteenth century when production techniques in England had improved and tile makers could make thinner tiles suitable for walls that the manufacture of tiles in London became a more substantial industry again.

During the eighteenth century tiles were not only manufactured in London but also in other centres like Bristol and Liverpool; some tiles were also produced at the Delftfield factory in Glasgow. Until about 1750 many English delftware tiles were often closely based on Dutch examples, particularly those made in London. Factories in Lambeth produced single tiles depicting flower vases, landscapes, pastoral scenes, ships and biblical subjects (fig. 173). The Dutch influence is perhaps not surprising given the Dutch potters who had settled in London in the seventeenth century. However the uses of tiles in Britain were not as varied as they were in Holland: they were mainly used in fireplaces or sometimes for tiled alcoves with washbasins or in dairies of large country houses. Occasionally English delftware tiles were also used as signs for eighteenth-century inns or coffee houses. Special tin-glazed tiles called 'pill tiles' were produced for pharmacists for making pills and powders because of the tiles' smooth and hygienic surfaces.

Tile production in Bristol dates from about 1720 and started at the Limekiln Lane and Redcliffe Bank potteries. Biblical tiles and tiles with figures in landscapes were produced, often strongly reminiscent of Dutch work in their choice of subjects and corner motifs. But over time Bristol tile makers began to make more unusual and uniquely English tiles with birds and chinoiserie figures painted in polychrome set within *bianco-sopra-bianco* borders. The term *bianco-sopra-bianco* comes from Italian and means 'white on white'. It is achieved by painting with saturated white tin glaze on a tin glaze that has less tin oxide in it and is therefore slightly bluish.

The effect of white on white is very subtle and was reserved for more upmarket tiles. It is a particular English feature normally not found on Dutch delftware tiles.

The Liverpool tile industry dates from 1710 when Richard Holt set up a pottery in Lord Street. During the eighteenth century Liverpool became a leading production centre and a great variety of tiles was made consisting of landscapes, harbour scenes and biblical subjects as well as tiles with *bianco-sopra-bianco* borders (figs 174, 175). It was also in Liverpool that in 1756 the first experiments with transfer printing on white tin-glazed tiles were carried out by the printer John Sadler and his partner Guy Green. Their tiles show an intriguing range of subject matter. Their images were first taken from wood blocks and then from engraved copper plates, making them the harbingers of the Industrial Revolution and posing a direct challenge to hand-painted tiles.

English and Dutch delftware tiles have a closely interwoven history and to the uninitiated it can sometimes be difficult to tell them apart, particularly the more common blue-and-white variety. There are differences, however, which can be seen if a close examination is made of the structure of the tile body, the glaze and the way in which the tiles have been painted. Generally speaking Dutch tiles are painted in a more assured manner and with greater deftness. The tin glaze of Dutch tiles is usually whiter because it often contains more tin oxide. English tin glaze is somewhat bluish and much glossier and smoother than Dutch glaze and does not craze easily. On English tiles the blue decorations have sometimes sunk below the level of the glaze, creating perceptible hollows. This is a particular feature of some tiles from Liverpool. The clay body of English tiles tends to be harder and denser than that of the Dutch, which is softer with a more sandy texture. This made Dutch tiles easier to trim and for that reason it seemed builders sometimes preferred Dutch tiles to English ones. Nail holes left on the front of the tile as part of the cutting and trimming

ABOVE LEFT [fig. 173] Tile with a biblical scene showing John the Baptist baptizing Jesus in the river Jordan. Tin-glazed earthenware. London, England, *c*.1750. 12.8 x 12.8 cm. Private collection.

ABOVE RIGHT [fig. 174] Tile with a *bianco-sopra-bianco* border with a floral motif in the centre. Tin-glazed earthenware. The tin glaze is slightly bluish which helps to create a more effective contrast with the white border. Liverpool, England, 1760–75. 12.8 x 12.8 cm. Private collection.

process are very common on Dutch tiles, but less common on English tiles, which sometimes have nail holes on the back.

During the second half of the eighteenth century English delftware potters and their counterparts in Holland began to suffer from the competition of industrially made tableware produced at well-organized factories in Staffordshire under the direction of progressive potters like Josiah Wedgwood and Josiah Spode. Their products were superior to delftware, and Wedgwood's creamware and Spode's blue-and-white under-glaze printed ceramics had driven most traditional delftware pottery makers out of existence by about 1800. A few delftware factories in London survived into the early nineteenth century but by 1850 they had all closed down.

DANTE

FROM INDUSTRY TO ART

So we must be a law to ourselves, and when we get a tile or a plate to ornament remember two things: first, the confined space or odd shape we have to work in; and second, the way in which the design has to be executed.

William Morris

Some Hints on Pattern-Designing, 1881

The Industrial Revolution began in Britain during the second half of the eighteenth century and reached its climax in the nineteenth century. In Britain the necessary economic and institutional conditions were found that allowed entrepreneurs to capitalize on inventions bringing the transformation from hand power to mechanized production, resulting in the greater and faster production of goods. These goods, previously produced by hand in small workshops, were now manufactured in factories on a production line basis with the aid of machinery driven by water or steam power. Raw materials and the finished products were transported to and from the factories via a newly built canal and road system and later in the nineteenth century also by rail. The resulting economic prosperity meant that factory-made products were in demand in a growing domestic market as well as in new markets worldwide.

The changes in tile production were typical of the Industrial Revolution. Until the middle of the eighteenth century tiles were made and decorated by hand. Then the development of new decoration techniques like transfer printing and inventions like dust pressing resulted in larger scale, faster and cheaper production. Tile manufacture shifted from small to large purpose built factories where tiles were fired in huge bottle kilns with the aid of cheap coal (figs 177, 178). Although tile factories were located in areas rich in clay materials and coal, improved transportation systems meant that special clays could be brought in from further afield when needed.

The Industrial Revolution also resulted in the rapid growth of towns and cities, bringing with it increased demand for tiles. In the home, industrially produced tiles were used for their hard-wearing qualities in hallways and on floors and for their waterproof and hygienic properties in kitchens, bathrooms and lavatories, while their

OPPOSITE [fig. 176] Detail of one of the tiled walls in the former reading room of Leeds Central Library, West Yorkshire, England, opened in 1884. The walls are covered with dust-pressed relief tiles by E. Smith & Co., Coalville, Leicestershire. The terracotta roundel of the poet Dante was made by the sculptor Benjamin Creswick.

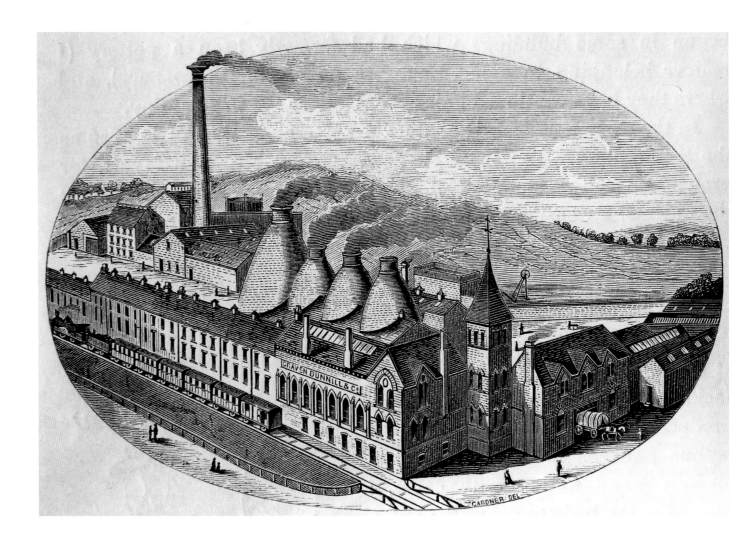

resistance to fire made them well suited for fireplaces. Tiles were not only used in domestic settings but also in various types of buildings in the expanding cities and towns including churches, schools, hospitals, hotels, theatres, shops, railway stations and civic buildings such as town halls, museums and libraries. Increasingly stringent building regulations stipulated that buildings should be more hygienic and fireproof and this led to an increased use of tiles on floors, walls and ceilings to meet these new requirements. Enterprising tile manufacturers who understood the market potential invested in new patents and built factories to satisfy the huge demand for tiles.

The adoption of the methods of mass production also brought about an increased awareness of the limitations inherent in machine manufacture. Some considered the cheapness of mechanical production to be matched by the nastiness of the designs. Throughout the nineteenth century there were a number of attempts to address this problem. One of these, the Arts and Crafts Movement, proved unrealistic as its adherents completely shunned the machine and advocated the return to good design via old-fashioned hand work. More fruitful was the employment of trained artists and designers by large-scale industry which saw tile manufacturers taking on prominent designers either 'in-house' or on a freelance basis and making high quality design possible within the constraints of mechanical processes.

British industrial tile production methods also influenced tile making on the

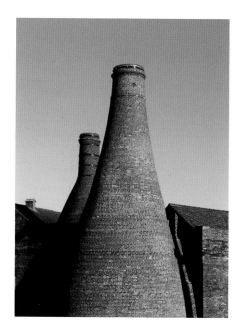

ABOVE [fig. 178] Two nineteenth-century bottle kilns at what is now the Gladstone Pottery Museum in Longton, Stoke-upon-Trent, England.

ABOVE RIGHT [fig. 179] Tile printed by John Sadler. It depicts a scene from Molière's *Le Dépit Amoureaux* based on a print by the French engraver Laurent Cars (1699–1771). Tin-glazed, with an on-glaze transfer print. Liverpool, England, 1756–7. 12.8 x 12.8 cm. British Museum 1905,1018.6. Donated by Thomas Boynton.

European continent and in the United States where British tile technology was either adapted or further developed to suit local conditions, while several new factories were set up with the help of immigrant British tile makers. In this way the new production methods quickly spread worldwide and made the nineteenth century arguably the most important in the history of tiles. It was the age when tiles were transformed from ornaments for the elite to objects of everyday use and became artefacts available to all.

British tiles

British tiles produced during the second half of the eighteenth and throughout the nineteenth century show how the impact of new production methods and decoration techniques created many new types of tile for use on floors, walls and even ceilings. The industrial transformation of tiles was manifold: as objects they were mass produced, as artefacts they were used for an infinite variety of practical and decorative purposes, and as images they depicted a large range of designs and subject matter. Huge new markets opened up and millions of tiles were produced to satisfy an ever growing demand. Tiles from this period show enormous diversity in how they were made and decorated and were aimed at a multi-layered market determined by the purchasing power of the client.

Early transfer printed tiles

An early instance of the adoption of new industrial processes in the decoration of tiles was the method of transfer printing. Painting tiles by hand was labour intensive and costly and in the middle of the eighteenth century attempts were already being made to decorate tiles more quickly. Experiments with transfer printing on tiles were undertaken as early as 1756 by the printer John Sadler of Liverpool who used white glazed but otherwise undecorated tiles obtained from local delftware potteries. An affidavit of 27 July 1756, sworn in front of witnesses, states that John Sadler and his assistant Guy Green printed more than twelve hundred tiles within the space of six hours, many more than any painter could do by hand. The novelty of the technique lay in transferring an image from an engraved copper plate to a plain white tin-glazed delftware tile with the aid of a thin sheet of gelatine (bat printing), although the first experiments were achieved by taking prints from wood blocks. Some of the printed tiles were later coloured by hand with on-glaze enamels, but most of them are without extra colour and were printed in monochrome black, red or blue. The decorations were fired onto the surface of the tile in a muffle kiln at a low temperature (between 600 and 800 Celsius.)

The range of subjects on Sadler & Green tiles is considerable. There are numerous open-air scenes with figures of fashionable society as well as scenes from rustic life.

ABOVE [fig. 180] Tile printed by Guy Green. The figure represents the famous actor David Garrick (1717–79) in the character of Don John in *The Chances*, an early 17th-century play by John Beaumont and Francis Fletcher. Earthenware, tin-glazed with on-glaze transfer print from a copper plate. Liverpool, England, *c.*1777–80. 12.8 x 12.8 cm. British Museum 1887,0307,E.166.19. Donated by Sir Augustus Wollaston Franks.

Other themes are ships, games, fables, biblical scenes, romantic ruins, chinoiserie subjects and classical vases. But perhaps the most interesting of all are the portraits of contemporary actors and actresses of the English theatre (fig. 180). They are usually portrayed in their famous stage roles and each tile often bears the name of the actor or actress and the title of the play.

The next steps in technical innovation were taken by Josiah Wedgwood and Josiah Spode, leading figures in the industrialization of the British ceramics industry. During the second half of the eighteenth century Wedgwood developed new clay bodies which were much harder and stronger than delftware. One of these improved clay bodies was creamware which was made of fine pale clay and calcified flint and fired at temperatures between 1,100 and 1,150 Celsius. It was then covered with a clear lead glaze showing the cream colour of the clay body. Creamware was very different from delftware as the latter has a white opaque tin glaze covering a red or yellow earthenware body that was fired at around 1,000 to 1,050 Celsius and was therefore less strong then creamware. Creamware was extensively used for the manufacture of tableware but tiles were also made, particularly for use in dairies.

At the end of the eighteenth century Josiah Spode was instrumental in introducing under-glaze transfer printed decoration which was printed under the glaze instead of on top of it as John Sadler had done. Transfer printed designs on the glaze are very vulnerable to wear but if they are put under a transparent glaze they last as long as the piece of ceramic they decorate. Decorations were often printed in blue derived from cobalt oxide, a suitable and stable colour to be fired at the same temperature as the transparent glaze that covered it. Transfer prints taken from copper plates were now transferred via a piece of special paper and no longer with the aid of vulnerable gelatine bats as John Sadler in Liverpool had done. When transfer paper is used, the copper plate and the piece of paper placed on it have to go through a printing press with steel rollers to force the paper into the engraved lines to make sure they pick up all the inked pigment. Bat printing is suitable for printing small areas but when larger areas have to be covered, such as in the production of transfer printed tableware, paper is a more stable medium in the transfer process.

During the first quarter of the nineteenth century there was limited production of transfer printed tiles by firms like Spode in Stoke-upon-Trent and W. Smith & Co. in Stockton. They made tiles from fine quality white earthenware with scenes reminiscent of the kind of decoration that was also printed on dinner plates. It made sense at that time, when there were no special patterns designed for tiles, to use the available stock of copperplate engraved images made for tableware and adapt them for the small output of wall tiles when these were required. It was not until the 1830s that Copeland & Garrett, the successors of Spode, created transfer printed designs which seem to be specifically created for square tiles. At that time Copeland made tiles of various sizes ranging from 5 inches to 9 inches square (c. 12.5 to 23 centimetres). They showed carefully arranged floral designs or chinoiserie motifs with designs borrowed from Chinese porcelain. Transfer prints could be executed in a single colour like blue or black, or they could be hand decorated with extra colours in a process known as 'print and tint', where parts of the transfer printed design were painted. However, it was not with the manufacture of wall tiles that the age of mass production began but with floor tiles for use in Gothic Revival churches.

Encaustic tiles

The term 'encaustic' was used in the nineteenth century to describe floor tiles of red-brown clay indented with an ornamental clay pattern of a lighter colour. The word 'encaustic' comes from the Greek meaning 'burnt in' and it became the type of tile associated with the movement known as the Gothic Revival. This stemmed from the eighteenth-century romantic interest in medieval ruins and the study of Gothic architectural ornament, which at that time was occasionally applied to domestic interiors like Horace Walpole's Strawberry Hill House near Twickenham. At the beginning of the nineteenth century the interest in the medieval period became more academic and antiquarians began to study and excavate medieval sites and record their findings. In the case of tiles this interest was first linked to the 'rediscovery' of medieval tiles in cathedrals and parish churches and excavations by antiquarians at the sites of monastic ruins, for example the tiled floors at Jervaulx Abbey in Yorkshire which were excavated and recorded in 1807 on the orders of the owner, the Earl of Aylesbury. Unfortunately the floors, with their impressive circular tile arrangements, were left exposed to the ravages of the weather and the pilfering activities of collectors, and most of the pavements had disappeared soon after their discovery.

Interest in medieval tiles was further stimulated by books that combined informative text with reproductions of medieval tiles like John G. Nichols' important work *Examples of Decorative Tiles* published in 1845 with descriptions of medieval sites and many illustrations of medieval tile designs. This was followed in 1858 by Henry Shaw's outstanding *Specimens of Tile Pavements* with fine colour plates of complete floors from such places as Jervaulx Abbey, Winchester Cathedral, Westminster Abbey and Gloucester Cathedral. The illustrations of the Jervaulx pavements have proved particularly important in view of the subsequent loss of the original tiles.

ABOVE LEFT [fig. 181] Tile with an under-glaze transfer print from a copper plate with coloured pigments added by hand. White earthenware. Copeland & Garrett., Stoke-upon-Trent, England, 1833–47. 20. 5 x 20.5 cm. Private collection.

ABOVE RIGHT [fig. 182] Floor tile with an inlaid design showing two lionesses with their tails intertwined, copied from a 13th-century medieval floor tile still in situ at Westminster Abbey Chapter House, London. Unglazed encaustic. Minton & Co., Stoke-upon-Trent, England, 1841–42. 15 x 15 cm. Private collection.

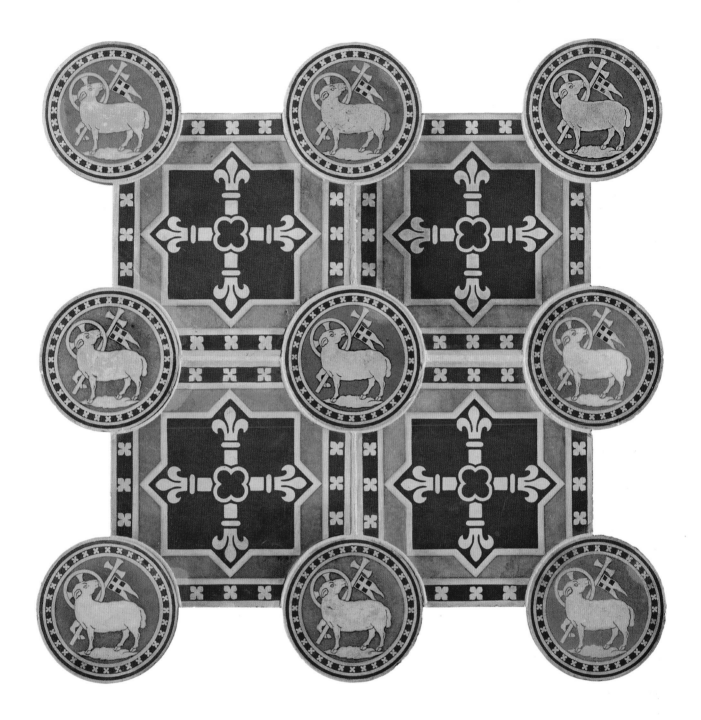

ABOVE [fig. 183] Panel of floor tiles with round tiles showing the Holy Lamb, and polygonal tiles with fleur-de-lis motifs. Parts of the design have been painted with yellow enamel which contrast vividly with the unglazed blue and brown sections. Encaustic and enamel. Designed by A. W. N. Pugin for Minton & Co., Stoke-upon-Trent, England, c.1845. Round tiles: 15.8 cm in diameter. Polygonal tiles 27 x 27 cm. British Museum 1980,0307.30.

The Gothic Revival was also associated with the religious revival in the nineteenth century. Architects such as A. W. N. Pugin (1812–52) advocated an architectural Gothic revival style based on the careful study of the medieval past. As a staunch Roman Catholic Pugin denounced classical architecture as pagan and advocated that buildings of all kinds such as churches, schools, hospitals, civic buildings and private homes should be erected in the Gothic style, which best expressed the religious and moral ideas of a Christian society. Pugin's own churches and houses in the Gothic style such as St Giles in Cheadle and The Grange in Ramsgate had strikingly ornate interiors, and on the floors he used decorative inlaid floor tiles made to his own designs which were derived from the study of medieval examples. These were made for him by the ceramics manufacturer Herbert Minton in Stoke-upon-Trent (figs 183, 184).

Herbert Minton (1793–1858) was an entrepreneur and an expert at spotting trends in the market. The successful owner of a ceramics factory in Stoke-upon-Trent that made tableware and ornamental ceramics, he also had an interest in tiles. He saw the great potential of a patent taken out by Samuel Wright (1784–1849) of Shelton, Stoke-upon-Trent, in 1830 for the manufacture of ornamental floor tiles. In the mid-1830s Minton struck a deal with Wright that allowed him to operate the patent under licence in return for royalties. It took five years of developing suitable methods of production using plaster moulds and small screw presses until the point was reached when the tiles could be mass produced.

The ornamental or encaustic tiles covered by Wright's patent were made from ordinary malleable or plastic clay with a design of different coloured clays laid into the body using plaster moulds and a small screw press. This is the defining hallmark of an encaustic tile which has a design of different coloured clay burnt into the body. The screw press was used to force the clay into the moulds and indent a design into the clay, which was then filled with clay of a contrasting colour, either by pouring or pasting. After drying the surface was scraped level to reveal the inlaid design and then the tiles

ABOVE LEFT [fig. 184] Panel of nine floor tiles with a central Gothic quatre-foil motif enclosed within a circular frame with fleur-de-lis and leaf designs. Tiles like this were used on church floors throughout Britain and were also exported abroad. Unglazed encaustic. Designed by A. W. N. Pugin for Minton & Co., Stoke-upon-Trent, England, c.1850. Each tile: 15 x 15 cm. British Museum 1980,0307.8.

ABOVE RIGHT [fig. 185] Tile depicting the stoning of St Stephen who was one of the first Christian martyrs to die for his faith in Jerusalem in c. AD 35. Unglazed encaustic. Minton & Co., Stoke-upon-Trent, England, c.1860. 30.5 x 30.5 cm. British Museum 1994,0707.1.

ABOVE LEFT [fig. 186] Four floor tiles with an inlaid design based on medieval tiles. Glazed encaustic. Chamberlain, Worcester, c.1840. Each tile: 15 x 15 cm. British Museum 1995,0910.1.a-d.

ABOVE RIGHT [fig. 187] Floor tile with a classical motif. Unglazed encaustic. Maw & Co., Benthall Works, Broseley, Shropshire, England, c.1870. 15 x 15 cm. British Museum 1992,0510.5. Donated by Judy Rudoe.

were placed in ceramic boxes called saggars for firing in large bottle kilns. Minton's encaustics were usually left unglazed but during the 1840s the white inlaid parts would often be painted with a yellow enamel glaze which created a vivid contrast with the unglazed background colour. One of the greatest technical problems to overcome was to produce clays which all contracted at the same rate during the firing. All this development work was costly but Minton was a well-established china manufacturer who had the financial resources to support experiments in developing Wright's patent. Minton's persistence with making encaustic floor tiles paid off as in the early 1840s he successfully met the requirements of his first important order. In 1841 Temple Church in London needed to be re-paved and he was asked to make replica tiles based on the recently rediscovered medieval tiles in Westminster Abbey Chapter House. This commission was a great success, and led to further orders.

Throughout the 1840s Minton cooperated closely with the architect A. W. N. Pugin and it was probably with Pugin's encouragement that Minton began to experiment with using other colours in his encaustic tiles beyond the traditional yellow and brown-red of medieval times. The addition of blue and green created richer polychromatic effects and this, together with Pugin's numerous designs for encaustic tiles, led to Minton paving not only Pugin's churches but also prestigious commissions like the new Houses of Parliament that were built in a Neo-Gothic style. Minton's encaustic floor tiles, designed by Pugin, were laid there in large numbers between 1847 and 1852. The encaustic tiles for churches had designs with ecclesiastical emblems like the Paschal Lamb, the Evangelists, the pelican and Christian monograms and symbols, whereas the encaustic tiles for the Houses of Parliament were given a wide range of Gothic ornamental motifs such as fleur-de-lis, quatrefoil and trefoil as well as royal monograms and coats of arms.

Minton's encaustic tiles were also a huge success at the Great Exhibition of 1851. An article entitled 'Encaustic tiles' in the *Art Journal* of that year said 'Those who

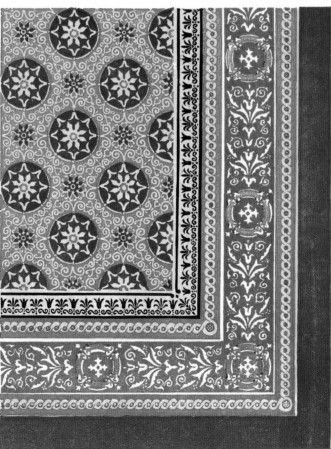

166

have not sought out the court within the Palace of Industry which is devoted to mineral manufacture, should not fail to do so, for the purpose of inspecting the choice examples of Mr Minton's tiles and tesserae it contains. The varieties of which we have given illustrations and many others of great beauty are there.' Minton's encaustic tiles became famous throughout Britain and were laid in many churches and other buildings. He was also a generous man and donated tiles not only to churches, but also to parsonages, schools and hospitals. Between 1844 and his death in 1858 numerous such gifts were made to churches and allied institutions in Britain and abroad.

Herbert Minton was not the only ceramics manufacturer who had taken a share in Samuel Wright's patent. Walter Chamberlain who ran a porcelain works in Worcester also became involved at the same time as Minton and came on board with encaustic tiles in or about 1837. Chamberlain was friendly with Harvey Eginton, County Surveyor of Worcestershire, who was an antiquarian with a strong interest in medieval tiles. This explains why so many encaustic tiles made by Chamberlain show patterns copied from medieval examples (fig. 186). They were used either in the building of Gothic Revival churches or in the refurbishment of medieval churches such as Malvern Priory in the town of Malvern, where there are still splendid Chamberlain encaustic tiles in situ in the back wall of the sanctuary. Chamberlain's encaustics remained much closer to the rougher work of medieval tiles and did not strive for the mechanical perfection that Minton achieved, nor did he introduce new colours as Minton had done, and in this sense they did not rival each other. In 1840 Chamberlain & Co. amalgamated with Flight, Barr & Barr. Porcelain production was concentrated at Chamberlain's old works and the encaustic tile making was moved to a factory at Palace Row in Worcester run by George Barr and Fleming St John. When Samuel Wright was granted an extension of his patent for a further seven years on 5 July 1843, he also extended his business arrangements with Herbert Minton and Fleming St John who, according to an Assignment of Letters Patent dated 29 April 1844, jointly paid Wright the sum of £612. This was a large sum of money in those days which shows how lucrative the business of encaustic tile manufacture must have been.

By 1850 Samuel Wright's patent had run out and the field was wide open for others to compete in supplying encaustic tiles for the growing market. Maw & Co. began the manufacture of church tiles in 1850 after buying the remains of Walter Chamberlain's tile works in Worcester. In 1852 they moved to Broseley in Shropshire where there were plentiful supplies of clay and coal. Their catalogues of the 1850s and 1860s show a good range of Gothic Revival tiles but also tiles derived from other design sources. These catalogues are at pains to stress the prominent architects who designed encaustic tiles for them. These included Matthew Digby Wyatt (1820–77), George Goldie (1828–87) and Henry Bayly Garling (1822–1909) whose tiles with classical designs were aimed at the domestic market or to floor public buildings (fig. 188). They also developed a special type of dust-pressed encaustic tile where the surface of the tile was indented with lines that created mosaic patterns. When the tiles were laid on the floor and the indented lines were filled with cement they looked convincingly like Roman mosaic, and the firm took out a patent for the process in 1864.

Another important manufacturer who came onto the scene specializing in church tiles was Godwin. It was set up in Lugwardine, near Hereford in 1852 by William Godwin (1813–83), aided by his brother Henry (1828–1910) who had gained useful practical experience of encaustic tile making at Maw's in Worcester. At first their

ABOVE [fig. 189] Three dust-pressed tiles impressed with superimposed pseudo-mosaic patterns showing a female head and bearded man in the classical style and a foliate design. Unglazed encaustic. Maw & Co., Benthall Works, Broseley, Shropshire, England, c.1880. Width of each tile: 18.4 cm. British Museum 2010,8009.1.a-c.

encaustics were made of plastic clay employing the usual techniques, and they produced some very fine floors including the one at Worcester Cathedral, but they also made stunning circular pavements as can be seen in the Lady Chapel at Chichester Cathedral. Sometimes their tiles have distressed surfaces creating an effect close to that of medieval tiles, like the fine pictorial tiles in the sanctuary at St Mary's Church, Shrewsbury. They took advantage of the invention of the process of dust pressing encaustic tiles that had been patented by William Boulton and Joseph Worthington in 1863 inspired by the technical introduction of this process in 1852 on the European Continent by Villeroy & Boch in Mettlach, Germany and Boch Frères in La Louvière, Belgium. In many ways this opened up the church tile market for true mass production and other firms like Maw also took advantage of this new process. Many churches throughout Britain, for instance Leeds Parish Church, feature dust-pressed Godwin tiles and their smaller $4\frac{1}{4}$ by $4\frac{1}{4}$ inch (c. 10.75 centimetre) size became very popular rather than the standard 6 inch (c. 15.25 centimetre) square tile. Godwin's tiles were in great demand with many Gothic revival architects with whom the company had good relations and the firm stressed this in company literature and advertisements. In a late advertisement by Godwin in *The Architects', Surveyors' and Engineers' Compendium* of 1891 the company took a full page showing testimonials from eminent architects including Sir Arthur Blomfield who endorsed the firm's encaustic tiles with the words 'Messrs. William

ABOVE LEFT [fig. 190] Dust-pressed floor tile with a Neo-Gothic bird motif based on a medieval design. Glazed encaustic. Godwin, Lugwardine, Herefordshire, England, *c*.1875. 10.4 x 10.4 cm. Private collection.

ABOVE RIGHT [fig. 191] Floor tile with a dove within a circular border and star motifs in the corners. Unglazed encaustic. Robert Minton Taylor, Fenton, Stoke-upon-Trent, 1869–75. 15 x 15 cm. British Museum 1980,0307.126.

Godwin & Son have laid floors for me with their Encaustic tiles in many churches. The tiles and workmanship have been invariably satisfactory.'

Although new firms like Maw and Godwin had now become rivals, Minton & Co. remained a dominant force in the field of encaustic tile making. After the death of Herbert Minton in 1858, his nephew Colin Minton Campbell ran the china business and another nephew Michael Daintry Hollins took over the tile business. In 1863 they acquired an additional partner in the shape of Robert Minton Taylor who was the son of Herbert Minton's sister Catherine. This arrangement continued until 1868 when all partnerships were dissolved. Hollins built a new tile factory in Stoke in 1869 and Robert Minton Taylor started his own factory in Fenton, although Hollins was not happy that the name Minton appeared in Robert Minton Taylor's factory mark. When Colin Minton Campbell bought the Robert Minton Taylor tile works in 1875 and set up a new company under the name of the Minton Brick & Tile Co., Hollins began legal proceedings about the use of the name Minton. He won his case and Campbell was forced to change the name of his company to the Campbell Brick and Tile Co., with Robert Minton Taylor staying on as manager. In 1882 they became known as the Campbell Tile Co. All this may explain why after the court case of 1875, Minton, Hollins & Co. were very protective of the name Minton and in the company catalogues brought out after this date they often stressed their exclusive right to the name Minton. On the front of many tile catalogues it stated quite clearly that 'The patents of the manufacture of encaustic and plain tiles belonged exclusively to and were carried out by the firm who have the sole right to the use of the name Minton in the manufacture and sale of these tiles'.

ABOVE [fig. 192] Panel of four floor tiles with
the monogram IHS, an abbreviation of the
Greek word for Jesus. Unglazed encaustic.
Campbell Brick & Tile Co., Stoke-upon-
Trent, England, c.1880. Each tile: 15 x 15 cm.
British Museum 1980,0307.50.a-d.

RIGHT [fig. 193] Engraving of a 19th-century tile press for the production of dust-pressed tiles from W. J. Furnival, *Leadless Decorative Tiles, Faience, and Mosaic*, Stone, Staffordshire, 1904.

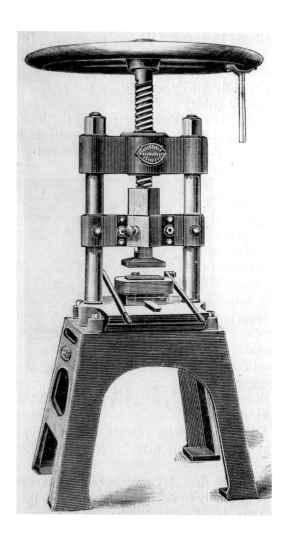

Dust-pressed tiles

The invention by the Englishman Richard Prosser that led to the industrial mass production of tiles was initially not related to tile making. In his patent of 17 June 1840 mention is made of 'Improvements in manufacturing Buttons from certain materials: the which improvements in manufacturing are applicable in whole or in part to the production of Knobs, Rings and other articles of the same material.' The material used was finely powdered clay with a low moisture content. It was compacted under great pressure between the surfaces of two steel dies in a metal mould with the aid of a hand operated screw press and was used by Prosser for making ceramic buttons. As was the case with encaustic floor tiles, it was again the ceramics manufacturer Herbert Minton who saw the potential of this invention for the large-scale production of wall tiles and, with the encouragement of the London-based manufacturer John Marriott Blashfield (1811-82), also for the manufacture of small tesserae for mosaic floors, and he therefore bought a stake in Prosser's patent. In August 1840, less than two months after Prosser had been granted his patent, Minton had six presses in operation for the production of white glazed tiles. More tile presses were constructed and by September 1842 Minton had sixty-two presses in operation. Minton dust-pressed tiles made in the 1840s always carry an acknowledgement of Prosser's patent on the back.

Minton's tile presses had a square metal mould with an adjustable plate at the bottom which could be set at a certain depth for the required thickness. The cavity of the mould was completely filled with slightly moist dust clay and the surface levelled. By turning the great flywheel, the screw, which had a square plate at its lower end, was brought down and compressed the dust clay slowly to allow the air to escape. It was then raised slightly only to be brought down again with great force compressing the clay and forming the tile. The tile was removed from the press and then fettled to remove the thin feather edge or burr along the edges of the tile. When dry, tiles were biscuit fired (fired but not glazed) and were ready for decorating and glazing. Dust-pressed tile production had many advantages over the traditional manufacturing process of handmade tiles. A skilled operator could make up to a thousand tiles per day and it was possible to manufacture perfectly formed tiles which were subject to little or no warping and required much less drying time than tiles made from ordinary clay. For plain tiles, metal dies with flat surfaces were used but it was also possible to make relief tiles using a die with an intaglio (incised) design. This became the most cost effective production method because forming and decorating the tile were done in one single operation. Dust pressing also allowed for a key pattern to be imprinted on the back of the tile to assist adhesion to cement and to show the name of the manufacturer and place of manufacture.

Dust-pressed tiles with relief patterns were decorated with three kinds of glaze: transparent, translucent and opaque. The simplest method was an application of transparent glaze over the relief decoration to make it waterproof. Sometimes the clay was slightly stained with a colour so that the colour of the tile was the colour of the fired biscuit seen through a clear glaze. The second method was to use a translucent or semi-transparent glaze that, when it was run over the relief

ABOVE LEFT [fig. 194] Dust-pressed tile decorated with a print of a basket with flowers. The tile carries an acknowledgement of Prosser's Patent on the back and this together with the transfer printed design on the front makes it one of the early examples of mass-produced wall tiles in Britain. Under-glaze transfer. Minton & Co., Stoke-upon-Trent, England, 1845–50. 15 x 15 cm. Private collection.

ABOVE RIGHT [fig. 195] Dust pressing a tile at Craven Dunnill Ltd, Jackfield, Shropshire, England. The operator is lifting the compressed tile out of the metal mould ready for fettling, drying and biscuit firing.

decoration, would settle as dark pools in the hollows and be much lighter at the top of raised areas where the glaze had run off and was thinner. The light coloured body of the tile would shimmer through and create interesting nuances of tone. Such tiles were either covered with a single translucent glaze or more than one could be used on a single tile. The third way was to cover the relief design with opaque glazes of different colours completely hiding the colour of the clay body. With these tiles the polychromatic effects that were created were the main ornamental feature. Colourful opaque glazes that became known as 'majolica' glazes were introduced at Minton's around 1850 following the appointment of the French ceramist Léon Arnoux as Art Director in 1849. Dust-pressed relief tiles show a wide range of subject matter with such things as flowers, animals, landscapes and human portraits as well as various ornamental patterns based on Gothic, Classical and Middle Eastern designs.

Dust-pressed tiles were also transfer printed in great numbers and there were various ways of doing this. The most commonly used method was printing from an engraved or etched metal plate. The copper plate was inked with an oily ceramic pigment and covered with transfer paper. Once this had gone through a printing press, the paper with the oily sticky design was transferred to the surface of the biscuit tile and was rubbed down vigorously for maximum adhesion. The transfer paper was then soaked off in water and the transfer printed design was left on the surface of the tile. Transfer printed tiles came in different colours like black, green or purple but sometimes a little colour was added by hand between the printed lines. The printed images on the the tiles were given a 'hardening on' firing to drive out the oil and then given a transparent glaze before being fired again. Applying a clear transparent glaze helped to protect the printed decoration, but also made the tile impervious to water and dirt and transformed it into an object fit for use in various

ABOVE LEFT [fig. 196] Dust-pressed glazed relief tile bearing the letter H. The letter H stands for Hollins and this tile once formed part of a tiled dado of the office staircase at the Minton Hollins factory. Painted with opaque glazes. Minton, Hollins & Co., Stoke-upon-Trent, England, 1869. 15 x 15 cm. Private collection.

ABOVE RIGHT [fig. 197] Dust-pressed tile with a moulded relief design of an Alhambra style arabesque motif. Painted with opaque glazes. Maw & Co., Benthall Works, Broseley, Shropshire, c.1875. 15 x 15 cm. British Museum 1980,0307.143.

LEFT [fig. 198] Dust-pressed tile with a print from a copper plate with children's scenes from a series of 12 tiles. Under-glaze transfer print. Minton, Hollins & Co., Stoke-upon-Trent, England, *c*.1880. 15 x 15 cm. Private collection.

architectural settings, particularly cast-iron fireplaces. The range of images found on transfer printed tiles is very wide. Many show naturalistic flowers and fruit, but there are also tiles with animals and landscapes and noted historic locations. Manufacturers like Minton, Hollins & Co., Maw & Co. and Wedgewood brought out series of picture tiles, often as sets of twelve to fit the metal frame of fireplaces. These have themes like nursery rhymes, the months of the year, signs of the zodiac, Aesop's Fables, British song birds, wayside flowers and sporting subjects. Minton, Hollins & Co. was particularly profilic in its output of pictorial tiles (fig. 198). Between 1870 and 1900 it brought out sixty-six series of picture tiles as well as numerous single pictorial tiles covering a wide range of those subjects that appealed to Victorian taste.

Herbert Minton again played a leading part in developments in the technology of transfer printing. In 1848 he took a share in the new printing method invented by F. W. M. Collins and A. Reynolds. They had discovered a method of printing flat colours on ceramics using transfer paper taken from metal plates, which was very different from the already well-established technique of transfer printing from line-engraved copper plates. Minton even employed Alfred Reynolds in his design department so he could be responsible for developing his printing method, which became known as 'block printing'.

If transfer printing from engraved and metal plates was the most common method, it was also possible to take prints from lithographic stones. Lithographic printing is

ABOVE [fig. 199] Dust-pressed tiles with Gothic motifs designed by A. W. N. Pugin, Minton, Hollins & Co. Although the architect Pugin had died in 1852 his designs were kept in production throughout the second half of the 19th century. Under-glaze transfer print (with some additional hand painting). Stoke-upon-Trent, England, 1870–75. Each tile: 15 x 15 cm. British Museum 1994,0711.1-2.

done with the aid of special stones that have a very smooth flat surface which is water absorbent. A design was created on the dry stone using greasy wax. The stone was then wetted and gone over with a roller coated with greasy ink containing ceramic pigment. This stuck to the wax design on the stone but not the wet areas which repelled the oily ink. This method was undertaken by firms like Craven Dunnill in Jackfield near Ironbridge in Shropshire (fig. 200). This firm was a latecomer to the Victorian tile industry, becoming active from 1870 onwards and building a new state-of-the-art factory in 1874. There is a well-known illustration of the new Craven Dunnill factory in Llewellynn Jewitt's *Ceramic Art of Great Britain* (1878) that shows the tile works with four smoking bottle kilns which also became the trademark on the back of their tiles (fig. 177).

A special type of lithography known as photolithographic printing was developed by George Henry Grundy and Arthur Lingard between 1895 and 1900, for which they were granted a patent in 1897. They produced tiles with photographic images of topographical landscape scenes and historical locations printed in black and white or sepia on dust-pressed blanks (fig. 201). In a way these were the ultimate example of industrial tile production whereby a mechanically produced image made by a camera was transferred to a machine-made tile.

Marking a tile with the manufacturer's logo, name and location on the back became standard practice as part of the tile production process and special metal plates were made to do this. This was often part of a raised grid pattern which was embossed to give extra grip to cement. Some manufacturers like Sherwin and Cotton even devised a special 'lock back' method that created slightly undercut indentations on the backs of tiles to ensure even better cement adherence. In addition to all this, firms would sometimes print diamond-shaped registration marks on the back indicating the particular date when an image or pattern on the front had been

registered with the patent office for design protection and this was occasionally accompanied by a design pattern number.

Since the great majority of firms making dust-pressed tiles were concentrated in the Stoke-upon-Trent area, that was where the support industries grew up which processed raw materials and provided specialist machinery for tile and pottery production. One such firm was A. Wenger, who from the 1870s onwards supplied ready-made clays, glazes and production equipment like tile presses from its Helvetia works in Hanley. In a catalogue of 1883 it described itself as 'Merchant in Articles of every description for Potters' use'. It also supplied firms abroad who wanted to buy British tile making equipment and its export business seems to have been big enough to make it worthwhile having its catalogues printed in foreign languages like French. Firms like Wenger enabled small tile makers to buy everything in ready-made form and just focus on the decoration of tiles. One such firm was the Decorative Art Tile Company who operated in Hanley between 1881 and 1907. They specialized in making transfer printed tiles using blanks from other manufacturers and decoration material and equipment obtained from firms like Wenger (fig. 202).

ABOVE [fig. 200] Dust-pressed tile with a printed pattern of an Art and Crafts inspired floral design. The design was lithographically printed, a process well suited for patterns made up of bold flat lines. Under-glaze transfer print. Craven Dunnill, Jackfield, Shropshire, England, c.1890. 15 x 15 cm. Private collection.

RIGHT [fig. 201] Dust-pressed tile with an image of the West Pier in Brighton executed on a Pilkington's tile blank. Under-glaze photographic image. Photo Decorative Tile Co. Ltd., Derby, England, c.1901. 15 x 15 cm. Private collection.

RIGHT [fig. 202] Dust-pressed tile with added hand-colour of a Scottish Highland scene depicting Loch Long. Under-glaze transfer print. Decorative Art Tile Company, Stoke-upon-Trent, England, c.1890, executed on a blank from the firm Lea & Boulton. 15 x 15 cm. Private collection.

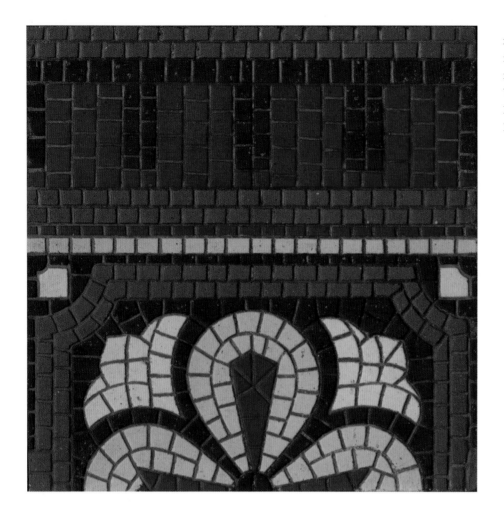

LEFT [fig. 203] Dust-pressed floor tile impressed with a superimposed pseudo-mosaic pattern with classical motifs. Unglazed encaustic. Villeroy & Boch, Mettlach, Germany, c.1880. 16.5 x 16.5 cm. Private collection.

The spread of British mass production techniques abroad

British industrial techniques for making floor and wall tiles had a marked influence on the manufacture of tiles in Continental Europe. The European scene during the nineteenth century was complex and varied. On the one hand there were countries such as Holland, Spain and Portugal where much of the production of tiles remained firmly within the tradition of hand craft and workshop production while in contrast, Germany, Belgium and France began to follow the of lead of Britain in mechanizing tile production and decoration. On the Continent changes in industrial techniques first manifested themselves in the making of floor tiles and it was not until the last three decades of the nineteenth century that dust pressing became one the principal methods of wall tile manufacture.

Germany took the lead in the industrial production of floor tiles and in the late 1830s the earthenware manufacturer Ernst March in Charlottenburg had even found a way of pressing coloured dust clay into small simple shapes to make geometric mosaic floors. Although it was used for a few prestigious commissions in Berlin and Potsdam the method did not develop further in the way that Richard Prosser's patent did in the early 1840s. In Germany true industrialization of tile production came via the initiatives of the Boch family, who during the second half of the eighteenth and first half of the nineteenth century created a ceramics empire not only in Germany but also in Luxembourg, Belgium and France.

ABOVE [fig. 204] Dust-pressed wall tile with a print of a town along a lake. Under-glaze transfer print. Villeroy & Boch, Mettlach, Germany, c.1890. 14.5 x 14.5 cm. Private collection.

François Boch began the production of ceramic ware at Audun-le-Tiche in Germany in 1748 and on his death in 1754 the factory was continued by his three sons, the twins Jean-François and Dominique, and the youngest Pierre-Joseph. In 1767 a new factory was set up at Septfontaines in Luxembourg. The Bochs were innovators and interested in maximizing production by building bigger kilns and using coal for fuel instead of wood. In 1823 Pierre-Joseph's son, Jean-François, visited England to study industrial pottery production methods and on his return set up a transfer printing workshop at the Septfontaines factory.

The Bochs also started a new factory at Mettlach in Germany in 1809 which was to see important developments in the industrialization of tile production. In Mettlach the firm became known as Villeroy & Boch and it was here in the mid-1840s that the antiquarian and architectural historian August von Cohausen encouraged the Mettlach factory director Eugen Boch to begin experiments with tile production. By 1846 single-coloured tiles were made using the dust-pressing technique, in which for the first time screw presses were used. The great breakthrough came in 1852 with the production of multicoloured encaustic tiles in the dust-pressed technique that became known as 'Mettlacher Platten'.

Production was based on technical advances such as using metal moulds and coloured dust clays stained with oxides. The coloured clay powders were placed in a raised metal stencil within the tile mould. The raised stencil was carefully removed

and the mould was then filled up with the body colour powder and the back of the tile covered with a metal plate. The filled mould was now pushed into a hydraulic press, which under high pressure compacted the dust clay into a tile. The design was embedded up to half a centimetre into the tile body which after firing became a very durable and hard-wearing tile. During the 1850s the making of encaustic floor tiles in Mettlach remained a sideline to the production of tableware and ornamental ceramics, but in 1869 a special factory was set up that specialized in making floor tiles, and mass production now started in earnest for tiled floors in public buildings, churches, schools and hospitals.

After Belgian independence in 1830 the brothers Victor and Eugen Boch expanded their operations to this new country, setting up a factory in Saint-Vaast in 1841 which was in full production by 1844 making all kinds of household goods and tableware. This became known as Boch Frères Kéramis, and began the production of dust-pressed encaustic floor tiles in the 1850s. The instigator was probably the Neo-Gothic architect Jean Baptiste Bethune who in some of his earlier work had had to rely on encaustic tiles imported from Britain and was keen to use floor tiles made in Belgium. Boch Frères encaustic floor tiles proved a success at the World Exhibition of 1862 in London and found a ready market amongst Belgian church architects.

In France the industrial manufacture of encaustic floor tiles started at the brick factory of Joseph-Achille Boulenger in Auneuil in 1854 using the malleable clay method of pressing plastic clay into plaster moulds developed by Herbert Minton. By 1855 it was achieving success at the World Exhibition in Paris. Its encaustic tiles were also used on walls and a remarkable set of nineteenth-century buildings have survived in Auneuil that still show the enormous variety of encaustic tiles it produced and their different applications.

ABOVE LEFT [fig. 205] Floor tile with a medieval design of a fantastic sea monster. Unglazed encaustic made from plastic clay. Boulenger, Auneuil, France, *c*.1880. 14 x 14 cm. Private collection.

ABOVE RIGHT [fig. 206] Dust-pressed wall tile with a landscape after the Dutch 17th-century painter Jan van Goyen. Under-glaze transfer print. Boch Frères Kéramis, La Louvière, Belgium, *c*.1895. 15 x 15 cm. Private collection.

RIGHT [fig. 207] Dust-pressed floor tile with a geometric design and central leaf motif, Unglazed encaustic. Doezies, Maubeuge, France, c.1890. 15 x 15 cm. Private collection.

The dust pressing technique of encaustic tile making was introduced to France in 1862 when the Belgian firm Boch Frères Kéramis set up a factory just over the Franco-Belgian border in Louvroil near Maubeuge (Nord). After the Franco-Prussian war of 1870–71, France experienced strong industrial growth and this led to the founding of more factories making floor tiles including Sand & Cie in Feignies in 1872, Paul Charnoz & Cie in Paray-le-Monial in 1877 and S. A. Produits Céramique de Maubeuge in Douzies-Maubeuge in 1882.

The technical development of wall tiles was much slower in Germany, Belgium and France than in Britain. During the 1860s industrial production of wall tiles began in Germany, although many tiles were initially still made from plastic clay. Around 1875 the dust-pressing technique was introduced and this led to the making of relief tiles as well as stencilled and transfer printed tiles. Initially Villeroy & Boch in Mettlach led the way but in the 1880s more firms came on to the scene such as the Norddeutsche Steingutfabrik in Grohn near Bremen. In 1888 Wessel in Poppelsdorf near Bonn began large-scale tile production, while in southern Germany Ernst Teichert began making dust-pressed wall tiles in Meissen in 1889. In Belgium Boch Frères in La Louvière made transfer printed wall tiles in the 1890s in addition to encaustic floor tiles. In 1897, George Gilliot set up the firm Gilliot Frères in Hemiksem, which became one of the largest manufacturers of floor and wall tiles in Belgium. It expanded phenomenally and the number of kilns increased from four

LEFT [fig. 208] Dust-pressed wall tile. It shows a painted landscape with a windmill copied from a picture by the Dutch artist J. G. Vogel, whose name is acknowledged in the bottom left corner. The tile was dust-pressed with equipment bought from Wenger in Stoke-upon-Trent, England in 1891. Painted under the glaze. Made by the firm Rozenburg, The Hague, Holland, 1895. 15 x 15 cm. Nederlands Tegelmuseum, Otterlo, The Netherlands.

in 1900 to twenty in 1904 and continued to grow thereafter. In France the dust-pressing technique for wall tiles was first introduced in 1860 by the eartheware factories at Creil and Montereau followed by Hippolyte Boulenger & Cie. This company became an important producer of wall tiles with its contract in around 1898 to supply tiles for the Paris metro. It produced a special tile with bevelled edges, which is still known as a 'metro tile'.

In Holland, at end of the nineteenth century, the tableware manufacturer Louis Regout – later known under the name Mosa – in Maastricht was the first to begin the manufacture of dust-pressed wall tiles in 1888. A number of newly established Dutch ceramics factories also brought decorative pottery onto the market and, after mastering the inherent technical production problems, they started to produce dust-pressed tiles in the 1890s. These factories were Rozenburg in The Hague, De Porceleyne Fles in Delft and the firm Holland in Utrecht. One of the directors of the Rozenburg factory, Herman van de Sande, even undertook a special mission to Stoke-upon-Trent in 1890 to learn about and see for himself industrial tile production and he bought equipment to make dust-pressed tiles from the firm Wenger in Hanley, Stoke-upon-Trent (fig. 208).

In Spain, British tile design exerted a direct influence on tile decoration during the late nineteenth century. Mass produced tiles were often decorated with stencils which, although a hand process, still allowed much more rapid production than the hand painting that had been the predominant method of tile decoration in Spanish

Of a certain Prince who delivered a King's daughter from a sleep of a hundred years, wherein she & all hers had been cast by enchantment

ABOVE [fig. 209] Panel of tiles illustrating the story of *Sleeping Beauty* designed by Edward Burne-Jones. The background tiles have been painted with a 'swan' pattern. This panel is one of three made as over mantels for bedrooms in the house of the painter Myles Birket Foster, The Hill in Witley, Surrey, England. Tin-glazed, painted with on-glaze enamels. Morris, Marshall, Faulkner & Co., England, 1864–5. W. 121 cm. Victoria and Albert Museum, London.

factories until that time. Tile designs by A. W. N. Pugin and Christopher Dresser proved very popular and were freely copied by tile makers like La Campana in Onda and Pickman in Seville, while other factories copied Belgian and German tile designs.

Tiles of the Arts and Crafts Movement

The art critic John Ruskin (1819–1900) often spoke out strongly against the effects of industrial capitalism on the lives of ordinary workers. In his *Stones of Venice* published in 1851–3, he argued how men were debased by machines because they were enslaved by the division of labour and mechanical forms of production. He wrote: 'It is not that men are ill fed, but that they have no pleasure in the work by which they make their bread and therefore look to wealth as the only means of pleasure.' In contrast he believed that medieval craftsmen had joy in their labour as they were part of and in control of the whole manufacturing process from beginning to end. This gave them more satisfaction in the things they made rather than the money they earned.

Ruskin's writing and ideas had an enormous influence on William Morris (1834–96) for whom it became a lifestyle philosophy that drove him in all the facets of his career as a designer, craftsman, printer, writer and socialist. The idea of becoming a designer came to him when he furnished his own home, the Red House, in Bexley Heath, designed by his friend the architect Philip Webb in 1859–60. More importantly, the Red House became a centre for social gatherings of artists and

LEFT [fig. 210] Tile with an on-glaze stylized artichoke set within swirling leaves. Painted on a Dutch tin-glazed tile. Morris & Co., 1865–70. 15.5 x 15.5 cm. British Museum 1994,1003.8.

RIGHT [fig. 211] Detail of the tiled reredos in Clapham Church, Sussex, with the hand-painted figure of the archangel Gabriel bearing a branch of lilies. Morris & Co., 1873–4.

poets such as Dante Gabriel Rossetti, Edward Burne-Jones, Charles Faulkner and his sisters Lucy and Kate, and Ford Maddox Brown. Morris and his friends set about designing and making many of the articles for the house by hand, including hand-painted tiles. In one of the outside porches there are still tiles painted by Morris showing designs with Tudor roses, his father's coat of arms and Morris's personal motto 'Si je puis' ('As I can').

This 'Red House experience' led to the foundation of the firm Morris, Marshall, Faulkner & Company in 1861. The firm produced hand-manufactured items such as wallpaper, stained glass, textiles and tiles. All those actively involved with the firm like Rossetti, Burne-Jones, Webb and Maddox Brown contributed designs. The tile output consisted of patterned tiles, with design motifs like daisies, sunflowers, floral scrolls and swans, as well as figurative tiles and panels depicting fairy tales, the labours of the month, saints, angels and minstrels. Rossetti, a founder of the Pre-Raphaelite Movement in 1848, was responsible for introducing tiles showing women with the long flowing red hair so characteristic of much Pre-Raphaelite painting of the period (fig. 211).

The style of painting on the tiles was simple, clear and direct in line with Morris' view of medieval hand work. He avoided Victorian naturalism and he was concerned that the figures, foliage and floral motifs should be in harmony with the flat surface for which they were designed. This is made clear in one of his lectures given at the

LEFT [fig. 212] Tile painted with William Morris' daisy pattern and made in Holland at the Ravesteijn Factory in Utrecht as a bespoke design for Morris & Co. Tin-glazed earthenware, *c*.1885. 15 x 15.4 cm. British Museum 1994,0709.1.

Working Men's College, London, in 1881 entitled *Some Hints on Pattern-Designing* in which he argued: 'In pottery-painting we are more than ever in danger of falling into sham naturalistic platitude, since we have no longer to stamp our designs with a rough wood-block on paper or cotton, nor have we to build up our outlines by laying square by square of colour, but, pencil [brush] in hand, may do pretty much what we will. So we must be a law to ourselves, and when we get a tile or plate to ornament remember two things: first, the confined space or odd shape we have to work in; and second, the way in which the design has to be executed.'

In keeping with the Arts and Crafts ideal of hand work, Morris insisted that the firm's designs were painted on handmade tiles. Since many tiles commonly available at that time were dust-pressed tiles, Morris used undecorated glazed tiles imported from Holland where tile production had not yet been industrialized. The designs were painted on the already fired glaze and fired again in the firm's stained glass kiln. But these tiles left much to be desired technically, which was already noticeable at the time. This is perhaps the reason why the manufacture of the patterned tiles was franchised to the Dutch firm Ravesteijn in Utrecht (fig. 212). Not only did the Dutch make and decorate tiles by hand, but the delftware technique they employed consisted of an in-glaze method which was much more durable than the on-glaze technique of Morris & Company.

Tile with red lustre decoration featuring a large cornflower with swirling foliage. This design is known as the 'BBB pattern' and the letters stand for Barnard, Bishop and Barnard, makers of cast-iron fireplaces in Norwich, England. Glazed earthenware. William De Morgan, Sands End Pottery, Fulham, London, England, 1888–97. 15.4 x 15.4 cm. British Museum 1980,0307.47.a-b.

The link with Dutch tile firms was probably brought about by Murray Marks, the son of a Dutch Jew who had settled in London. Marks ran a shop in Oxford Street, London, where he sold oriental blue-and-white porcelain and Dutch tiles to prominent members of the Aesthetic Movement such as the shipping magnate F. R. Leyland, the painter James McNeill Whistler, the artist Birket Foster and the artist and poet Dante Gabriel Rossetti, and Marks certainly knew Morris personally. Morris must have approved of the Dutch versions of his firm's designs as he not only used them in houses he was commissioned to decorate, but also in his own rural retreat Kelmscott Manor, Kelmscott, near Lechlade, where he and his family spent time after 1871.

Morris & Company tiles were used in churches, educational institutions and houses, like Clapham Church in Sussex, the dining rooms of Queens' College and Peterhouse in Cambridge, Stanmore Hall in London, and Birket Foster's house The Hill at Witley, Surrey. These commissions were carried out for an educated and well-to-do elite who appreciated well-designed hand work. As well as the medieval style craftsmanship of Morris & Company, their taste extended to oriental design, particularly Japanese and Islamic ceramics. The latter was much favoured by the potter and tile maker William De Morgan who was greatly inspired by Iznik pottery and tiles.

William De Morgan (1839–1917) was a close friend of William Morris, and first became associated with Morris & Company in 1862 when he designed some stained

glass and tiles for it. By 1869 he decided to branch out on his own and specialize in the manufacture of tiles at his house in Fitzroy Square, London. After a fire De Morgan moved to new premises in Cheyne Row, Chelsea, in 1872, where he established himself as an important independent tile maker. It was here that some of the early lustre tiles were made which became such a major feature of his later output. Like Morris he used Dutch tile blanks for some of his lustre tiles but he also used dust-pressed blanks from firms like Wedgwood and Minton, Hollins & Co., which shows that he was in some ways less averse to using machine-made products than Morris. In some cases he would execute designs by Morris: the panels made for Membland Hall in 1876 which were designed by Morris and painted by De Morgan are a prime example. In return Morris & Company stocked De Morgan tiles for sale in its shop.

De Morgan's successes meant his business expanded and soon bigger premises were needed. His tile business moved to Merton Abbey, Surrey in 1882. A final move came in 1888 when the works moved to Sands End, Fulham where he formed a partnership with the architect Halsey Ricardo. This partnership was dissolved in 1898 when a final phase began in cooperation with three employees – Frank Iles and the brothers Charles and Fred Passenger – which lasted until 1907.

William De Morgan was a prolific designer whose range of patterns and motifs

ABOVE [fig. 214] Panel of three tiles with a design of a fanciful classical-style galleon with three sails and silhouetted figures on board, set against a sea with leaping fish and a setting sun. Earthenware with under-glaze colours. William De Morgan, Sands End Pottery, Fulham, London, England, 1888–97. Each tile: 20 x 20 cm. British Museum 1980,0307.170.

included flowers, birds and animals, as well as medieval style sailing boats. Many tiles were executed in ruby lustre which was stencilled onto the surface of the tile before firing. This resulted in strong, bold, flat designs which shimmer with a metallic sheen when the light catches them at the right angle. However, the most glorious tiles are those painted in polychrome with exquisite blues, turquoises, greens, purples and yellows, which are most striking when combined with Islamic motifs.

De Morgan's tiles were used in fireplaces, bathrooms and even P & O ocean liners. One of the most spectacular examples of his work can still be seen at Debenham's House, Addison Road, London, designed by Halsey Ricardo in 1904–7. The exterior of the house is covered with green and blue glazed bricks, while De Morgan tiles were used on the wall of the outside passage leading to the front door and in the porch. Inside they decorate many fireplaces, the walls on the first floor landings and several bathrooms. Ricardo was a leading advocate of polychromatic faience on and in buildings and Debenham's House is his tour de force.

An account of British Arts and Crafts tiles would not be complete without drawing attention to the Della Robbia Pottery, Birkenhead, near Liverpool which was in existence between 1894 and 1906. It was founded by Harold Steward Rathbone, a pupil of the Pre-Raphaelite painter Ford Maddox Brown, who believed in the

LEFT [fig. 215] Panel of eight tiles with two fabulous peacocks amidst foliage and flowers in the centre and fish above and below. The rich design reveals the influence of Iznik ceramics which was much admired by the adherents of the Arts and Crafts movement. Earthenware painted with under-glaze colours. William De Morgan, Sands End Pottery, Fulham, London, England, 1888–97. 90 x 54 cm. British Museum 1980,0307.172.

[fig. 216] Tile depicting carnations and foliage. The elegance of this floral design was inspired by 16th-century Turkish tiles and pottery. Earthenware painted with under-glaze colours. William De Morgan, Sands End Pottery, Fulham, London, England, 1898–1907. 15.5 x 15.5 cm. British Museum 1980,0307.118.

principles of William Morris. Pottery, tiles and plaques were made by hand using local clays (fig. 219). Conrad Dressler, a sculptor, joined the firm in 1894 and was put in charge of the architectural department. He left the Della Robbia Pottery in 1897 and set up his own workshop based on Arts and Crafts principles at Marlow Common which became known as the Medmenham Pottery, Buckinghamshire. One of the catalogues of this firm tells us that 'we place ourselves in conditions approximating those of the old potteries whose ware delighted and inspired us. We therefore established our pottery right away in the country. We use our Marlow materials as much as possible and employ village work people. These elements are to influence our work to the fullest possible extent.' One of the main commissions that came its way was to supply polychrome ceramic tiled friezes for the Sunlight Chambers in Dublin built for the soap manufacturer Lord Leverhulme by the architect Edward A. Ould in 1901. The friezes show such things as the extraction of raw materials for soap and the soap manufacturing process and are interesting examples of the use of colour in architecture.

Another intriguing Arts and Crafts pottery venture was the establishment of the Compton Pottery at Compton near Guildford. It was set up in 1895 by Mary Watts, the wife of the artist George Frederick Watts, initially to make terracotta decorations for the Mortuary Chapel that was built as part of a new cemetery for the people of Compton. With the aid of local villagers and using local red clays, extraordinary

LEFT [fig. 217] Panel over the doorway of a rural cottage at Westfield Farm near Medmenham, depicting a man threshing corn. Polychrome faience. Designed by Conrad Dressler as part of a series of 12 Labours of the Month made by the Medmenham Pottery, Medmenham, Buckinghamshire, England, c.1908.

terracotta ornaments were made for the exterior of the chapel in an eclectic mixture of Byzantine and Celtic design (fig. 218). The panels show Pre-Raphaelite style female figures amidst interlacing knots and patterns of intricate complexity and sinuous line work that can be regarded as foreshadowing Art Nouveau. After the completion of the chapel in 1898, the Compton Pottery specialized in making terracotta garden ornaments such as benches, sundials and garden vases.

Artists and designers like William Morris, William De Morgan and to a certain extent Conrad Dressler and Mary Watts had retreated into an anti-industrial world of romantic medievalism characterized by honest hand work, community living and socialist ideals. This world was brought to life by Morris in his novel *News from Nowhere* published in 1890. This was a utopian romance about a society based on common ownership with no big cities or monetary system. It was a simple agrarian society where things were done by hand and where people enjoyed nature but above all found pleasure in their labour undertaken for the common good. Although Arts and Crafts designers had shown to the world the beauty of craft work and good design, doing things by hand resulted in limited production which was ultimately expensive and could only be afforded by the rich, and it was therefore never within the grasp of the ordinary working people they professed to champion.

Tiles of the Aesthetic Movement

During the last three decades of the nineteenth century the Aesthetic Movement embraced the culture of beauty and the notion of 'art for art's sake'. It sought to cultivate refined tastes in art and design as a reaction against the philistinism and vulgarism of the industrial world and drew on many different sources for its inspiration: the paintings of the Pre-Raphaelites, the designs of the Arts and Crafts Movement, and also the exotic arts of the Far East and in particular Japanese art. One of the tenets of aestheticism was that art was not to be confined to the Fine Arts like painting and sculpture but that it should also embrace everyday design, including tiles. Manufacturers responded to this new fashion phenomenon by making what they called 'art tiles' which were tiles that were admired more for their beauty than their utility.

OPPOSITE (TOP RIGHT) [fig. 218] Handmade panels on the exterior of the Mortuary Chapel in Compton, near Guildford, Surrey, England. The sinuous designs are imbued with mystical and spiritual meanings. The two angels on the left symbolize Service and Joy; the two angels on the right symbolize Peace and Purity. Terracotta. Designed by Mary Watts, Compton, England, 1895–98.

OPPOSITE (BOTTOM RIGHT) [fig. 219] Panel of handmade glazed relief tiles over the porch of a house in Hoylake, Wirral, Cheshire, England. It represents brownies at work and reflects the fascination of the period with the world of gnomes, fairies and elves. Glazed earthenware. Della Robbia Pottery, Birkenhead, England, c.1900.

LEFT [fig. 220] Dust-pressed tile painted under the glaze with the image of the ancient Roman goddess Proserpine picking flowers. Designed by Sir Edward Poynter for the Grill Room of the South Kensington Museum, now the Victoria and Albert Museum. The tile was painted on a Minton, Hollins & Co. blank by female students at the Minton's Art Pottery Studio in London, England, early 1870s. Glazed earthenware. 26 x 26 cm. British Museum 1980,1010.10.

Some of the prominent firms like Minton's China Works, Doulton and Maw set up special studios or departments for the manufacture of art pottery and art tiles staffed by well-qualified in-house designers, and also engaged prominent freelance artists like Christopher Dresser, Walter Crane, John Moyr Smith and Lewis Day. Lesser firms supplied a diverse market with mass-produced 'art tiles' that consisted of transfer printed products with sunflowers, lilies, peacocks and oriental design motifs which were the popular symbols of the Aesthetic Movement.

Colin Minton Campbell, owner of Minton's China Works in Stoke-upon-Trent, had fruitful connections with the South Kensington Museum in the 1860s and helped to set up Minton's Art Pottery Studio in South Kensington in 1871 under the directorship of William Stephen Coleman. In addition to the production of fine hand-painted pottery and tiles by Coleman and his assistants, the studio gave an opportunity for students at the South Kensington Schools' painting classes to practise pottery painting on biscuit ware and biscuit tiles supplied by Campbell from his factory in Stoke-upon-Trent. After they had been painted, these were fired in the glaze kiln of the Art Pottery Studio. The studio also continued the decoration of the tiles designed by Edward Poynter for the Grill Room at the South Kensington Museum (fig. 220). Tiles for this extensive project executed in the studio were given the distinctive round Art Pottery Studio back mark. The Art Pottery Studio was a point of contact for prominent freelance designers working in London such as

ABOVE [fig. 221] Two dust-pressed tiles transfer printed under the glaze. They depict a design of blue tits perched on foliage with bulrushes on either side of a stylized flower. Designed by Christopher Dresser, Minton's China Works, Stoke-upon-Trent, England. The backs carry a registration mark for 28 February 1870. Each tile: 20 x 20 cm. British Museum 1993,0508.1-2.

Christopher Dresser and John Moyr Smith who designed tiles for Minton and, as it turned out, were more than happy to use mechanical printing processes to realize their designs.

Christopher Dresser (1834–1904) was one of the most prominent industrial designers of his age and executed many commissions for Minton's China Works during the 1870s for both pottery and tiles. The tile designs were usually executed as block printed designs (colours were sometimes added by hand) that emphasized his sensitive yet strictly disciplined approach. Much of his work showed an underlying sense of abstraction and a clear grasp of form which is always the hallmark of a great designer. He went to Japan in 1876–7 where amongst other things he visited scores of Japanese potteries and was instrumental in popularizing the craze for Japanese art which was so clearly visible in his own tile designs.

John Moyr Smith (1839–1912) who had worked in Dresser's studio in London during the 1860s was clearly influenced by him and, like his mentor, engaged in many freelance commissions for Minton's China Works between 1870 and 1880. He usually designed tiles in sets of twelve. One of the earliest was The Trades, which was soon followed by other series like The Old Testament and The New Testament, Shakespeare, Tennyson's Idylls of the Kings, Classical Figures with Musical Instruments, Early English History and scenes from the Waverley novels. They were executed as block printed images for 6 by 6 inch (c. 15.25 centimetre) dust-pressed tiles but at times they were given an extra border so that they could be made as 8 inch (c. 20.3 centimetre) tiles. The designs are mainly round set within a square border which made it possible for the central round designs also to be used as the centre pieces of ceramic plates. Moyr Smith not only designed tiles for Minton's China Works but also undertook commissions for tile series for Minton, Hollins & Co., which since 1868 had been a totally separate firm. His tiles were often used in

cast-iron fireplaces and cast-iron stoves but were also used in Victorian furniture such as hall stands and hall chairs as well as sideboards.

The ceramic manufacturer Henry Doulton had followed Minton's example and set up a special design studio in 1873. He had already made his fortune by making salt glazed ceramic bottles, sanitary ware and drainpipes and was now able to invest some of his wealth in setting up an art pottery studio at the Lambeth factory in London where students from Lambeth School of Art were encouraged to come and work and experiment with pottery and tile making. Female artists with flair and talent like Hannah Barlow soon made their name with well-made pots and decorated stoneware tiles with finely executed incised decorations known as 'scratch blue'. During the 1870s Doulton also engaged outside artists like Helen J. A. Miles the painter and book illustrator to undertake commissions for hand-painted tiles. At that time Doulton did not make its own dust-pressed blanks but bought them ready made from other firms for use in its studio. Helen Miles would sign her work on the front and the name of Doulton was put on the back of the tiles.

Maw & Co. also quickly capitalized on the growing market for art tiles. It engaged Walter Crane (1845–1915), a leading book illustrator, designer, painter and writer, in the mid-1870s. He created several series of tiles on the subjects of nursery rhymes, the seasons and the elements (fig. 224). The company devoted several pages to his work in its tile catalogues of the time and it was always proudly announced as 'Picture Tiles Designed by Walter Crane'. Crane's elegant female figures are dressed in classical garb that evoked the world of genteel classicism found in the paintings of Lord Leighton. Maw also engaged Lewis Foreman Day (1845–1910) who like Crane was an influential designer at the time. In 1887 he designed a special fireplace for the company, as well as an intriguing set of red lustre tiles depicting grotesque animals (fig. 225). Lustre was a rare and difficult technique that had been re-introduced into British tile making by William De Morgan but had been taken up with success by

ABOVE LEFT [fig. 222] Dust-pressed tile transfer-printed under the glaze with an image of a Greek musician playing a tambourine. Part of a series of eight tiles entitled 'Classical Figures with Musical Instruments'. Earthenware. Designed and signed by John Moyr Smith, Minton's China Works, Stoke-upon-Trent, England, 1876. 20 x 20 cm. British Museum 1996,0206.1-3.

ABOVE RIGHT [fig. 223] Tile depicting a fox-hunting scene. The tile is decorated with hand-incised lines, with blue-black pigment rubbed in. Glazed stoneware. Designed and executed by Hannah Barlow, Doulton, Lambeth, England, c.1875. 20 x 20 cm. Private collection.

RIGHT [fig. 224] Dust-pressed tile transfer printed under the glaze with added hand colour depicting the Greek personification of Nox (Night). One of a series of four tiles depicting the four times of day. Earthenware. Designed by Walter Crane, Maw & Co., Benthall, Shropshire, England, 1878. 20 x 20 cm. British Museum 1980,0307.165.

some commercial manufacturers like Maw. The designer Owen Gibbons also worked for Maw & Co. in a freelance capacity. He had spent his student days in London where, during the 1870s, he had contributed to the internal decorative schemes of the South Kensington Museum. He came to Shropshire in 1880 to take up the position of head of the Coalbrookdale School of Art and established close links with Maw & Co. His time as a student in London had brought him into contact with leading artists and designers of the day, and his feel for the aesthetic taste of the time is amply shown by the tiles he designed for Maw featuring kimono clad ladies and floral patterns derived from Japanese porcelain, which were executed as transfer printed designs and used in cast-iron fireplaces (fig. 226).

In the mid-1870s 'aesthetic' style tiles with figures wearing Japanese dress were being made by Wedgwood using transfer printing accentuated with hand colour. They represent Japanese actors and are based on a series of prints by the nineteenth-century Japanese artist Utagawa Kunikazu (fig. 228). In 1880 Wedgwood also took a stake in George Marsden's patent for making tiles with low-relief coloured slip decorations which were used for designs showing Japanese style branches with blossom or stylized floral motifs (fig. 227). Some of these were designed by Lewis Foreman Day, and they also had their own in-house designer Thomas Allen who produced high quality tile series such as six patterns for Greek musicians inspired by the classical style paintings of Albert Moore.

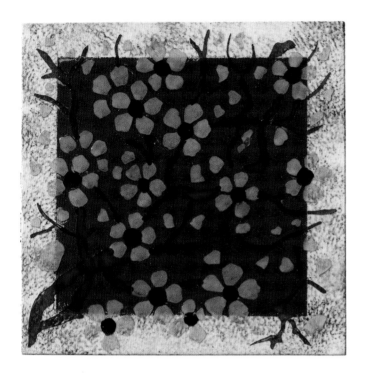

Some design firms specialized in art interior tile decorations but were not themselves tile manufacturers. W. B. Simpson & Sons was a firm of painters and decorators with premises in London who made the supply of hand-painted tiles, mosaics and stained glass a speciality (fig. 229). In 1862 it became the sole agent in London for the tile manufacturer Maw & Co. and involved the latter in commissions where encaustic floor tiles or relief-pressed wall tiles were needed. In 1878 the entire business moved to new premises at 100 St Martin's Lane where the whole of the upper floor was used as a painting studio. Simpson & Sons painted its own tile commissions on blanks which were probably supplied by Maw & Co. or firms like Minton, Hollins & Co., but did its own firing in kilns under the South Western Railway arches at Vauxhall. Its tiles carry various marks on the back which can be just the logo WBS&S, but sometimes fuller marks were used with the words 'Art tiles painted by W. B. Simpson & Sons'. A large business was done in hand-painted tile decorations for churches, theatres, restaurants and public houses, some of which can still be seen today. Examples are the hand-painted panels for the Criterion Theatre in London undertaken in 1870–74 and the tile decorations at Clapham Church in Sussex in cooperation with Morris & Co. in 1873–4. The latter undertook the tile panels with the archangels behind the main altar, while Simpson made the tile panels with hand-painted images of saints for the walls of the deeply recessed windows.

Stores like Liberty, which opened in Regent Street, London in 1875, were also instrumental in commercializing the 'refined tastes' of the Aesthetic Movement and bringing artefacts which had previously been reserved for the rich to a much wider public. Initially Liberty sold mainly imported oriental goods, particularly those from Japan, but it widened its range in the 1880s and 1890s to include designer goods of every description made in Britain and sometimes imported from the European Continent. These products had the word 'art' in front of them like 'art furnishings', 'art fabrics' and 'art pottery and tiles', and were often sold at affordable prices.

The store stocked, for example, art pottery and tiles made by the firm Burmantofts in Leeds, who like Doulton had made its fortune by manufacturing heavy clay products like bricks, chimney pots and architectural faience, but had set up a studio in 1880 producing high quality handmade pottery and tiles to capitalize on the growing market for such products. Its art tiles were made from plastic clay and painted with thick coloured slips under a transparent glaze or were moulded with relief decorations taken from plaster moulds and painted with monochrome translucent glazes. In the mid-1880s the company even employed a French artist, Pierre Mallet, to design relief tiles for it. He specialized in designs of animals, including exotic species like parrots; this kind of subject matter was created especially for use in the 'aesthetic' interiors of well-to-do middle class homes.

The tiles of the Aesthetic Movement showed that it was possible to unite industry and art by hand painting decorations on industrially made tile blanks which offered good flat surfaces to work on, or producing high quality relief tiles made from plastic clay modelled with the aid of plaster moulds, or designs with aesthetic style decorations which were executed as plain or hand-coloured transfer printed tiles for use in fireplaces and furniture. In these ways 'beauty' was brought into many more homes than had previously been possible.

American tiles

During the first three-quarters of the nineteenth century, America was mainly dependent on imported British tiles, but after 1870 it began to manufacture its own. Initially the American tile industry made use of the skills of European immigrants from Britain and Germany and adopted the mass production techniques developed in Britain. This is clearly evident in the output of firms such as the American Encaustic

ABOVE [fig. 228] Set of six dust-pressed tiles with added hand colour depicting Japanese theatrical figures. The designs were copied from a series of prints by Utagawa Kunikazu (active 1849–67). Under-glaze transfer prints. Wedgwood, Etruria, Staffordshire, England c.1875. Each tile: 15 x 15 cm. British Museum 1995,0713.1-8.

OPPOSITE [fig. 229] Panel of hand-painted tiles decorated by W. B. Simpson & Sons. The central plaque of solid buff clay is painted on the glaze with the figure of a woman in classical garb in the style of Alma Tadema. The surrounding buff dust-pressed tiles are painted under the glaze with a pattern of daisies influenced by the floral designs of Lewis F. Day. London, England, 1875–80. H. 108 cm. British Museum 1994,0720.1.

Tiling Company, Low Art Tile Works, Hamilton Tile Works and the Trent Tile Company. But by the turn of the century some highly individual tile makers and manufacturers had come on the scene like Mercer, Grueby and Rookwood who began to produce handmade tiles with matt glazes in the spirit of the American Arts and Crafts Movement. As had happened earlier in Britain, there was a shift in taste from industrially made tiles to hand-decorated and handmade tiles and it is with the latter that American tile making made its unique contribution to the history of tiles.

American industrial tiles

It was a mark of the determination and resolve of the pioneers of the nineteenth-century American tile industry that they managed to assert themselves so quickly in competition with the major British tile manufacturers who had dominated the American market until the early 1870s. The legacy of British tile firms can still be seen throughout the big towns of the East Coast. The enormous Minton floor in the Capitol in Washington laid in 1856–9 and the beautiful Minton floor tiles in the entrance of Lichfield Mansion in Brooklyn, New York, built in 1855 are cases in point.

The Philadelphia Centennial Exhibition of 1876 is regarded by many as the turning point for the American tile industry. It came in the aftermath of the American Civil War which had ended in 1865 and within the twelve-year Period of Reconstruction that followed it. The exhibition was visited by more than ten million people. In the Women's Pavilion visitors were introduced to aesthetic ideas on how to decorate the home and there is no doubt that it helped to create a new interest in domestic interior decoration. It also coincided with the growth of the aesthetic movement in America which encouraged 'good taste' in the home, of which tiles were a part. Already in 1868 the English writer on interior design, Charles Eastlake, had published his influential *Hints on Household Taste* which also became very popular in America. He considered tiles for use in the home 'a means of decoration which for, beauty of effect, durability, and cheapness, has scarcely a parallel.' In similar vein, the American writer, Clarence Cook, published *The House Beautiful* in 1878. It was illustrated with a frontispiece by Walter Crane showing a woman pouring tea in a tastefully decorated room with a large fireplace with blue-and-white tiles that match the oriental porcelain on the mantelpiece. To reinforce the 'aesthetic' message, the aesthete Oscar Wilde began a lecture tour of America in 1882 promulgating the pursuit of beauty. Even American artists got involved with tiles with the formation of the Tile Club in New York in 1877 (the club existed until 1887). This was a group of twelve artists, including Winslow Homer, who began to meet weekly on Wednesday nights to paint on 8 inch (20.3 cm) square white tiles. It showed that fine artists took tiles seriously as an aesthetic medium and in that way helped to promote the fashion for tiles.

All these various factors taken into consideration made clear to any American entrepreneur that there was huge scope for American expansion in this field.

One of the first great pioneering firms was the American Encaustic Tiling Company set up by Benedict Fischer and George R. Lansing in Zanesville, Ohio, in 1875. Its early efforts were in the field of floor tiles and the business got going with the aid of an English tile maker in the shape of Gilbert Elliot who was taken on in 1876 to put the production of encaustic floor tiles on a sound commercial footing. One of the firm's first successful commissions was the paving of the Muskingham County Courthouse in Zanesville, executed at the beginning of 1877. The company made encaustic tiles from plastic clay in the British manner but also manufactured dust-pressed encaustics. After a tentative beginning under the direction of the general manager George A. Stanberry, large-scale tile production took off in the early 1880s and the company became one of the major producers of encaustic floor and dust-pressed wall tiles in America. Much of its success was due to the employment of well-qualified German immigrants like the sculptor and modeller Herman Mueller and the glaze chemist Karl Langenbeck. They helped to establish one of the specialities of the firm which was dust-pressed relief tiles decorated with translucent glazes executed in the form of classical figures and portraits, as well as naturalistic animal and floral designs. In 1892 the American Encaustic Tiling Company built a completely new factory in Zanesville to expand production. To commemorate this

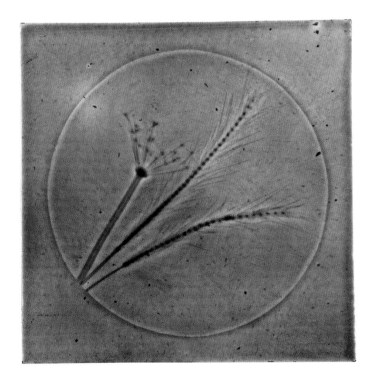 

ABOVE LEFT [fig. 231] Moulded and glazed dust-pressed tile with imprints of plant forms. This is a so-called 'natural process tile' and is one of the earliest tiles made by John Gardner Low. Earthenware. J. & J. G. Low Art Tile Works, Chelsea, Massachusetts, United States, 1879. 15 x 15 cm. Smithsonian Institution, Washington, DC.

ABOVE RIGHT [fig. 232] Moulded and glazed dust-pressed tile with two flowers and leaves. Earthenware. J & J. G. Low Art Tile Works, Chelsea, Massachusetts, United States, 1881. 15.5 x 15.5 cm. Smithsonian Institution, Washington, DC.

event a special dedication tile designed by Herman Mueller was brought out showing the head of a girl amidst swirling ribbons. The British designer Walter Crane also contributed to the firm's output with two series of transfer printed tiles, Baby's Own Aesop Fables and Baby's Own Opera. One of the most interesting companies amongst the larger firms was J. & J. G. Low Art Tile Works in Chelsea, Massachusetts. The firm was set up in 1877 by John Gardner Low with his father John Low who provided some of the capital. In 1883 the name of the company changed when John Gardner Low's father John left the business and his son, John Farnsworth Low took his place and the name of firm changed to J. G. & J. F. Low Art Tile Works. The artistically gifted John Gardner Low had studied painting and drawing in the studios of Thomas Couture and Constantine Troyon in Paris between 1858 and 1861, and on his return he had become an apprentice at the Chelsea Keramic Art Works where he was able to observe the decoration of vases with the imprints of natural flowers. The Philadelphia Centennial Exhibition of 1876 opened his eyes to tiles and in 1877 he began his first experiments with the production of what he called 'natural tiles'.

Instead of copying existing figures or ornaments he began to imprint natural objects such as leaves and grasses straight into the clay. In an interview printed in the *Century Magazine* in April in 1883 he described how 'it occurred to me that it might be possible to stamp a figure or a letter, or indeed, any form whatever, upon the face of the tile, just as the manufacturer's name is stamped on the back. ... I naturally thought of leaves as the material nearest at hand, and rushing out of the shop, down behind there, towards the brickyard, I found a mullein leaf. I hurried back, put the dust in the press, flattened it down by light pressure of the screw, then laying on the leaf, gave the screw a hard turn. I pressed the juice all out of the leaf, but I got my imprint perfectly'. This account gives an idea of the excitement of some of these early experiments which initiated Low into the art of tile making (fig. 231).

By 1879 commercial production began and his tiles won a Silver Medal at the Cincinnati Industrial Exposition. The following year Low entered an exhibition of British and American tiles at Crewe, near Stoke-upon-Trent, England, which opened on 2 September 1880. After the judging, the firm received a cablegram saying: 'Low won Gold Medal.' This upstaging of the British tile industry was recalled in 1895 by the American C. T. Davis in his book *A Practical Treatise on the Manufacture of Brick, Tiles and Terra-cotta*: 'The development of tile making in the United States has been the most remarkable instance of rapid progress of an industry in any country or age, and our tile makers may be relied upon to hold the place they have gained against all the competition of Europe.'

Low Art Tile Works produced a considerable range of mainly dust-pressed tiles which it marketed as 'art tiles' (fig. 232), not only for fireplace surrounds, stoves, walls, ceilings and furniture panels, but also for soda fountains. The term 'art tile' clearly indicated that its tiles were not merely functional products but were also meant to serve a higher aesthetic purpose. Much of its success in this field was due to its employment in 1879 of a talented designer from the 'old country', Arthur Osborne, who had studied at the South Kensington Schools in London. He was also responsible for the firm's so called 'plastic sketches' showing subjects like farm animals and portraits, often signed by Osborne with an A inside an O. Low Art Tile Works stopped making tiles in 1902 and went into liquidation in 1907.

Other firms of note were the Trent Tile Company and Hamilton Tile works. The Trent Tile Company, in Trenton, New Jersey, was set up in 1882 and by the beginning of the twentieth century was a large company employing over 300 workers. The firm produced a fine range of dust-pressed embossed tiles many of which were designed by their in-house artists Isaac Broome and William Wood Gallimore. Broome joined the firm in 1883 and became a prolific designer of embossed tiles. He left in 1886 and was replaced by the Englishman Gallimore who, despite having only one arm, produced notable designs for tiles. Trent tiles are beautifully embossed with decorations of finely modelled heads, plants and flowers which show a distinct feel for organic and sinuous forms of nature. The Hamilton Tile Works in Hamilton, Ohio, was opened by the German immigrant Adolf Metzner in 1883 and despite a turbulent history produced some fine monochrome glazed relief tiles with striking portraits (fig. 235), wild and domestic animals, and classical subjects.

American Arts and Crafts tiles

Although dust-pressed tiles with glazed relief decorations were useful products that fulfilled important architectural needs, industrial production had forced a visual uniformity on them which did not match up to the ideas of a new generation of tile makers and designers who began to emerge around 1900 and who were influenced by the principles of the British Arts and Craft Movement. These had been transmitted to America during the last quarter of the nineteenth century via the writings of Ruskin and Morris and through visits by Arts and Crafts designers like Christopher Dresser and Walter Crane. There were strong reactions and responses to this in America as can be seen in the activities of the craftsman Gustav Stickley in Syracuse in the state of New York. Stickley had made a trip to Europe in 1898 where he had met the Arts and Crafts architect C. F. A. Voysey in London and the style guru Siegfried Bing in Paris. On his return he began publication of a magazine called *The Craftsman*, the

first issue of which came out in 1901. The magazine paid homage to the work and ideas of Morris and Ruskin and in 1903 published an article by Bing on the new European style phenomenon of Art Nouveau. Siegfried Bing had already shown a lively interest in American design during his stay in 1894 when he had visited the workshops of Louis Comfort Tiffany in New York and the Rookwood Pottery in Cincinnati. Also in Syracuse lived Adelaide Alsop Robineau, a ceramist who began the publication of a magazine called *Keramic Studio* which was launched in 1899 as a design magazine for the pottery trade.

However the man who gave American Arts and Crafts tiles their proper foundation was Henry Chapman Mercer (1856–1930). He was a gentleman of

independent means who had been educated at Harvard and lived in Doylestown near Philadelphia. He had a strong interest in archaeology and anthropology and had travelled extensively in Europe and South America to look at art and culture, all of which influenced his tiles. His interest in ceramic manufacture was aroused when he began collecting tools used by Pennsylvanian settlers, which for him illustrated the history of American pre-industrial technology. In his searches he came across a disused local pottery and this led him to study more closely the manufacturing processes used in pottery and tiles. He first began to experiment with tile making in 1897–8 using local red clays and after a time he felt confident enough to set up his own business under the name Moravian Pottery and Tile Works. Between 1908 and 1912 he constructed a purpose built pottery on a new site in Doylestown, building his own residence, Fonthill, next to it.

Mercer produced three types of handmade tiles: plain and moulded relief tiles, mosaic tiles and 'brocade' tiles, a type of tile of his own invention. His plain tiles were cut from slabs of plastic clay and were often used in combination with moulded relief tiles. The latter were hand pressed in moulds and coloured with slips and glazes (fig. 237). Mosaic tiles meant cutting flat shapes of different sizes which after colouring and firing were assembled to make up a picture. The method was not unlike the making of stained glass but instead of joining the pieces of glass together with lead he used bands of cement to fill the spaces between the variously cut pieces, creating contour lines. Brocade tiles were three dimensionally modelled individual units of such things as figures, animals, trees or letters, which were assembled into larger compositions embedded in concrete (fig. 238). Mercer's own residence Fonthill was a show case for his own tiles. The plain exterior belies the extraordinary interior where every wall and ceiling is covered with various kinds of Mercer tiles with scenes drawn from medieval sources, or showing depictions from the four seasons or the Bible. One of the most intriguing installations is the Columbus Room where the

ABOVE LEFT [fig. 234] Moulded and glazed dust-pressed tile with head of Michelangelo. Earthenware. Trent Tile Co., Trenton, New Jersey, United States, c.1885. 15 x 15 cm. Smithsonian Institution, Washington, DC.

ABOVE RIGHT [fig. 235] Moulded and glazed dust-pressed tile with the head of a Native American. Earthenware. Hamilton Tile Works, Hamilton, Ohio, United States, c.1895. 10 x 10 cm. Smithsonian Institution, Washington, DC.

ABOVE [fig. 236] Tile mosaic floor panel in the corridor of the Pennsylvania Capitol Building showing a woman making candles. Harrisburg, Pennsylvania. Earthenware. Designed by Henry Chapman Mercer, Moravian Pottery and Tile Works, Doylestown, Pennsylvania, United States, 1903.

ceiling is covered with brocade tiles telling the story of the discovery of America.

Mercer's travels in Europe in his youth had made him acquainted with its rich history and in his designs for tiles he drew on the history of medieval tiles and on Hispano-Moresque *arista* tiles for inspiration. This showed in his production of relief tiles with medieval knights on horseback and medieval bird designs or the line-impressed tiles he made with the Spanish motto 'Plus Ultra' that became so popular in Spain after Charles V became king of both Aragon and Castile in the early sixteenth century. Both types of tile were created by pressing plastic clay into moulds with either positive or negative impressions. This method allowed production in quantity and yet the tiles retained a strong handmade look which according to Mercer made them 'cheap enough to sell and artistic enough to rival the old ones'. This indicated that despite his ideological bias towards hand-craft production, he realized that it had to be done in such a way that it became economically feasible.

Mercer's most important outside commission was undertaken in 1903 when he was asked to pave the corridors of the State Capitol Building in Harrisburg which covered 1,486 square metres. He used his mosaic method for the creation of 400 different tile pictures depicting scenes from Pennsylvanian history, industry, agriculture and local species of animals (fig. 236). Each mosaic was set in a background of red 3 inch (7.62 centimetre) terracotta tiles which harmonized well with the tile mosaics. In 1908 Mercer published his *Guide Book to the Tiled Pavement*

LEFT [fig. 237] Peacock relief panel above the basement entrance in 139 East 19th Street, New York. Glazed earthenware. Moravian Pottery and Tile Works, Doylestown, Pennsylvania, United States, *c*.1909.

in the Capitol of Pennsylvania in which he wrote about his own creations: 'Varying considerably in size, but generally not more than five feet in diameter, or gauged so as to focus the human eye at a distance of five or six feet, the mosaics may stand for mere patches of harmonious colour to the individual who rapidly walks across them, while it is only to him who pauses and studies them carefully that their full significance gradually appears. What the observer sees is less a picture than a decoration. The drawing is simplified so as to satisfy the clay process. The colors of men, animals and objects are fantastic and not realistic.' Mercer's tiles were unique creations that have a strong homespun and vernacular feel to them which is unlike anything else done at that time. His work was certainly original and must rank amongst the great tile experiments of the New World. He also exercised considerable influence on other American Arts and Crafts tile makers such as Grueby and Batchelder.

William Henry Grueby (1867–1925) was very different from Mercer. If Mercer was a Harvard trained gentleman archaeologist turned tile maker then Grueby had come up through the ranks in the tile business with little formal education. He learned his trade at Low Art Tile Works but eventually became dissatisfied with the many machine-made dust-pressed tiles with their monochrome glossy glazes which he helped to produce. In 1894 he set up the Grueby Faience Company in Boston and began to experiment with making pseudo-Chinese and Moorish style tiles, some of which were exhibited at the Arts and Crafts Exhibition in Boston in 1897. He also studied the tiles made by Mercer: it is well known that in 1902 he ordered a batch of Mercer tiles just for this purpose. Grueby tiles were made from plastic clay with hand pressed moulded designs which could be covered with matt glazes, and the development of matt glazes, particularly matt green, for use on tiles and pottery is

one of the great contributions of Grueby to the history of American ceramics at the turn of the century (figs 239, 240). Tiles and panels with matt glazes were produced by Grueby for the New York underground stations.

The second important Arts and Crafts tile maker who took his cue from Mercer was Ernest Allan Batchelder (1875–1957). He was a trained art teacher who taught at the Throop Polytechnic Institute in Pasadena on the West Coast. It seems he used Mercer tiles as teaching aids in the classroom and had some of them in his own house. This may have been what inspired him to try his hand at tile making. His first tiles were produced in the studio behind his home in 1910. In 1912 he went into partnership with Frederick L. Brown and set up a small factory at South Broadway in Pasadena. In one of their early catalogues they set out their adherence to Arts and Crafts principles when they say: 'Our tiles are hand wrought, by processes peculiar to our own factory. They have slight variations of shape and size – just sufficient to relieve the monotony of machine pressed tiles.' The tiles, made from local clays, were relief pressed by hand and decorated with matt coloured slips in tune with the vogue for tiles with matt surface decorations (fig. 243). They showed scenes from the American West, the Californian landscape or animals, birds and fruit.

The Art Nouveau style that had such a great impact on European tile design only caused few reverberations in America. Perhaps in a young country like America there was less need for a new style, and if anything they wanted to keep their links with their European roots and hence the past, which may explain their preference for Arts and Crafts ideals rather than Art Nouveau. However, a few firms like Rookwood showed the influence of Art Nouveau in the tiles they made shortly after the turn of the century. The Rookwood Pottery in Cincinnati, Ohio, was founded by Maria Longworth Nichols in 1880 with financial support from her father Joseph Longworth. Between 1880 and 1900 it made high quality vases and bowls which

ABOVE LEFT [fig. 239] Moulded tile with a tulip. Earthenware with matt glazes. Grueby Pottery, Boston, United States, *c.*1902. 15.2 x 15.2 cm. Cooper-Hewitt National Design Museum, New York, 1983-88-11. Gift of Marcia and William Goodman.

ABOVE RIGHT [fig. 240] Moulded tile with a lake scene and pine trees. From a frieze called 'The Pines'. Earthenware with matt glazes. Designed by Addison B. LeBoutillier, Grueby Pottery, Boston, United States, *c.*1902. 15.4 x 15.2 cm. Cooper-Hewitt National Design Museum, New York, 1983-88-12. Gift of Marcia and William Goodman.

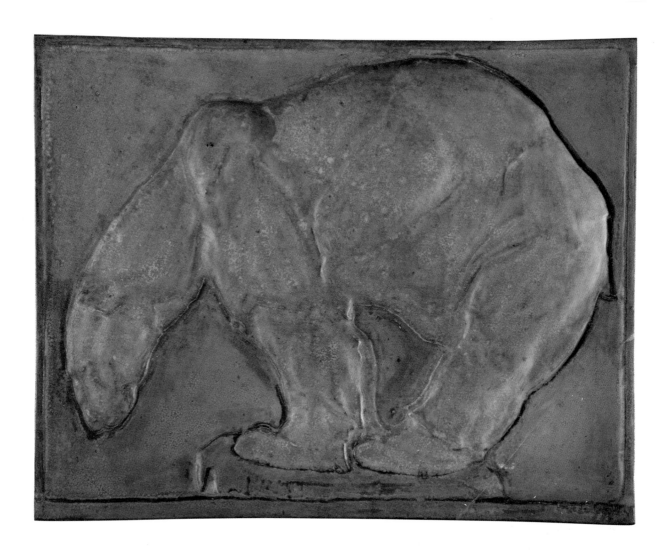

ABOVE [fig. 241] Moulded tile with a polar bear. Earthenware with matt glazes. Designed by Frederick G. R. Roth, Grueby Pottery, Boston, United States, c.1906. 17 x 22 cm. Smithsonian Institution, Washington, DC.

became famous throughout America and Europe. Rookwood architectural faience and tiles were not made until 1902 when William Watts Taylor who was Rookwood's business manager established the company's architectural and faience department. Its tiles and faience products were painted with matt glazes which the firm had developed a few years earlier for its pottery and with which it had such great success at the International Exposition in Paris in 1900 when it captured the Grand Prix. An early important commission was the decoration of Fulham and Wall Street underground station in New York in 1905. A promotional catalogue of 1907 shows Rookwood tiles with flowers, plants, birds and landscapes, all with the sinuous lines characteristic of Art Nouveau (fig. 242).

An unusual Arts and Crafts venture of a very different nature developed in Boston in 1906 in a Saturday Evening Girls' Club to educate immigrant girls organized by Boston's North Bennet Street Industrial School. The club arranged all sorts of classes and the librarian Edith Guerrier promoted the girls' interest in books and ideas. The venture also attracted the attention of the philanthropist Helen Osborne Storrow, who was particularly interested in the education and empowerment of girls. It was Guerrier who approached her with the request for funding to set up a pottery class which began to make simple decorative tiles and offer them for sale. The initial venture was a success and it moved to bigger premises at 18 Hull Street in Boston

LEFT [fig. 242] Tile showing a wooded landscape with rooks. This is a Rookwood advertising plaque designed by Sarah Toohey whose initials are incorporated at the bottom left. Earthenware with matt glazes. Rookwood Pottery, Cincinnati, United States, 1903–13. 37.8 x 20 cm. Cooper-Hewitt National Design Museum, New York, 1984-84-22. Gift of Marcia and William Goodman.

ABOVE LEFT [fig. 243] Moulded tile with a Dutch boy carrying milk pails. Earthenware with matt glazes. Batchelder Tile Co., Pasadena, California, United States, c.1914. 15 x 15 cm. Smithsonian Institution, Washington, DC.

ABOVE RIGHT [fig. 244] Tube-lined tile showing Mather-Eliot House, on the corner of Hanover and North Bennet Streets in Boston. Earthenware with coloured glazes. The tile was made as part of the activities of the Saturday Evening Girls' Club. Designed by Edith Brown and decorated by Fanny Levine for the Paul Revere Pottery, Boston, United States, c.1910. 9.3 x 9.3 cm. Cooper-Hewitt National Design Museum, New York, 1983-88-20. Gift of Marcia and William Goodman.

where Guerrier persuaded Edith Brown who was an artist and illustrator to take on the artistic direction of the pottery. The venture operated under the name of Paul Revere Pottery, named after Paul Revere, the famous eighteenth-century American patriot. It was an example of true Arts and Crafts ideals in practice: poor immigrant girls making tiles by hand while working reasonable hours in a clean studio for a decent wage. The tiles were tube lined and this also helped keep the glazes separate on firing. Some charming tiles were made showing animals, landscapes and historic locations in Boston (fig. 244).

American Arts and Crafts tiles were a real alternative to decorative dust-pressed relief tiles for customers with discerning taste and enough money. The handmade look of the Arts and Crafts tiles made them popular for fireplaces and as splashbacks for drinking fountains and they were also used as floor tiles. However, in a domestic context, they were normally not installed in bathrooms and kitchens where dust-pressed tiles were preferred for reasons of hygiene because they were exact in size and could be fitted very closely together on the wall. Art and Craft tiles, being made from plastic clay, shrank much more unevenly than dust-pressed tiles and this had to be compensated for by increasing the width of the grouting joints which, in an unintended way, became an appealing characteristic of handmade tiles in architectural locations.

By the beginning of the twentieth century all the main industrial production and decoration techniques pioneered and developed during the nineteenth century were firmly in place. Although the handmade tiles of the Arts and Crafts Movements both in Britain and America proved an interesting diversion and helped to raise the aesthetic quality of tile design, industrially made dust-pressed tiles were still the future. In the twentieth century the focus was with few exceptions on the design of industrially made tiles, as would be seen with Art Nouveau, Art Deco and Modernist tiles.

THE CENTURY
OF DESIGN

There is no danger that standardisation will force a choice upon the individual, since due to natural competition the number of available types of each object will always be ample to provide the individual with a choice of design that suits him best.

Walter Gropius

Bauhaus Dessau: Principles of Bauhaus Production, 1926

The technical and economic history of tile making in the twentieth century was in many ways a continuation and a reaffirmation of the dominance of industrial production which had begun in the nineteenth century. Tiles were manufactured in ever more machine-efficient ways and plain tiles in particular were mass produced in increasing numbers and used for utilitarian purposes in all kinds of buildings. Production was increased by innovations like the switch from traditional coal-fired bottle kilns to gas-burning or electric tunnel kilns, and the introduction of semi-automatic and fully automatic tile presses. Starting in the nineteenth century the machine production of tiles had brought prices down and in the twentieth century, with the rise in living standards in the industrial world, almost everybody could afford tiles.

It is, however, not the plain tiles but the decorative tiles of the twentieth century that are the most interesting. They show the influences of many different styles and design approaches that have marked the design history of the twentieth century, often regarded as the 'century of design' because of the myriad of rapidly changing movements that saw design become the stamp and hallmark of modern society. The decorative styles of European Art Nouveau followed by European and American Art Deco dominated the first half of the century. In the second half abstraction and minimalism became the major trends of the 1950s, 1960s and early 1970s. After this the pendulum swung back towards more figurative art and design as part of the phenomenon known as 'post-modernism'. Twentieth-century decorative tiles strongly reflect this rich tapestry of successive design movements, trends and fashions. They show not only how innovative architects and designers have been in their use of tiles but also the contribution made by prominent fine artists to the design of tiles.

OPPOSITE [fig. 245] Detail of a hospital tile panel depicting a scene from *Sleeping Beauty*. Designed by Margaret E. Thompson, Doulton & Co., London, *c*.1905. See p. 229 for full view and caption.

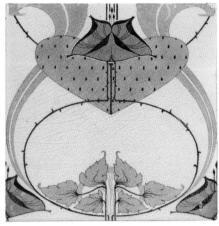

ABOVE [fig. 247] Dust-pressed tile with an Art Nouveau design based on a blackberry and its leaves and thorny branches. Underglaze transfer print. Minton's China Works, Stoke-upon-Trent, England, c.1900. 15 x 15 cm. British Museum 1995,0719.9.a-d.

Art Nouveau

Art Nouveau was a late nineteenth and early twentieth century stylistic phenomenon that manifested itself particularly in Europe in art, architecture and design including tiles and architectural ceramics. Brussels and Paris – often regarded as the birthplaces of Art Nouveau – were where progressive artists, designers and architects created a new style based on fresh inspirations from nature and the art and design traditions of the Far East. A group of avant-garde artists in Brussels known as Les Vingt became associated with a publication called *L'Art Moderne* and in 1884 began to call themselves 'the believers in Art Nouveau'. However, the popular use of the name is associated with the gallery called L'Art Nouveau opened by Siegfried Bing in Paris in 1895. Until 1910, Art Nouveau became the iconic style of the period now known as the Belle Époque.

As a movement Art Nouveau was an attempt to give a new direction to architecture and design and to replace the prevailing historical nineteenth-century styles such as the Gothic Revival and Neo-Classicism with a new style inspired by nature, existing vernacular traditions and design sources from outside Europe such as the newly discovered art of Japan. The importation of Japanese porcelain and woodcuts proved particularly significant in opening the eyes of European artists to the purely formalistic qualities of strong line and colour. Art Nouveau aimed to be 'new' in a world of progressive developments. New forms of industrial production,

ABOVE LEFT [fig. 246] Dust-pressed tile with raised relief lines showing an Art Nouveau design of a water lily. Glazed earthenware. Henry Richards Tile Co., Stoke-upon-Trent, England, c.1905. 15 x 15 cm. British Museum 1994,0511.11.

ABOVE [fig. 248] Detail of the Art Nouveau facade of Louis Coilliot's ceramic showroom designed by the French architect Hector Guimard at rue de Fleurus, Lille, France, 1898–1900. The ceramic panels were made by E. Gillet in Paris.

ever increasing urbanization, breakthroughs in science and technology, and worldwide trade all contributed to a new world view marked by a sense of ever accelerating progress and change. This is perhaps why the French name for Art Nouveau highlights the sense of 'renewal', which can also be seen in the names for it in other countries. In Holland it was called *Nieuwe Kunst*, in Germany *Jugendstil*, in Austria *Sezession*, in Spain *Modernista*, in Italy *Style Liberty* and in Portugal *Arte Nova*, all signifying affinity with ideas of the 'new', 'youth' and 'modernity', and indicating that art was poised on the threshold of a new era.

From a stylistic point of view Art Nouveau was characterized by the dominant use of line and the emphasis on flat areas of colour which added vitality to the linear design. These lines and flat colours were applied to organic design motifs such as plants and flowers with slender sinuous stems and tendrils, insects with their delicate wings, legs and antennae, amphibians and lizards with their strange curvilinear body shapes, different varieties of exotic birds and their bright plumage, and last but not least young women in long dresses with free flowing hair. Drawing on such diverse sources and themes, designers were able to create striking and visually appealing images. However Art Nouveau could also be geometric rather than organic. Geometric Art Nouveau designs characterized by angular abstract forms became an important aspect of the work of a number of artists in Glasgow and Vienna at the beginning of the twentieth century.

LEFT [fig. 249] Detail of a tile mosaic panel showing the barter of a woman in exchange for weapons, by the Dutch artist Jan Toorop in the vestibule of the Amsterdam Stock Exchange, The Netherlands, built in 1898–1902. It is part of series of symbolic tile panels representing past, present and future on the theme of labour and commerce made by De Porceleyne Fles in Delft.

ABOVE [fig. 250] Floor tile with a small spiral motif in the corner. The simple spiral motif with a square represents the geometrical side of Art Nouveau as opposed to the curvilinear. Unglazed encaustic. Designed by the German architect Peter Behrens, made by Villeroy & Boch, Mettlach, Germany, 1903–1904. 16.7 x 16.7 cm. British Museum 1990,0408.1.

Art Nouveau architects

Art Nouveau emerged everywhere in Europe and no country remained untouched. It became an important phase in the work of prominent architects such as Hector Guimard in France, Hendrik Petrus Berlage in Holland, Peter Behrens in Germany, Joseph Olbrich and Otto Wagner in Austria, and Antoni Gaudi in Spain, who all used architectural ceramics and therefore played a seminal role in the development of the Art Nouveau style in tiles.

The French architect Hector Guimard (1867–1942) is the best-known representative of French Art Nouveau during the late nineteenth and early twentieth century. One of his most famous commissions was Castel Béranger in rue de la Fontaine, Paris, built in 1898. The entrance in particular shows how his sinuous abstract design vocabulary suggests plants and organic matter and how he integrates different materials like stone, wrought iron, ceramic panels, glass and plaster into a coherent overall design. At the turn of the century he also became involved in designing the famous entrances of the Paris Metro with their exotic roofs of glass and iron reminiscent of dragonfly wings. One of Guimard's most striking Art Nouveau houses is Maison Coilliot at 14 rue de Fleurus in Lille (fig. 248). The whole facade, built in 1898–1900, is alive with extreme curvilinear lines and shapes, and above the windows and door are ceramic panels designed by Guimard showing extraordinary ornamental Art Nouveau lettering. The ceramic panels were made of a special

material known as *lave émaillée* created from crushed volcanic rock and clay and were produced by E. Gillet in Paris.

Hendrik Petrus Berlage (1856–1934) was the most important architect working in the Nieuwe Kunst in Holland but his designs are less flamboyant when compared with French Art Nouveau. His architecture shows restraint and he makes much use of bricks (unglazed and glazed) and tile panels. One of his most famous buildings is the Stock Exchange in Amsterdam constructed between 1898 and 1903 where his use of tiles is not merely decorative but has underlying meaning relating to the building. In the brick entrance hall are three large tile mosaic panels by the Dutch Symbolist artist Jan Toorop representing the past, the present and the future, made by the ceramics firm De Porceleyne Fles in Delft (fig. 249). Toorop's allegorical figures are delineated with black outlines and are conceived as flat shapes without three-dimensional modelling – a stylistic device taken from Japanese woodcuts. The ceramic panels were made in a special *sectiel* technique where the figures are outlined in black as in stained glass panels.

In Germany it was the architect and designer Peter Behrens (1868–1940) who became the leading exponent of the Jugendstil. In 1899 he was invited by the Grand Duke of Hesse to become a member of his recently established artists' colony in Darmstadt, where Behrens built his own house. In 1907 he helped to set up the German Werkbund which sought to establish links between architects, designers

ABOVE [fig. 251] The house of the Austrian architect Joseph Olbrich, Darmstadt, Germany. The exterior has been decorated with Art Nouveau tiles with spiral motifs probably made by Villeroy & Boch in Mettlach, Germany, 1901.

and manufacturers to improve the quality of the design of everyday objects, including
tiles. At the beginning of the twentieth century Behrens designed tiles for the firm
Villeroy & Boch with geometric motifs. These tiles were patterned with black or
dark-brown lines on a white background. In some he used a spiral motif, similar to
those he used for book covers and wall decorations (fig. 250).

The Austrian architect Joseph Olbrich (1867–1908) was also invited by the Grand
Duke of Hesse to become a member of his artists' colony and he too was given the
opportunity to design and build his own house in Darmstadt in 1901. The white
stuccoed exterior walls of his house were decorated with panels of white and black-
blue tiles arranged in chequerboard fashion and decorated with spiral motifs – an
iconic pattern of Austrian Art Nouveau also seen in the work of artists like Gustave
Klimt. These tile panels show two different facets of Art Nouveau: the alternating
dark and light square tiles represent the abstract side and the spiralling tendrils
refer to organic forms from the natural world (fig. 251).

The spiral motif was also a favourite of the Austrian architect Otto Wagner
(1841–1914). He made striking use of Art Nouveau tiles in his Majolica House built on
one of Vienna's grand streets, the Linke Wienzeile, in 1898–9 (fig. 252). Its six-storey
facade is covered from top to bottom with Art Nouveau tiles showing brightly
coloured flowers and tendrils and probably made by the firm Zsolnay in Pécs,
Hungary. The composition of the huge facade has been carefully planned. There is a

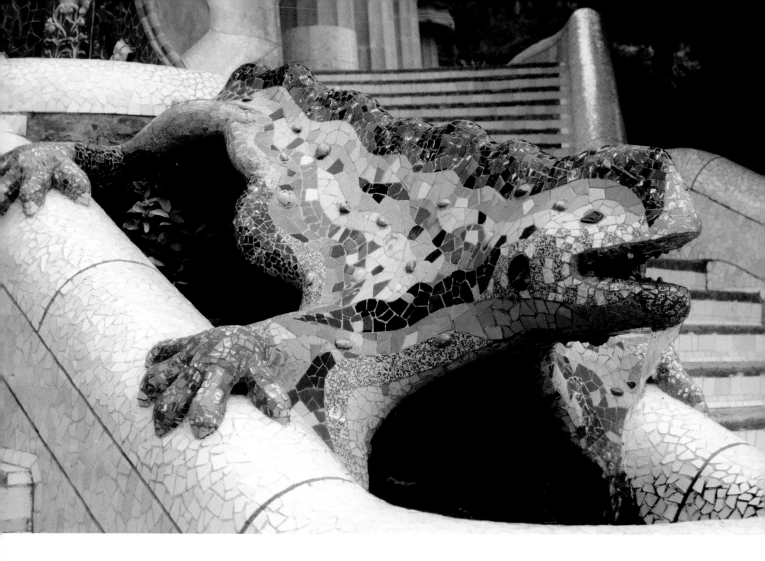

gradation of detail and colour from red to green from the ground floor upwards and an increase in the complexity of the floral pattern towards the roof, which is finally capped with lion heads in relief and elaborate overhanging eaves. The curvilinear tendrils that snake their way up the facade link up with the heavily embossed decorative window sills emphasizing the carefully integrated nature of the design.

Of all the architects who made use of Art Nouveau tiles in their work, Antoni Gaudi (1852–1926) is in a league of his own. His uniquely creative inventiveness has come to epitomize the Catalan Modernista movement and he was without doubt the most famous and celebrated architect of his time, representing a unique facet of Spanish Art Nouveau. His buildings in Barcelona using Spanish Gothic forms integrated with European modern movements like Art Nouveau are world famous and show the revival of Catalan culture that began in the second half of the nineteenth century. Park Güell, built between 1900 and 1914, is recognized as his most memorable endeavour. The main entrance is on Carrer d'Olot where the high walls of the park are decorated with large round medallions with the words 'Park Güell' highlighted in tile mosaic. The entrance is flanked by two gate lodges built of stone that have wondrous fairy tale roofs with biomorphic towers and turrets covered with a skin of colourful tile mosaic. Once through the gate visitors enter an enclosed space leading to a tiled staircase flanked on either side by curved and crenellated walls all covered with broken tiles. In the middle of the staircase the visitor is greeted

ABOVE [fig. 253] Fountain in the shape of a colourful tiled dragon on the staircase of Park Güell in Barcelona, Spain, designed by the Spanish architect Antoni Gaudi between 1900 and 1914. The sinuous shapes of the dragon blend in well with the amorphous shapes of Gaudi's architecture in the park.

by a large tiled dragon acting as a fountain (fig. 253). Eventually the staircase leads to the market hall with its Doric columns and its ceiling covered in plain white tile mosaic interspersed with colourful tile mosaic roundels of great complexity. The columns of the market hall support the great platform which looks out over Barcelona. It is here that we find the famous curvilinear Serpentine Bench that marks the perimeter of the platform.

Art Nouveau tile designers

The Art Nouveau style was also embraced by noted designers and ceramic artists who made it an important part of their own creative output. This can be seen in the work of Privat Livemont in Belgium, the Czech artist Alphonse Mucha, Max Läuger and Carl Sigmund Luber in Germany, and Léon Victor Solon, William Neatby, Charles Francis Annesley Voysey and Margaret E. Thompson in Britain.

OPPOSITE [fig. 255] Detail of a hand-painted tile panel showing a woman holding roses. It is part of a series of four panels known as *Les Fleurs*. Designed by the Czech artist Alphonse Mucha for Pilkington's Tile and Pottery Co., Manchester, England, 1901. Each tile: 15 x 15 cm. Formerly in a shop entrance in Glasgow, Scotland, the location of the panel is now unknown.

ABOVE [fig. 256] Tube-lined tile panel with a peacock made by the German ceramic artist Max Läuger. Glazed earthenware. Kandern, Germany, 1907–1911. It was originally made for the villa Kareol House in Aerdenhout in The Netherlands. 104 x 156 cm. Nederlands Tegelmuseum, Otterlo, The Netherlands.

Privat Livemont (1861–1936) was a successful Belgian commercial designer who created stunning posters in the Art Nouveau style and also designed tile panels. His poster style of flat colours and clear but sensuous outlines translated well to the medium of tiles as can be seen in the sumptuous series of tile panels designed by him and made by the firm Boch Frères Kéramis in La Louvière for the facade of Grande Maison de Blanc in Brussels (fig. 254). The building was designed by the architect Oscar François who was given the commission for a department store on rue Marché aux Poulets in Brussels in 1897–8. The panels show women in long loose flowing dresses and elaborate hairstyles who pose as personifications of industry and commerce or the seasons. Although the panels bear Privat Livemont's name he did not paint them himself as this requires expertise in ceramic techniques and the panels were therefore executed by Georges De Geetere the artistic director of Boch Frères Kéramis at that time.

The Czech artist Alphonse Mucha (1860–1939) was, like Privat Livemont, a celebrated poster designer who also designed tile panels in the Art Nouveau style. He created a series of four panels called *Les Fleurs* around 1900 for Pilkington's Tile & Pottery Co. in Manchester, England showing female figures who personify four types of flower (rose, carnation, iris and lily). On the panel called The Rose, for example, is a woman in a long dress standing among intertwining roses with her long hair piled high and threaded with wild roses (fig. 255). Like Livemont, Mucha did not

paint these ceramic panels himself and his designs were executed on tiles by Pilkington's own in-house artists like John Chambers and Thomas F. Evans. Pilkington's was obviously taken with Mucha's tile panels as they were shown proudly at trade exhibitions in Glasgow in 1901 and in Wolverhampton in 1902.

In Kandern in Germany the ceramic artist Max Läuger (1864–1952) became well known for his tube-lined Jugendstil tiles. Characteristic of much of his work is the special turquoise glaze he used, which became known as 'Läuger blue'. One of his largest and most interesting commissions was the tile panels for Kareol House in Aerdenhout in Holland, built between 1907 and 1911 to a design by the Swedish architect Anders Lundberg. The designs for the panels were inspired by Richard Wagner's opera *Tristan and Isolde*. On the outside of the house were more than twenty large tile panels, and on the facade were tiles in the form of friezes, as well as tiles covering the columns at the top of the tower. In the bathroom the floor and walls were covered with large tiles representing a forest with flowers, birds and a squirrel. Sadly this eccentric villa was demolished in 1979 but some panels were rescued and are at present in the Nederlands Tegelmuseum in Otterlo and in the Town Hall of Heemstede (fig. 256).

ABOVE LEFT [fig. 257] A woman standing amongst sunflowers and poppies. Designed by the German artist Carl Sigmund Luber for the firm Johann von Schwarz. Dust-pressed tile with lines in relief and coloured glazes with added hand painting. Nuremburg, Germany, *c.*1900. 16.2 x 27.5 cm. Private collection.

ABOVE RIGHT [fig. 258] Tube-lined and hand-painted panel of woman holding a flower with a peacock at her side, by Léon Victor Solon for Minton's China Works. It was originally made for the Dutch tile dealer A. M. A. Heystee in Amsterdam. Glazed earthenware. Stoke-upon-Trent, England, 1900–1905. 82 x 123 cm. Nederlands Tegelmuseum, Otterlo, The Netherlands.

ABOVE [fig. 259] Detail of a tube-lined and hand-painted tile panel of a woman playing a flute in situ on the proscenium of the theatre at the St Nicholas Hospital, Gosforth, Newcastle-upon-Tyne, England. Designed by William Neatby, Doulton & Co., London, England, 1898. Each tile: 15 x 15 cm.

In Germany the firm Johann von Schwarz in Nuremburg also made high quality artistic Art Nouveau tiles between 1896 and 1906. Many of these were designed by the painter and artist Carl Sigmund Luber (1868–1934) who became the technical director of the firm in 1896. Most famous were his tiles with female figures set against the background of an idealized landscape (fig. 257). The design on these tiles was pressed on, producing raised outlines, and the areas between were then filled with glaze, with the details of the faces painted in by hand. The technical quality of these tiles was so high that many were used as ornamental tiles in furniture, and they were also made into fashionable serving trays. Luber's female figures have some affinity with Mucha's work, but if Mucha's women often emanate an aura of the erotic, Luber's females look more demure and contemplative.

Britain also produced notable Art Nouveau tile designers such as Léon Victor Solon (1872–1957), son of the eminent Marc Louis Solon who had left the Imperial Manufactory at Sèvres in 1870 to come to England to work for Minton's China Works. Léon Victor Solon followed in his father's footsteps and became one of the most outstanding Art Nouveau tile designers of his generation. He trained first at Hanley School of Art and in 1893 became a student at the South Kensington Schools in

London. He joined Minton's China Works in 1895 where he was responsible for the design of some fine Art Nouveau plaques and tiles showing floral designs and female figures (fig. 258).

Some of Solon's luxury designs were executed painstakingly by hand in tube-line technique and painted with colourful glazes enhanced at times with gold lustre. At Minton's China Works he worked with the designer John Wadsworth who had joined the firm in 1901, and they developed a particular range of hand-decorated Art Nouveau ware known as Secessionist ware aimed at a more discerning clientele, but he also produced designs for tiles with pseudo tube-line effects which were dust pressed and destined for the wider popular market.

William J. Neatby (1860–1910) was one of Britain's most prolific designers of Art Nouveau tile panels as can be seen from his output between 1895 and 1902. One of his early schemes was the terracotta decorations for the South Building of the Royal Observatory in Greenwich, London in 1895 which featured the female heads with long flowing hair that were to become a hallmark of the Art Nouveau period. A year later, in 1896, he made tile panels for the Winter Gardens in Blackpool depicting colourful full-length female figures in ornate flowing robes showing the influence of the Pre-Raphaelites and graphic designers like Aubrey Beardsley. This was followed in 1898–9 by an unusual commission for the Jubilee Theatre in St Nicholas Hospital in Gosforth, Newcastle, where the whole proscenium of the stage was tiled in a design executed in bright colours, showing long-robed female musicians sitting amid flowers and tree branches (fig. 259). He also worked with local architects from all over England, like George Skipper the designer of the Royal Arcade in Norwich built in 1898–9. It is decorated inside and out with Doulton faience and tiles designed and executed by Neatby. One of the most striking elements in this scheme are the female figures in the spandrels of the glass roof of the arcade. One of these panels is actually signed with Neatby's name leaving no doubt as to who designed them.

Perhaps Neatby's most spectacular ceramic work was done for the Everard Printing Works in Bristol designed by the architect Henry Williams for the

ABOVE [fig. 261] Hand-painted tile panel depicting a scene from *Sleeping Beauty,* designed by Margaret E. Thompson. Tile panels with fairy tales were often used to brighten children's wards in hospitals. Glazed earthenware, Doulton & Co., London, England, *c.*1905. 105 x 139 cm. Private collection.

printer Edward Everard. The building has a facade made up of rounded arches and decorative columns topped by a triangular gable flanked by two turrets. The architecture is not very Art Nouveau in style, but its strikingly colourful Art Nouveau tiled facade celebrates the printer's craft. At the top of the building is a female figure representing the spirit of light and truth, while between the ground floor and the first floor one can see the printers Johann Gutenberg and William Morris at their printing presses on either side of a winged figure representing the spirit of literature. There is also much Art Nouveau style detailing and lettering which help to accentuate the facade and make it visually striking. When the building was opened in 1901, so great were the crowds that came to see it that the police had to be called to control them. One of Neatby's last schemes was for Harrods' Meat Hall in London, which was completed in 1902. It has an extensively tiled ceiling showing flat stylized trees below which are hunting and animal scenes in circular frames. The whole design is accentuated by strong black outlines and vivid colours. The tiled pillars supporting the ceiling have beautiful abstract Art Nouveau tiles finished with gold which help to create a suitably opulent shopping environment.

Although Charles Francis Annesley Voysey (1857–1941) began his career as an

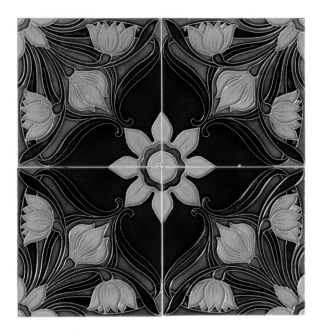

Arts and Crafts architect and became a member of the Arts Workers Guild in 1884, he was also a prolific designer of interior furnishings. At the beginning of the twentieth century he became involved with tile design and worked as a freelance artist for Pilkington's Tile & Pottery Co. His sensuous and elegantly linear designs of water lilies, seaweed, flowers and birds have a clear affinity with the prevailing Art Nouveau style at that time (fig. 260). His tile designs were executed as dust pressed relief tiles which were decorated with translucent glazes. Despite his Arts and Crafts origins, he was quite happy to see his tiles mass produced as this allowed high quality designs to find a much wider audience than if his designs had been manufactured purely as handmade tiles.

Not all Art Nouveau tile designers were men. Margaret E. Thompson was a highly trained London-based artist who had studied at the Royal College of Art and who specialized in book illustration. She became a freelance designer for Doulton about 1900 and was particularly at home with nursery rhyme subjects for tile panels which were used in hospital wards for children (fig. 261). One of the first commissions of this kind was the panels for the Lilian Ward at St Thomas's Hospital in London. It is most likely that as a freelance artist she was only responsible for the design of the panels as her drawings were easily adapted for ceramic tiles with their bold black outlines and lack of fine surface modelling and shading, and could be executed by the in-house artists in Doulton's tile department. Her panels have great charm and visual appeal and are an important part of early twentieth-century Art Nouveau tile design.

Techniques, themes and subjects

Architects and tile designers were important in establishing the fashion for Art Nouveau tiles but their work was ultimately only available to those who could afford their specialist services as part of upmarket commissions for prestigious locations. There was also widespread demand for Art Nouveau tiles for use in bathrooms, hallways and porches in ordinary homes. To respond to this demand for affordable tiles many manufacturers branched out into making Art Nouveau tiles that were

ABOVE LEFT [fig. 262] Four tiles with moulded decorations showing a stylized composition of yellow flowers (*Leucojum*). Dust-pressed buff coloured, with coloured glazes. Gilliot & Cie, Hemiksem, Belgium, 1904–1910. Each tile: 15 x 15 cm. British Museum 1995,0719.11.a-d.

ABOVE RIGHT [fig. 263] Tile with a stylized design of a yellow water lily. Dust-pressed relief, with translucent glazes. Minton, Hollins & Co., Stoke-upon-Trent, England, 1905–1910. 15 x 15 cm. British Museum 1995,0719.7.

OPPOSITE [fig. 264] Detail of a panel with peacocks and sunflowers. It is part of a series of four panels in the entrance vestibule of Hotel Jan Luyken, in Amsterdam. Dust-pressed tiles with tube-lined and painted decorations under a transparent glaze, made by Plateelbakkerij De Distel, Amsterdam, The Netherlands, *c*.1905. Each tile: 15 x 15 cm.

machine moulded and dust pressed and decorated with translucent glazes. In Britain were firms such as Minton's China Works, Pilkington's Tile & Pottery Co., Henry Richards Tile Co. and J. H. Barratt & Co.; in Belgium Gilliot & Cie and Maison Helman Céramique; in Germany the Norddeutsche Steingutfabrik, Boizenburger Wandplattenfabrik, Wessel's Wandplattenfabrik and Villeroy & Boch; and in France Faïencerie de Sarreguemines and Hippolyte Boulenger & Cie. The production of dust-pressed Art Nouveau tiles was big business: the German firm Villeroy & Boch opened new factories in Leipzig, Lübeck and Dresden; in 1912 the Dresden factory alone employed around 1,500 workers.

Mass produced Art Nouveau tiles were made in standard 15 by 15 centimetre and 15 by 7.5 centimetre formats and were dust pressed in metal moulds so that after pressing the raised lines of the design stood out on the surface. After the first biscuit firing, the tiles would be painted with translucent glazes. A variation of this process was to create machine pressed tiles with shallow relief decorations accentuated by raised or hollow lines and areas lying above as well as below the surface which, after glazing, appeared as dark lines and areas because the glaze 'pooled' in them. Some Art Nouveau tiles have both raised lines and sunken lines in the same design. This method worked best when a single dark translucent glaze was used which created subtle variations of tone and interesting contrasts between dark and light. This technique is sometimes called *émaux ombrants* from the French for 'shadow enamels'.

Another popular method was tube lining (sometimes the expression slip trailing is also used). It involved the piping of lines onto the biscuit surface of the tile much in the manner of a cook icing a cake. A small bag filled with liquid clay with a nozzle at the end was used to pipe thin lines onto the surface of the tile to make a pattern or design. When this process was completed, translucent coloured glazes were added between the lines, which acted as barriers to stop the glazes from running into each other. With tube-lined tiles, either dark or light coloured clay slip was used to delineate the design. The tube-line method is characterized by thin lines and little dots of clay, which form where lines intersect or change direction or where the tile decorator paused momentarily, which adds an attractive handmade look to this type of decoration that is absent from dust-pressed tiles with imitation tube-lined lines. At times Art Nouveau tiles were also transfer printed as this technique gave more scope to express delicate line work but these tiles lack the impact of dust-pressed tiles with raised lines and brightly coloured glazes (fig. 247).

The stencil technique was also used to decorate dust-pressed tiles and was favoured by some manufacturers on the Continent like the Dutch firms De Porceleyne Fles in Delft and Rozenburg in The Hague. It was a very common method in Spain where it was used on a large scale by tile manufacturers like Pujol i Bausis in Barcelona and Juan Bautista Segarra Bernat in Onda. Spanish 'Modernista' tiles can be very elaborate in their design and the intricate patterns can run over many tiles resulting in sinuous line work of great complexity.

Floral designs were one of the most popular themes on Art Nouveau tiles, on both single tiles and panels, and an important source for these designs was *La Plante et ses applications ornamentales* by the Swiss designer Eugène Grasset (1845–1917) published in 1897. Although Art Nouveau tile designers approached floral designs differently, two main stylistic directions can be discerned: an organic, sinuous and

ABOVE [fig. 265] Two tiles with stylized water lilies. These tiles would have been used as a horizontal border for tiled wall dadoes. Dust-pressed relief decorated with coloured glazes. Villeroy & Boch, Mettlach, Germany, c.1900–1910. Each tile: 15 x 15 cm. British Museum 1995,0719.14.a-b.

dynamic style, and a more geometric, simplified and restrained style. The organic approach was often applied to design motifs like plants and flowers with long sinuous stems and tendrils. When Walter Crane reviewed the Turin Exhibition of 1902 for *The Magazine of Art* of that year, he wrote 'A prevalent motive in the new art is a long drawn-out stem, often multiplied, and varied with "kinks" and elbows, and terminating in formal rows of disks or floral forms.' The design approach he described was the result of a gradual process of abstraction. The designer started with the actual plant or flower and gradually pared away inessential details until only the most characteristic lines were left. Although designers always turned forms to some extent into stylized compositions, the original subject could usually still be recognized, but occasionally some designers went further and created patterns of a completely abstract biomorphic nature.

When a designer used the geometric approach, a similar process of abstraction took place, but in this case it was a matter of simplification until the underlying geometric essentials were clearly exposed. During the period immediately before the First World War, this abstract geometric approach was affected by the growing interest of some architects and artists in a severe rectilinear style, which is seen particularly in the work of the Scottish architect Charles Rennie Mackintosh as well as Austrian designers like Josef Hoffmann.

Particular species of flowers lend themselves well to the Art Nouveau design treatment, including poppies, lilies, roses, cyclamen, pansies, honeysuckle, tulips, sunflowers, irises and water lilies. The water lily motif became one of the most popular designs for Art Nouveau tiles in Germany, Belgium and Britain and almost all the major tile manufacturers had one or more tiles with this motif in production (fig. 265). Birds such as herons, storks, swans, parrots, birds of paradise and peacocks also were favoured by designers because of their graceful long legs and necks or their colourful array of feathers, and were popular Art Nouveau motifs for tiles. The

LEFT [fig. 266] Tile with a pressed relief design of two butterflies by Rafael Bordalo Pinheiro. Earthenware with coloured glazes. Caldas da Rainha, Portugal, 1900–1905. 19 x 19 cm. British Museum 2005,1105.1.

peacock in particular was a much used design because of the splendour and colours of its long tail feathers and it was used on tile panels as well as single tiles (fig. 264).

Tile designs with amphibians like frogs and salamanders and insects such as butterflies and grasshoppers were in demand because of their peculiar body parts or long tails that could be exploited so effectively as Art Nouveau design elements. The Portuguese potter and tile maker Rafael Bordalo Pinheiro (1846–1905) excelled in the production of this type of tile (fig. 266). At the beginning of the twentieth century he made remarkable relief tiles at his factory in Caldas da Rainha depicting insects and amphibians. They were made from plastic clay in plaster moulds and decorated with opaque and translucent coloured glazes.

Art Nouveau tiles with animal designs are less common than tiles with floral, bird, insect and amphibian motifs but there are some noted examples such as the design by the German Otto Eckmann called *Fuchsenkopf* (fox head) printed in a lithographic technique by the German firm Villeroy & Boch in 1902 (fig. 267). In Belgium the firm Gilliot & Cie made some remarkable Art Nouveau tube-lined tiles with animals like squirrels whose curvy bushy tails fitted well into the Art Nouveau design idiom.

By 1910 the great vogue for Art Nouveau began to wane and other progressive 'isms' began to emerge such as German Expressionism, French Cubism, Italian Futurism and British Vorticism, while Dutch artists of the De Stijl group and Russian painters of the Suprematist movement were beginning to experiment with pure

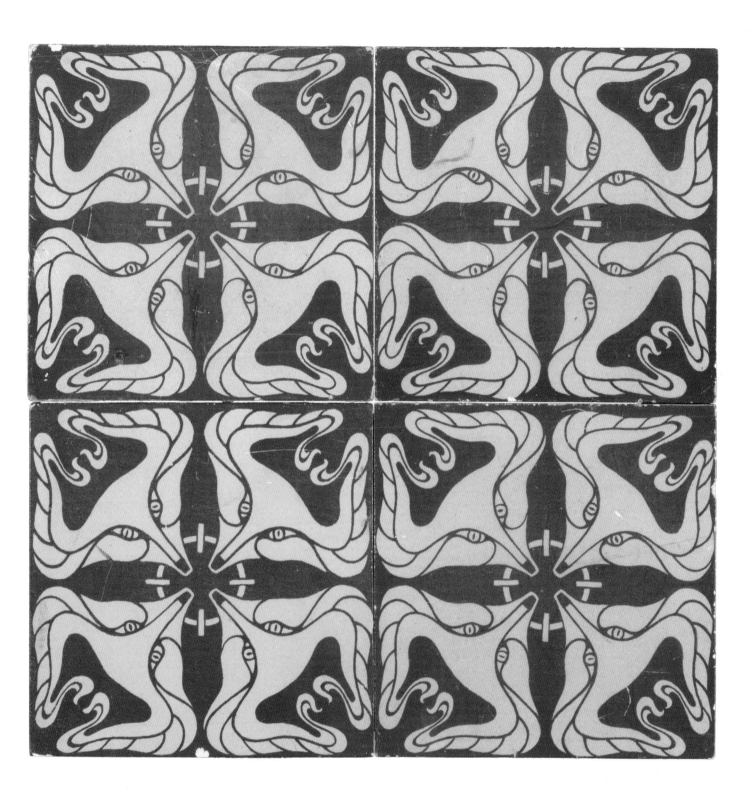

ABOVE [fig. 267] Four dust-pressed tiles decorated
under the glaze with lithographic transfer prints
of a fox's head, by the German Jugendstil designer
Otto Eckmann. Earthenware. Villeroy & Boch,
Mettlach, Germany, *c.*1902. Each tile: 15 x 15 cm.
British Museum 2004,1220.1.a-d. Purchase funded
by British Museum Friends.

geometric abstraction. The radical changes in art and design were augmented by the upheavals of the First World War. When peace returned in 1919 there was a different world, and in art and design this found expression in the 1920s and 1930s through exotic, semi-abstract and completely non-representational forms. These changes were driven by a new breed of designers who were the products of a revolutionary type of art education epitomized by the German Bauhaus first in Weimar and later in Dessau and by progressive artists and designers in communist Russia. Many of these new revolutionary strands met in the design world of Art Deco.

From Art Nouveau to Art Deco

Even before the First World War, reactions against Art Nouveau and its excess of decoration were clearly discernible. These were given voice by architects such as the Austro-Hungarian Adolf Loos (1870–1933) who wrote a controversial essay in 1910 about the nature of design called *Ornament and Crime* in which he repudiated the florid style of Art Nouveau and advocated the abandonment of excessive decoration. He wrote: 'Evolution of culture is equivalent to the removal of ornament from utilitarian objects.' He practised what he preached and in 1910 he built the Steiner House in Vienna, Austria with plain stuccoed walls on the outside and greatly reduced ornamentation in the interior.

His exhortations and architectural examples were not necessarily followed but

ABOVE [fig. 268] Tile panel above the doorway of an apartment block on rue Belliard in Paris, France, by the French architect Henri Deneux, built in 1910. The striking geometric tile patterns around the figure of an architect at his drawing board can be regarded as precursors to Art Deco.

RIGHT [fig. 269] Detail of the tiles arranged in zigzag shapes on the facade of the home of the English architect Edgar Wood in Hale, near Manchester, England, built between 1914 and 1916. The zigzag design foreshadows the Art Deco style of the 1920s and 30s.

they were part of a general trend that led to the use of more simplified forms in architecture and this also affected the design and use of tiles. This can be seen in the work of the French architect Henri Deneux (1876–1969) who built an apartment block for his own use on rue Belliard in Paris between 1910 and 1913. Although the exterior is completely ornamented with tiles, he used undecorated square, triangular and round tiles set in concrete, creating abstract patterns across the wall surfaces which seem to foreshadow Art Deco. This abstract use of tiles was a far cry from the intricate and at times fussy organic and sinuous style of Art Nouveau. The only representational design element was a tile panel with the figure of an architect at his drawing board in a simplified flat style above the main entrance (fig. 268).

In Britain there was also an architect whose work was ahead of his time. This was the Manchester-based Edgar Wood who worked on some groundbreaking commissions just before and during the First World War. He came from Middleton near Manchester and by the beginning of the twentieth century had become a respected local architect. Wood had dealings with the Manchester tile firm Pilkington's and he designed its exhibition stand for the Franco-British Exhibition in London in 1908. For the exterior of the stand he used a creative interplay of abstract chevron patterns made of plain tiles. In 1914–16 he built his own house in Hale just outside Manchester. The house was constructed of brick but it has a flat roof and a concave facade with stone dressings. On the facade above the front door (fig. 269) is

a large panel of striking patterned tiles in the form of the strong zigzag design which was to become such a major feature of Art Deco during the 1920s and 1930s.

The Dutch painter and architect Theo van Doesburg (1883–1931), who founded the abstract De Stijl movement in 1917, was a strong advocate of elementary form and colour in painting, sculpture and architectural design. He participated in the decoration of a newly built holiday home for children called De Vonk in Noordwijkerhout designed by the architect J. J. P. Oud between 1917 and 1919. Van Doesburg designed the tiled floor for the entrance hall consisting of machine-made square black, white and buff tiles, and for the exterior he created coloured ornamental brick panels to decorate the main entrance (fig. 270). These abstract panels were executed in white, black, blue, yellow and green glazed bricks of different sizes and resemble the kind of abstract painting advocated by the De Stijl artists. The horizontal and vertical cement lines between the polychrome bricks are an important part of the overall abstract geometric composition.

The revolutionary De Stijl movement was only one facet of various developments in art and design in Holland at that time, and an opposing design strand known as Expressionism was also much in vogue. In Amsterdam there was a specific group of architects called the 'Amsterdam School' who advocated a more individual, subjective and spontaneous approach to architecture and design. Although they used abstract forms they tended to be more organic in their derivation and stylized naturalistic forms were also part of their design repertoire. This can be seen in the famous Tuschinksi theatre and cinema in Amsterdam. It was designed by Hijman Louis de Jong (1882–1942) and was built between 1918 and 1921 in cooperation with a number of designers who were responsible for the exotic interior and exterior

ABOVE [fig. 270] Panel of polychrome bricks designed by the Dutch artist Theo van Doesburg on the exterior of De Vonk, a house in Noordwijkerhout, The Netherlands, 1917–1919. The composition of the coloured bricks corresponds closely to Van Doesburg's geometrical abstract paintings when he was leader of the groundbreaking Dutch art group De Stijl.

RIGHT [fig. 271] Tile on the exterior of the Tuschinski theatre in Amsterdam, The Netherlands, built between 1918–1921. The tiles and architectural faience were made by Plateelbakkerij Delft in Hilversum and feature an Expressionist blend of semi-figurative and angular abstract forms. Glazed faience with relief decorations.

decorations. The faience decorations for the exterior were designed by Barend Jordens and were made by the ceramics firm Plateelbakkerij Delft in Hilversum (fig. 271). They show an extraordinary series of designs ranging from human and animal forms cowering under jagged thunderbolts and ornamental features borrowed from Hindu temples in Indonesia, including elephants' heads, to organic abstract motifs reminiscent of the scales of reptiles. The Tuschinksi theatre is now generally acknowledged as a unique piece of early Art Deco architecture.

Art Deco

Art Deco is now recognized as one of the most exciting design manifestations of the twentieth-century interwar period. The term 'Art Deco' comes from the important international design exhibition held in Paris in 1925 under the name Exposition Internationale des Arts Décoratifs. It ran for six months and was seen by over fifteen million people. International exhibitions were important venues for the dissemination and exchange of new design ideas and this exhibition in particular was intended to give an overview of the best of modern design produced by the

EXPOSITION INTERNATIONALE DES ARTS DÉCORATIFS — PARIS - 1925
PAVILLON «LA MAITRISE» Atelier des ARTS APPLIQUÉS des GALERIES LAFAYETTE
(par Jean Hiriart, Georges Tribout, et Georges Beau, architectes)   A. P

industrialized nations of the post-war world. With the notable exceptions of Germany and the United States many countries were represented. France, the host country, not only had a national pavilion but famous French manufacturers like Sèvres and fashionable Paris design stores such as Galeries Lafayette also had their own individual pavilions. The latter's pavilion was called *La Maitrise*, where the latest French fashions of the 1920s were on show with an emphasis on elegance, hand applied decoration and the use of expensive materials and processes. Visitors entered the pavilion by walking under a spectacular sunburst motif that was to become the iconic design symbol of the Art Deco style. The modernist architect Le Corbusier, who believed a house was a machine for living in, had his own pavilion called *L'Esprit Nouveau*. With its elemental and purist forms it became a showcase for his progressive ideas and was one of the most modern pavilions of the exhibition.

Art Deco was an eclectic style which came from many different sources including the work of European avant-garde artists and architects, classical architecture, the ancient civilizations of Egypt and South America, and exotic cultures from the Far East, but it also drew on the ideas of a contemporary world dominated by the machine. This myriad of sources clearly affected the design of tiles which showed the clean sleek lines, bold abstract forms and bright colours that became so characteristic of architecture and design in the interwar period. However the actual phrase 'Art Deco' was not coined in the 1920s and 1930s. Instead the words 'modern'

ABOVE [fig. 272] Postcard of the pavilion of the Galeries Lafayette at the Exposition Internationale des Arts Décoratifs et Industriels Modernes in Paris, 1925. It was one of the leading French pavilions in the show with a striking 'sunburst' motif over the entrance.

RIGHT [fig. 273] An abstract tube-lined Art Deco tile. The bold juxtaposition of the orange, black and white glazes is typical of ceramic design of the inter-war period. Glazed earthenware. Richards Tiles, Stoke-upon-Trent, England, 1937. 10 x 10 cm. Private collection.

or the French 'moderne' were used. The term 'Art Deco' was brought into use by the design critic Bevis Hillier in the late 1960s when he published a book in 1968 called *Art Deco of the Twenties and Thirties*. This was followed by a groundbreaking exhibition in 1971 at the Minneapolis Institute of Arts in the United States called *The World of Art Deco*.

Art Deco styles and themes

The wide range of styles and themes on Art Deco tiles came from many different sources in the history of art and design. Most of them were from the avant-garde art movements of the time like the French Cubists, the Italian Futurists and the English Vorticists, but tile designs were also influenced by contemporary design movements like the German Bauhaus, the Dutch De Stijl group and the Russian Constructivists who favoured elementary form and colour. In addition to these modern trends, inspiration was also drawn from the art and designs of ancient Egypt and South America and even African tribal art.

The use of abstract geometric form became one of the most memorable features of Art Deco design. Pure abstract form which had no reference to the natural world had already been explored by of a number of European painters such as Piet Mondrian in Holland, Wassily Kandinsky in Germany and Kasimir Malevich in Russia. In particular Mondrian and his fellow artists in the Dutch De Stijl group were important

LEFT [fig. 274] Design for an Art Deco entrance hall with a striking ceramic floor made of light and dark coloured tiles arranged in a geometrical abstract repeat pattern. Illustrated in Cyril Carter and H. R. Hidden, *Wall and Floor Tiling*, Caxton Publishing Co., 1937.

pioneers of abstract art and design. They pared down the shapes of the natural world to their basic geometric components and used the strong primary colours of red, blue and yellow in combination with white, grey and black. They had a marked influence on the German Bauhaus (1919–1933) whose students were taught to approach design from a standpoint of elementary form and colour. During the interwar period the principles of Bauhaus design education also began to influence art colleges in other European countries and it is therefore not surprising to see Art Deco tiles with abstract motifs in the 1930s.

Abstract Art Deco tiles fall into two categories, tiles with static forms and tiles with dynamic motifs. Tiles with static forms were usually composed of vertical and horizontal lines which intersected to create a composition of interlocking squares and rectangles that were then filled in with different colours. Tiles with dynamic motifs had intersecting diagonal lines and curves which created the suggestion of movement and jazzy shapes. Tiles with abstract motifs were also often grouped together to create zigzag and sunburst designs, and these were used with great effect as part of tiled fireplaces or above the main entrances of buildings. Strong colours were popular, particularly red, green, blue, orange and black, supplemented with metallic lustre colours like silver and gold. The latter in particular were used to add a glitzy element to upmarket Art Deco tile decorations.

Abstract Art Deco tiles were used with great effect on buildings in America and Europe. In America, architects applied them extensively to apartment buildings and skyscrapers. Between 1910 and 1930 the brothers George and Edward Blum designed many apartment and commercial buildings in New York extensively decorated with

RIGHT [fig. 275] The imposing facade of the Hoover Building, Perivale, London, was designed by Wallis, Gilbert & Partners in the early 1930s. Above the central door is a stunning sunburst motif made of tiles, metal and glass.

LEFT [fig. 276] Tiled entrance of Hilversum Town Hall, The Netherlands, designed by the architect W. M. Dudok and decorated with tiles made by De Porceleyne Fles in Delft, between 1923 and 1931. The gold, black and red tiles of the columns create a colourful contrast with the blue wall tiles in the background.

brick patterns, architectural ceramics and tiles. One of their best buildings in the Art Deco style is Gramercy House at 235 East 22nd Street in New York built in 1929–30. This has striking blue-green and buff faience tile friezes and other decorative bands of triangular tiles running along the entire facade.

In Britain Wallis, Gilbert & Partners, an architectural practice specializing in factory buildings, designed the Hoover Building in Perivale, London, which is now one of the most iconic Art Deco buildings in Europe. It was constructed in the early 1930s for the American firm Hoover Ltd and it has a long white fronted facade punctuated by tall columns with faience tiles at the base and the top which gives them an Egyptian air. The real glory is the main entrance with its sharply angled metal decorations on the doors and windows and a wonderful sunburst motif of coloured tiles, metal and glass above the main door (fig. 275). The red, green, blue and black ceramic tiles were made by Carter & Co. and create a vibrant splash of colour on the mainly white facade.

In Holland the architect Willem Marinus Dudok created an internationally acclaimed masterpiece of Art Deco architecture when he designed and built Hilversum Town Hall between 1923 and 1931 (fig. 276). Dudok was the contemporary of the modernist architects Walter Gropius, Le Corbusier and Mies van der Rohe and

ABOVE LEFT [fig. 277] Grill tile with a streamlined deer leaping through the air. Leaping and running deer were popular Art Deco motifs. Glazed earthenware. American Encaustic Tiling Co. Ltd, Zanesville, United States, 1925–30. Smithsonian Institution, Washington, DC.

ABOVE RIGHT [fig. 278] Tube-lined tile with semi-abstract streamlined seascape and flying seagulls. Glazed earthenware. Carter & Co., Poole. England, 1935. 10 x 10 cm. Private collection.

in some ways was sympathetic to their notion of 'less is more', but he did not shy away from ornamentation and with great subtlety and finesse integrated ceramics in the form of abstract colour fields made of tiles. Hilversum Town Hall is made of smooth yellow brick and the overall composition of the building is a sophisticated balance between high and low, vertical and horizontal, narrow and broad. Coloured glazed bricks and tiles have been used to accentuate the walkway towards the main entrance of the building. There are square columns clad with gold coloured tiles with black and red tiles at the top and bottom seen against a wall of azure blue tiles, creating abstract ceramic colour fields of great beauty. The floor of the walkway has been lined with red tiles creating a permanent red carpet. Inside the building gold coloured tiles have been used to decorate the inside of the window jambs, columns supporting the roof and, most striking of all, the wall behind the seats of the mayor and town councillors in the main council chamber. This profusion of colour and gold was inspired by one of Dudok's visit to Ravenna in Italy where the Byzantine mosaics in the churches made a deep impression in him.

Another feature of Art Deco was the streamlined and aerodynamic forms that became so symbolic of the interwar machine age. This had been explored earlier in the century in the painting and sculptures of the Italian Futurists, who had influenced the British rebel avant-garde group the Vorticists founded in 1914 who also experimented with these themes. When this was applied to design it meant stripping form down to its bare essentials with shapes expressing speed, dynamism and motion. Tiles depicted streamlined birds in flight, sleek deer running or the taut curved lines of billowing ships' sails (figs 277, 278).

An exotic element was introduced into Art Deco design following the discovery in Egypt of the tomb of Tutankhamun by Lord Carnarvon in 1922. This sparked great interest amongst designers and architects, and the contents of the royal tomb with its

furniture, sculptures and jewellery, and above all the mummy of the boy king wearing his famous golden mask, created a short lived frenzy in interwar art and design. Tiles and faience were also affected by this craze. Egyptian themes like sphinxes appeared and lotus buds and papyrus flower motifs became popular design elements, particularly for the colourful architectural faience decorations on cinemas in the 'Egyptian' style (fig. 279).

Representational landscape scenes executed in a highly stylized manner were also popular on Art Deco tiles. Trees and buildings were reduced to their essential outlines and clouds became a collection of circular shapes. Perspective was almost eliminated to make the scene look flat and strong colours were used to accentuate

ABOVE [fig. 279] Detail of the colourful neo-Egyptian glazed faience decorations on the facade of the Art Deco Carlton Cinema, Islington, London, England. Designed by the architect George Coles, 1930.

RIGHT [fig. 280] Art Deco tile panel executed in a tube-line technique. Designed by the Belgian designer Joseph Roelants for Gilliot & Cie. It is a preparatory study for a larger tile panel that formed part of the firm's stand at the World Exhibition in Brussels in 1935. It shows the head of Mercury, the Roman god of commerce, set against a stylized industrial landscape. Glazed earthenware. Hemiksem, Belgium, 1935.

different parts of the composition. This formalized way of representing rural landscape was also used to create industrial landscapes depicting factories with smoking chimneys and electricity pylons or industrial harbour scenes with ocean liners and cranes; this kind of landscape fitted well with the vogue for machine aesthetics in the 1930s.

A topical theme in Art Deco tiles was sporting subjects. Interest in outdoor pursuits and sport became increasingly common amongst the various classes in society in Europe in the interwar period. Shooting, sailing and horse riding for the upper classes; hiking, swimming, golf or taking the car for a spin for the middle classes; fishing, cycling, boating and football for the lower classes were activities with which to fill increasing leisure time. This was all reflected on interwar tiles. Edward Bawden, for example, designed several series of tiles for Carter & Co. in the 1920s showing a whole range of leisure pursuits executed in a simplified and comic way, offering an affectionate portrayal of British outdoor life (fig. 281).

Advertising panels

An interesting feature of tiles in the interwar period was how manufacturers of modern means of transport like bicycles, motorbikes and motorcars used tiles as a medium to promote and advertise their products. An amazing early example is the Michelin Building on the Fulham Road in London, a tailor-made headquarters for the Michelin Tyre Company which was opened in 1911. It was designed by the French architect François Espinasse and was a commercial palace dedicated to the world of the motor car with much use of faience and tiles on its exterior and interior decorations. The building's best features are its many tile panels showing famous motor car races (fig. 282). They celebrated a new and glamorous form of transport made quicker and more comfortable through the use of the pneumatic tyre. François Espinasse called on the French firm Gilardoni Fils et Cie based in Paris to design and produce the hand-painted panels and, although the various racing scenes are set within Art Nouveau style borders, some of the cars depicted showed the use of streamlining which looks forward to Art Deco.

ABOVE LEFT [fig. 281] Hand-painted tile from Edward Bawden's series 'The Chase', made by Carter & Co., Poole, England, 1935–40. This series was first designed in c.1922. Tin-glazed earthenware. 15.5 x 15.5 cm. British Museum 1980,0307.164.c.

ABOVE RIGHT [fig. 282] Detail of one of the hand-painted tile panels on the exterior of the Michelin Building in London, built in 1909–1911. The panels depict famous early 20th-century motor car races and were made by the French firm Gilardoni & Cie in Paris, France. Glazed earthenware.

ABOVE [fig. 283] Detail of a hand-painted tile panel in situ, with the logo of the Dutch Gazelle bicycle factory in Dieren, The Netherlands. Designed by André Vlaanderen and made by the Plateelbakkerij Delft in Hilversum, 1927. The leaping gazelle inside a bicycle wheel is meant to denote speed and the name Vael Ouwe is an old name for what is now the national park De Veluwe. Glazed earthenware.

The Studebaker Automobile Company was a major American car manufacturer based in Hamilton, Ohio, during the first half of the twentieth century. Although Studebaker cars now belong to the vanished world of great classic cars, in the 1920s and 1930s they were known worldwide for their quality and reliability. A rare surviving tiled advertising panel made in 1924 in Seville, Spain, shows an open topped Studebaker car filled with fashionably dressed young women enjoying 'a spin'. The panel was made by the Sevillian tile manufacturer Manual Ramos Rejano and is still in situ at Tetuan no. 9 in Seville.

The logo of the Dutch bicycle manufacturer Gazelle – a gazelle placed within a bicycle tyre – was created by the company's main designer, the graphic artist André Vlaanderen (1881–1955), who chose the gazelle because it is the fastest known deer and its shape lends itself to being depicted in a stylized aerodynamic way suggesting fast movement. The logo of the Gazelle factory executed in black on either a silver or a gold lustre background features prominently on two large tile panels in the entrance hall of the main office in the town of Dieren (fig. 283). Both panels were made by the Plateelbakkerij Delft in Hilversum in 1927 to commemorate the factory's thirty-fifth anniversary and were again designed by André Vlaanderen. They show various scenes relating to the history of the factory set within decorative Art Deco borders.

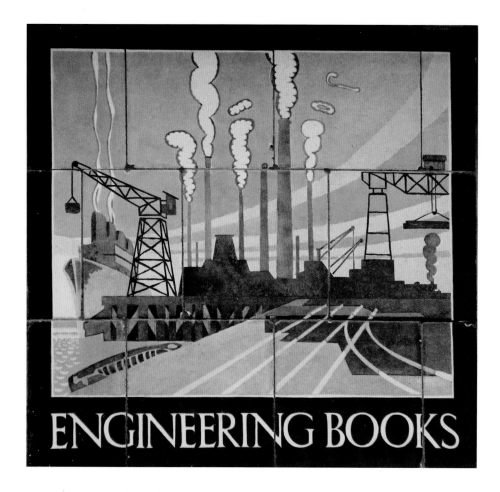

ENGINEERING BOOKS

Women tile designers

Another characteristic of the interwar period was that women designers became increasingly prominent. Previously women's role had been largely that of executing the designs made by men, but women had now become active as highly qualified and well-trained tile designers in their own right. In the British tile industry, Truda Adams (later Carter) and Dora N. Batty designed for Carter & Co.; Sylvia Packard and Rosalind Ord ran their own small firm Packard & Ord; and Polly Brace produced designs for the firm Dunsmore Tiles. There was also the interesting all-women venture of the Ceramic Studio at Olifantsfontein in South Africa.

Truda Adams (she became known as Truda Carter when she divorced the ceramic artist John Adams and married the manufacturer Cyril Carter in 1931) was an in-house designer at Carter & Co. in Poole and was responsible for many highly decorative floral and bird designs in the 1920s which show the influence of modernist painting and French Art Deco design. Her floral tiles can be bold and semi-abstract but are also at times minimalist. Some of her designs, executed in dashes of bright colour, are reminiscent of the colourful abstractions of Kandinsky.

Dora N. Batty was a freelance artist who undertook book illustration, poster and pottery design and she also taught at the London Central School of Art. For Carter & Co. she created a series of designs in the early 1920s called Nursery Rhymes and Nursery Toys (fig. 286) which were used on tiles and plates and seem to have been specifically aimed at the children's market. In Carter's catalogues they were

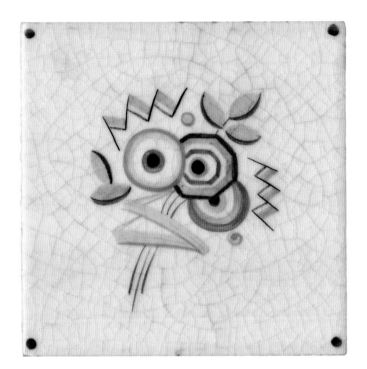

ABOVE LEFT [fig. 285] Tile with a hand-painted floral decoration in the Art Deco style by Truda Adams. Tin-glazed earthenware. Carter & Co., Poole, England, c.1925. 15 x 15 cm. Private collection.

ABOVE RIGHT [fig. 286] Tile with a hand-painted picture of Little Miss Muffet from a series of Nursery Rhyme tiles designed by Dora N. Batty. Tin-glazed earthenware. Carter & Co., Poole. England, c.1925. 12.7 x 12.7 cm. Private collection.

advertised as having 'been very successfully used in fireplace surrounds and to add colour and interest to simple wall tiling schemes'. The designs were cheerful and painted in vivid colours, capturing the figures of nursery rhyme characters and animals with playful yet precise linear definition.

Dunsmore Tiles was set up in the mid-1920s by Mary Brace (known as Polly) and Kathleen Pilsbury in Camden Hill, London. Most of the tiles they produced were designed by Polly Brace who had trained at the Central School of Art. She specialized in fish, bird and animal designs executed either as hand paintings or in a technique combining hand painting and stencil (fig. 287). Her hand-painted tiles show great dexterity and skill and fluent handling of the brush, and the stencilled and hand-painted tiles combine flat areas of colour with bold line work. One interesting series of designs based on the signs of the zodiac clearly shows the influence of Egyptian art which was so popular at that time in the bold flat forms of the star signs.

Sylvia Packard and Rosalind Ord were both qualified art teachers who had begun to decorate tiles in a small way in the early 1930s with tile blanks bought at Carter in Poole where their tiles were initially also fired. As their reputations grew and more commissions came in, they decided to set up a formal partnership in 1936 under the name of Packard & Ord. It had its base in Hungerford, where they were joined by a third woman designer Thea Bridges. They now had a kiln and could fire their own tiles but they still bought ready-made blanks from other firms like Rhodes Tile Company in Stoke-upon-Trent, so were tile decorators only. Their hand-painted designs ranged from flowers, birds and animals to nursery rhyme subjects painted in a charming, free, simplified style which was very popular in the 1930s. One series of tiles painted by Rosalind Ord in a streamlined style is known as Decorative Animals. They show deftly painted animals like hares, deer and dogs running along swiftly (fig. 288).

In South Africa in 1925 the artists Gladys Short and Marjorie Johnson established the Ceramic Studio where they made tableware, studio pottery and tiles. They rented

a kiln and workshop at an abandoned potter's village at Olifantsfontein. It was a remote location but good local clays were available and they built up a successful business. They were joined by other women like Joan Methley, Audrey Frank and Thelma Currie in 1926–7. This all female pottery commune was responsible for important tile installations throughout South Africa, such as the tiles painted with local subjects for the new railway station in Johannesburg in 1928 and the tiles with nursery rhymes designed by Audrey Frank for the children's ward and play rooms at the Groote Schuur Hospital in Cape Town in 1934.

Modern artists and tiles

Throughout the twentieth century tiles were not just the provenance of specialist tile designers. Well-known modern artists also turned to the medium of tiles to express their visual ideas. Artists such as Duncan Grant, Nikolai Suetin, Bernard Leach, Maurits Escher, Salvador Dali and Joan Miró, were all involved in making or designing tiles and ceramic plaques at some point in their distinguished careers, either as single tiles or panels or as commissions for specific architectural open air locations. Tiles are an extremely versatile medium that can accommodate very different artistic expressions and methods of working. Above all these artists discovered the exciting transformation of clay and pigments in the heat of a kiln which was so different from what they normally did with paint on canvas or prints on paper.

The Scottish born painter Duncan Grant (1885–1978) studied art in London and became part of the Bloomsbury group of artists which included the painter Vanessa Bell and the art critic Roger Fry. Grant's artistic talents found an outlet in the Omega Workshops set up by Roger Fry in 1913, which was a private venture to bring the sensibilities of modern art more in touch with daily life by the production of decorative designs. Fry discovered that his loose and free style of painting was very suitable for working on ceramics and tiles. Although the Omega workshops closed in 1919, Duncan Grant continued to paint tiles and some found practical uses in fireplaces and on stoves. A noted commission in the late 1920s was the tiled stove

ABOVE LEFT [fig. 287] Tile with a stencilled and hand-painted decoration of a heron by Polly Brace. Glazed earthenware, Dunsmore Tiles, London, 1929. 15 x 15 cm. British Museum 1980,0307.140.

ABOVE RIGHT [fig. 288] Tile with a hand-painted decoration of landscape with a running deer and a tree by Sylvia Packard. Glazed earthenware. Packard & Ord, Hungerford, England, c.1937. 15 x 15 cm. Private collection.

RIGHT [fig. 289] Ceramic stove with tiles painted by Duncan Grant. The freely painted decorations are reminiscent of the work of the French avant-garde painter Henri Matisse. Glazed earthenware. England, c.1929. Victoria and Albert Museum, London.

for Margaret Bulley who collected examples of modern decorative art. The tiles used on the stove were painted by Duncan Grant with fruit and foliage on the front and female figures carrying flowers on the sides (fig. 289). Grant employed a colourful and casual style of painting somewhat reminiscent of the French painter Matisse which he adapted cleverly to the confined spaces of the tiles.

The Russian artist Nikolai Mikhailovich Suetin (1897–1954) turned from painting to ceramics as part of a state-sponsored drive to get fine artists involved with practical design work. Suetin was a star pupil of the Russian Suprematist painter Kasimir Malevich (1878–1935). Suprematism was an abstract style of painting that developed in Russia between 1913 and the early 1920s. It began with simple shapes like squares and circles and moved to more complex compositions made up of variously coloured geometric forms and straight lines. The emergence of Suprematism coincided with the Russian Revolution of 1917 when easel painting was denounced as a decadent bourgeois activity and artists were encouraged to go and work in factories as designers and contribute in a useful way to the well-being

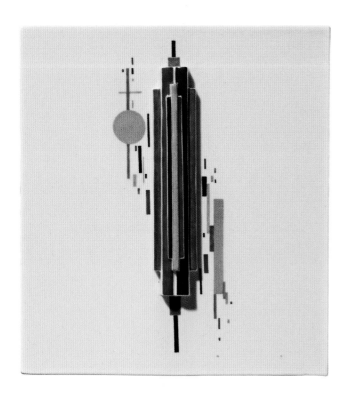 

of the newly founded communist state. Suetin started work at the State Porcelain Factory in Petrograd (formerly St Petersburg) in 1923 where he designed Suprematist compositions for use on ceramics, and under his direction they were applied to tableware and ceramic plaques. The ceramic plaques were known as *architektons*: abstract reliefs built up from thin rectangular ceramic strips of different lengths on a white ground painted with red, green, black and grey glazes (fig. 290). They were attempts to make Suprematism more useful by applying it to architecture, but in the end very few of these experimental plaques were made and those that have survived are now rare examples of the tile art of early communist Russia.

The well-known studio potter Bernard Leach (1887–1979) began his career as an artist by studying etching at the London School of Art in Kensington before settling in Japan where he worked as an artist. He became fascinated with Japanese raku pottery and then decided to take up making pottery himself. In 1920 he made his home in St Ives in Cornwall and set up a craft pottery, where from 1927 he also made tiles. The tiles had a definite handmade look about them and he referred to them as showing 'a certain degree of irregularity for which no apology is needed'. His stoneware tiles show bold and fluent brush work learnt in Japan which he used to paint primeval looking images of animals, fish, birds and trees or oriental scenes in the form of black silhouettes (fig. 291). His work fitted well with the fashion for hand-decorated tiles in vogue at that time.

Some artists became involved with tiles almost by accident, like the famous Dutch printmaker Maurits Escher (1898–1972) who became fascinated by tiles when he made a trip to Spain in 1922 and saw Moorish mosaic tiles in the Alhambra. He began to study their principles of tessellation, and used them as the foundation for his own work. He wrote: 'The Moors were masters in the filling of surface with congruent figures and left no gaps. In the Alhambra, in Spain, especially, they decorated the

ABOVE LEFT [fig. 290] Plaque with three-dimensional abstract relief ornaments in the form of clusters of thin rectangular rods of different lengths, designed by Nikolai Suetin. A rare plaque influenced by the abstract Suprematist movement of the Russian painter Kasimir Malevich. Hard-paste porcelain. State Porcelain Factory, Petrograd (St Petersburg), Russia, 1923–4. 22 x 20.1 cm. British Museum 1988,0609.1.

ABOVE RIGHT [fig. 291] Panel of tiles featuring a Japanese well, a Viking boat, a big cat and a Japanese wood-burning climbing kiln made by Bernard Leach. Stoneware painted with iron-oxide. St Ives, Cornwall, England, 1938. Each tile: 15 x 15 cm. Victoria and Albert Museum, London.

ABOVE LEFT [fig. 292] Black-and-white tile mosaic in the Alhambra, Spain. Moorish tile mosaic was a formative influence on the work of Dutch graphic artist Maurits Escher (see fig. 293). Glazed earthenware. Granada, Spain, 14th century.

ABOVE RIGHT [fig. 293] Detail of tiled column with black-and-white alternating tiles in the shape of swans in the entrance hall of a school in The Hague, Holland. Designed by the Dutch graphic artist Maurits Escher. The tiles were made by De Porceleyne Fles in Delft, The Netherlands, 1959. Inspiration for the black-and-white alternating shapes came from a visit to the Alhambra, Spain in the 1930s (see fig. 292).

walls by placing congruent multicoloured pieces of majolica together without interstices.' In the 1950s and 1960s Escher made designs for tiled columns for the entrance halls of two schools in The Hague (1959–60) and in Baarn (1968–70). They show alternating black-and-white images of fish, birds and reptiles made by the firm De Porceleyne Fles in Delft and add a touch of visual interest to the modern entrances of these schools (fig. 293).

The famous Spanish Surrealist painter Salvador Dali (1904–89) is better known for his paintings than his tiles, but his contribution to tile design is nevertheless worth noting. In the early 1950s Maurice Duchin in New York commissioned Dali to design a set of six tiles that were to represent three pairs of themes: War and Peace, Love and Music and Life and Death. Dali gave unique visual expression to these elemental themes. Life, for example, is shown as a sun from which emanate rays of heat but also branches with leaves signifying growth, while death is symbolized by a dead starfish lying on sand. In 1954 the tiles were executed as hand-stencilled images on factory-made blanks by the El Siglio factory of Miguel Pinon in Onda, Spain, and each tile shows Dali's signature (fig. 294).

Another Spanish Surrealist artist Joan Miró (1893–1983) made tiles a more significant part of his artistic output. In his painting he had sought to subvert the dominance of reason and logic with creative forms that emerged from the unconscious mind. In the 1950s he began to work with tiles and created several important murals amongst which are *Wall of the Moon and Wall of the Sun* for the UNESCO building in Paris in 1955–8; he also created a tiled mural for Harvard University in 1961. He undertook the creation of several public tile installations and sculptures in Barcelona of which *Dona I Ocell* (Woman and Bird) made in 1982–3 is one of his most famous (fig. 295). It was completed shortly before his death, and is situated on the edge of a pool in what is now Parc de Joan Miró in Barcelona. It is

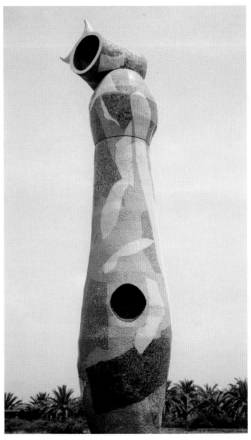

22 metres tall and covered with broken yellow, red, blue and green ceramic tiles which were applied to the sculpture by the ceramicist Joan Gardy Artigas with whom Miró had also collaborated on earlier murals. The impression this tiled sculpture makes varies greatly: some see it as a giant phallic symbol, others regard it as an elemental monolith on a par with the stones at Stonehenge. Whatever the impression it creates the coloured tiles add great impact to its memorable and striking form.

Modern and post-modern tiles

The second half of the twentieth century saw many changes and developments in tile production and design. In the aftermath of the Second World War there was much rebuilding in the so-called International Style, characterized by the use of steel, concrete and glass and influenced by the famous dictum of the architect Mies van der Rohe 'less is more'. It deliberately rejected historical precedents and local traditions, and the simple modern forms of the architecture were well suited to meet the complex building needs of an emerging post-war society. Although excessive decoration was shunned by modernist architects, tiles with abstract modernist designs, particularly screen printed tiles, found favour and were used with great effect in modern buildings of the 1950s and 1960s.

This was followed during the 1970s by a growing reaction against modernism and its dogmatic and narrow rules about what architecture should look like and the limited role assigned to ornamentation. These concerns were given voice by the American architect Robert Venturi who famously countered Mies van der Rohe's

ABOVE LEFT [fig. 294] Tile with a stencilled decoration symbolizing 'music' by the Spanish surrealist artist Salvador Dali. Part of a set of six tiles made by the El Siglio tile factory. Glazed earthenware. Onda, Spain, 1954. 20 x 20 cm. Museo del Azulejo, Onda, Spain.

ABOVE RIGHT [fig. 295] Tiled column named *Dona I Ocell* (Women and Bird), made by the Spanish Surrealist artist Joan Miró. Glazed tile mosaic. Barcelona, Spain, 1982–3. H. 22 m.

ABOVE LEFT [fig. 296] Two dust-pressed tiles with the screen printed 'Sun and Moon' pattern designed by Peggy Angus. This design was first introduced in *c*.1952 and remained in production throughout the 1950s, 60s and 70s. Glazed earthenware. Carter & Co., Poole, England, 1967. Each tile: 15 x 15 cm. Private collection.

ABOVE RIGHT [fig. 297] Tile with an English village scene designed by Sir John Bowman. Screen printed. Purbeck Decorative Tile Co., Dorset, England, early 1950s. 10 x 10 cm. Private collection.

dictum 'less is more' with 'less is a bore'. Venturi's stance became part of a trend that saw the return of historical styles, often in the form of pastiches or add-on elements which made buildings more 'fun' to look at. Tiles and terracotta also became part of this post-modernist revival of architectural ornament which saw the emergence of retro styles such as Victorian, Art Nouveau and even Art Deco that fed the demand for more decorative environments. This made the last quarter of the twentieth century a vibrant and diverse period for tiles in which both large and small firms as well as individual tile makers were able to flourish.

Screen printed tiles

Screen printing was a new method of tile decoration developed in the early 1950s. It is a stencil method of print making in which a design is imposed on a screen of polyester or other fine mesh, with the blank areas being coated with an impermeable substance. Ink is then forced into the exposed mesh areas with a blade or squeegee and then onto the ceramic surface of the tiles.

In Britain, firms like Carter and Pilkington's led the way in screen printing. It was particularly well suited for the bold abstract designs which came from noted artists like Peggy Angus who undertook freelance work for Carter. She developed an interest in abstract patterns during a visit to Russia in the 1930s where she learned about the geometric and machine inspired patterns of the Russian Constructivists. She often made bold lino-cut patterns which then became the basis for screen printed tiles, and were very effective as large-scale repeat patterns over extended areas. In the

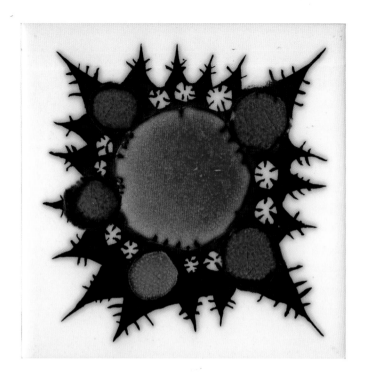

early days of screen printing tiles were marketed as 'hand printed' because each tile had to be screen printed individually by hand. This 'hand printing' and the fact that the patterns had been designed by professional artists bestowed on them an aura of real art. They fitted well with the modernist buildings of the 1950s and 1960s and were used for locations like schools, cafeterias, entrances of tower blocks, offices and airports.

At this time artistic screen printed tiles were also made by smaller firms like the Purbeck Decorative Tile Company who offered screen printed tiles designed by Sir John Bowman (fig. 297). Very unusual screen printed tiles were made by Kenneth Clark Ceramics; the firm was run by the husband and wife team Kenneth and Ann Clark who were both innovative tile designers. Ann Clark (nee Wynn-Reeves) designed many screen printed tiles with both abstract and figurative subjects that were created using a wax resist method (fig. 298). The black outline of the design was screen printed with wax-based ink and the remainder of the design filled with water-based coloured glazes which were kept from running by the wax-based outlines. In this way bold and painterly patterns and designs were created aimed at the 'modern' taste of the 1950s and 1960s.

In the 1960s and 1970s screen printing also became a significant method of tile decoration in the Italian tile industry, spearheaded by firms like Ceramica Gabbianelli and Ceramica Cedit, both located in Milan where they were part of a wider progressive Italian design industry. They commissioned designs from leading design groups such as the experimental Studio Alchymia run by industrial designers like Ettore Sottsass, who also created patterns for screen printed tiles. His work was flashy and daring and abstract tile patterns influenced by Op Art and Kinetic Art were cutting edge at that time (fig. 300).

Since then screen printing has become the most commonly used and cost effective method for the mass decoration of tiles. The manufacture of screen printed tiles is now part of a fully automated conveyor belt production system using both flat screen and

ABOVE LEFT [fig. 298] Tile with a 'Crystal' design by Ann Clark (nee Wynn-Reeves). Dust pressed with a hand-screen printed wax-resist. Kenneth Clark Ceramics, London, England, 1959. 15 x 15 cm. Private collection.

ABOVE RIGHT [fig. 299] Tile from the Aztec Deities series. Screen printed. Designed by Caroline Campbell, Florian studios, Suffolk, England, 1968. 15 x 15 cm. Private collection.

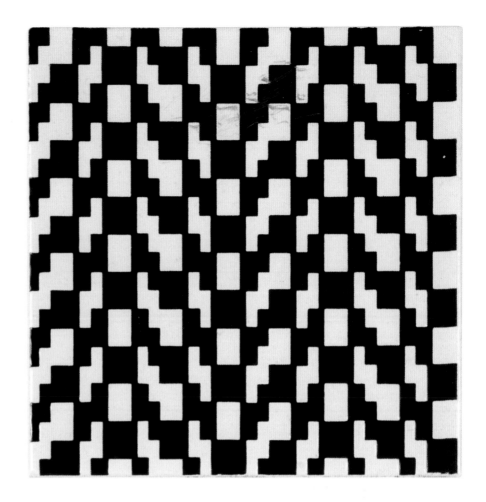

RIGHT [fig. 300] Tile designed by Ettore Sottsass, Ceramica Cedit. The black-and-white pattern shows the influence of 1960s Op Art and its penchant for 'optical' effects. Screen printed. Milan, Italy, 1968. 15 x 15 cm. International Ceramics Museum, Faenza, Italy.

rotary screen techniques that print tiles after glazing before they are subjected to a single firing process in a tunnel kiln at the end of the line. With the exception of a small element of quality control, human intervention has been totally eliminated from this production process which is guided and controlled by computer technology. This system has spread worldwide with Spain now one of the world's leading producers.

The revival of hand-crafted tiles

As a reaction against the automated mass produced tile industry of the twentieth century demand developed for a more individual type of tile that was either entirely handmade or at least had a handmade look. This has been met in various ways by large and small firms who have developed special tile products and tailor-made services. There is an echo here of what happened during the second half of the nineteenth century with the emergence of the Arts and Crafts and the Aesthetic Movements. However, when this parallel is looked at closely it is clear that the late twentieth-century phenomenon is led by tile entrepreneurs responding to market demands rather than being driven by idealistic or ideological concerns.

A novel and innovative approach was taken by the firm Fired Earth which began trading in 1983 and now has a chain of shops throughout Britain and abroad. It does not produce its own tiles but buys in handmade and hand-painted tiles from individual makers and small firms around the world, importing from countries like Holland, France, Spain, Tunisia and Mexico, as well as obtaining tiles from specialist tile makers

LEFT [fig. 301] Tile panel by the British tile artist Robert Jones showing a hand-painted design of an orange tree in a flowerpot standing on a ledge of traditional delftware tiles. Tin-glazed earthenware. Orleton, England, 1995. Each tile: 13 x 13 cm.

in Britain. To this it has now added paints and fabrics in order to offer integrated interiors as part of bespoke installation services aimed at a discerning clientele.

Individual tile makers during the 1980s and 1990s also offered a special type of hand-crafted tile, for example Robert Jones in Orleton near Ludlow and Stephen Cocker in Bedale, North Yorkshire, who both specialized in tin-glazed tiles. Jones produced hand-painted delftware tiles executed on dust pressed blanks. These were either copies of antique Dutch and English delftware tiles or, in true post-modern fashion, he would sometimes place designs of his own making within traditional border designs (fig. 301). He also made delftware style tiles employing various forms of stencilling or screen printing, showing his willingness to experiment with new decoration methods. Cocker made and decorated his own tin-glazed tiles in a variety of different styles and produced a striking hand-painted series of tiles called 'Cosmos' which were marketed by Fired Earth (fig. 303).

The emerging market for heritage tiles is catered for by Craven Dunnill Jackfield Ltd which is based in the former Victorian Craven Dunnill factory in Jackfield near

ABOVE LEFT [fig. 302] Tube-lined tile with a modern design marketed by H & R Johnson as a special hand-decorated range under the famous brand name of Maw & Co. Glazed earthenware. Stoke-upon-Trent, England, c.1985. 20 x 20 cm. Private collection.

ABOVE RIGHT [fig. 303] Hand-painted tile from the 'Cosmos' series designed and made by the British tile artist Stephen Cocker for Fired Earth. Tin-glazed earthenware. Bedale, North Yorkshire, England, 1991. 15 x 15 cm. Private collection.

Ironbridge, where the Jackfield Tile Museum is also located. Craven Dunnill is a well-established name in tile making as it started making tiles in 1872 and was a noted firm until 1950 when it stopped making tiles and became a tile distributor. In 2000 it entered the field of tile production again, specializing in heritage tiles. It makes faithfully manufactured period style tiles and where possible employs the original machinery, glaze recipes and hand decoration techniques. Its range comprises Victorian, Art Nouveau and Art Deco wall tiles, as well as encaustic and geometric floor tiles, and it caters for clients who want to restore original features or who want heritage tiles to decorate their homes. Craven Dunnill Jackfield Ltd is also involved with major restoration projects, requiring close liaison between architects and national conservation bodies such as the National Trust or English Heritage.

The big commercial firm Johnson Tiles in Stoke-upon-Trent, which has always been associated with large-scale industrial production, now also offers special ranges of tiles using the historical brand names Minton Hollins and Maw & Co., which bring together the famous tile names of the heyday of Victorian tile making. It also makes quality replica encaustic tiles reminiscent of the grand days of Minton encaustic tile production. Nostalgia for the designs and craftsmanship of the past play an overriding part here.

Tiles and terracotta panels as public art

During the second half of the twentieth century decorative tiles and terracotta panels were used with great effect on the facades of public buildings to add colour and decoration to the built environment or to display social or political messages. They were placed in public spaces where they could be seen and appreciated by large numbers of people and they gave many artists opportunities to create ceramic tile work for a wide public audience.

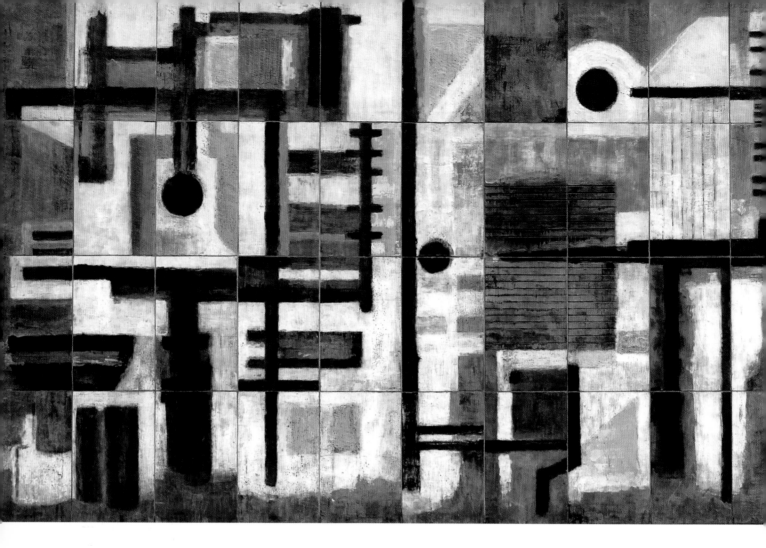

A fine example of public tile art from the 1960s is the work of the British artist. Dorothy Annan (1900–83) who worked as a painter, potter and tile muralist. In 1960 she was given a commission by the Ministry of Works to design and make a series of nine panels for the Fleet Building, Farringdon Street, at that time the largest telephone exchange in London (fig. 304). Appropriately they present images of pylons, cables, telegraph poles and generators and were made at the Hathernware pottery in Loughborough where she painted and hand-scored her designs into the wet clay. The nine panels were conceived on a large scale and when they are seen all together at street level they create a monumental area of colours, shapes and lines that brightens the bland modern facade for passers-by. Following the demolition of the Fleet Building in 2013, the panels were relocated to a new venue in the Barbican Centre, London.

Public tile art could also be employed for political propaganda purposes as was the case in Eastern Europe where it was used on a grand scale in communist East Germany. Huge tile propaganda murals extolling the virtues of communist society were put on public buildings. Lothar Scholz was one of the major artists of these murals. When working in East Berlin in the 1960s he became involved with their manufacture and execution, and oversaw the construction and installation of giant tile murals designed by other artists for various government and public buildings. This gave him the necessary background and expertise to undertake his own large-scale mural work and during the 1970s and 80s he was given many state commissions

ABOVE [fig. 304] Modernist semi-abstract tile panel painted by the British artist Dorothy Annan on the exterior of the Fleet Building, Farringdon Street, London. It is part of a series of nine panels depicting aspects from the world of telecommunication. Glazed earthenware, 1960. The panels have recently been removed and have been re-sited in a new location in the Barbican Centre, London.

RIGHT [fig. 305] Wall covered with tile mosaic created by the American artist Isaiah Zagar at his Magic Gardens at South Alder Street. Ceramic and glass mosaic. Philadelphia, United States, 1991.

for hospitals, swimming pools, hotels, and schools such as the mural for the exterior of the Rudolf-Tarnow School in Boizenburg, which was installed in 1971 (fig. 306). This is a large mural with a powerful decorative design augmented by lines taken from the poetry of famous German scholar Johann Wolfgang von Goethe. At the bottom the panel shows a heroic worker releasing the dove of peace set against an industrial landscape, while at the top there is a rocket and planetary symbols suggesting space exploration. The whole mural symbolizes peace and technological progress as well as the reaching out to the stars and all based on the endeavours of the proletariat. This mural was officially restored in 2000 in co-operation with the artist

and is now part of the protected heritage of buildings erected in East Germany during the communist era.

The work of the American artist Isaiah Zagar is in stark contrast to the state-sponsored public tile murals created by the German artist Lothar Scholz. Over a period of many years Zagar constructed a highly individualistic tiled environment now known as the 'Magic Gardens', located in a block on the corner of South Street and South Alder Street in downtown Philadelphia, United States. The actual tiled garden was begun in the early 1990s but Isaiah Zagar had been a part of the Philadelphia art scene in South Street since the late 1960s, when a group of young artists and entrepreneurs began renting derelict shops and apartments above the run-down stores in order to open galleries, cafes and music venues.

Zagar's Magic Gardens (fig. 305) are part of a phenomenon that is now labelled as 'visionary environments.' Such environments include buildings, gardens and parks created outside the boundaries of official culture that utilize organic forms and bright colours and reject straight lines. Tiled examples include Antoni Gaudi's Park Güell (1900–1905) in Barcelona, Spain and Friedensreich Hunderwasser's 'Kunst Haus Wien' (1991) in Vienna, Austria. Zagar's constructions are a wonderful mixture of broken tiles and pieces of mirror glass augmented with glass bottles and other found objects covering exterior walls and a labyrinth of passages and staircases inside existing buildings. This creates a visual world of striking personal intensity with a truly magical quality which has to be experienced at first hand to be fully appreciated.

Tiles as public art have also become a particularly strong feature of underground railway stations throughout the world. The early underground stations built at the end of the nineteenth and beginning of the twentieth century in capital cities like London, Paris and New York were often covered with plain tiles for purely practical reasons because tiles were hygienic, easily cleaned, fireproof and hard-wearing. Although the opportunity was sometimes taken to add ornamental ceramic features it was not until the second half of the twentieth century that metro stations were turned over to artists to decorate in a big way. They were given the opportunity to mark the station's history, or the cultural and commercial activities of the area above ground, while at the same time show what they could do as artists. It is normally part of the design strategy in refurbishment schemes, line extensions or the construction of completely new lines to give underground stations different levels of identity – corporate identity, line identity and station identity – and it is the latter that tile artists are mainly concerned with.

During the 1980s many underground stations in London were refurbished, creating opportunities for both well-known and new artistic talents. In 1984 the Pop artist Eduardo Paolozzi created his colourful quirky images in glass mosaic tiles inspired by the everyday city life and locations near the station at Tottenham Court Road. They show computer disks, gaming machines, musical instruments and the figure of a running man who could be a commuter in this brave new world. A different approach was taken by the artist Michael Douglas who designed the tiles for the newly refurbished Baker Street Station. He used screen printed images of the area's most famous 'resident', Sherlock Holmes, taken in profile wearing a deer stalker and smoking a pipe and presented in diverse and ingenious ways. Sometimes the images are shown as a repeat pattern with two faces on each tile, but there are also very large profiles of Sherlock Holmes made up of hundreds of very small profile images (fig. 308).

LEFT [fig. 307] The tiled platform of the Parque Metro station, Lisbon, Portugal, designed by the artist Françoise Schein, 1994. The blue vault is covered with letter tiles creating the words of the Declaration of Human Rights. Glazed earthenware.

RIGHT [fig. 308] Tiles with the image of Sherlock Holmes on the station platform at Baker Street underground station, London, England. The tiles were designed by Michael Douglas and screen printed by Pamela Moreton, 1984.

One of the best places to experience underground tile art is Lisbon where during the 1980s and 1990s massive refurbishment was undertaken along with new line extensions and the building of new stations. The most exciting new underground station is Oriente which was completed in 1998 in time for Expo '98. The various platforms were decorated with giant tile panels designed by a bevy of international artists from as far away as China and Japan who created spectacularly colourful tile murals. However the most memorable station is Parque on the Blue Line completed in 1994 (fig. 307). It was here that the artist Françoise Schein created a monumental work illustrating the moment when Europe developed a new understanding of the world. Along the two platforms are fifty large maps showing major moments in the history of Portuguese discoveries of the fifteenth and sixteenth centuries, while the ceiling of the station is a huge blue vault covered with the words of the Declaration of Human Rights. This is not mere tile decoration but a tile scheme with a serious underlying message.

LEFT [fig. 309] Detail of the tiled sculpture *Big Fish* by John Kindness at Donegall Quay, Belfast, Northern Ireland. It has become a celebrated landmark and the text and images printed on the tiles relate to the history of Belfast. 1999. Length 10 m.

Public tile art can also make a splash above ground as is the case with the giant *Big Fish* created by John Kindness in 1999 at Donegall Quay in Belfast in Northern Ireland (fig. 309). It is a 10-metre-long tiled sculpture of a salmon covered with blue and white tiles on which are printed images and texts that relate to Belfast's history. The tiled sculpture works on two levels. When seen from afar it is a striking monumental form that surprises and delights and when seen close up it holds the viewer's attention with intriguing images and text.

Another aspect of the renaissance of ceramic ornamentation on buildings has been the employment of figurative terracotta plaques to mark and emphasize the specific use of buildings. An early instance is the Cavern Walks shopping centre in Liverpool built in 1985 on the site of the Cavern Club made famous by the Beatles. It was decorated with terracotta relief sculptures designed by Cynthia Lennon, John Lennon's first wife, depicting peace symbols of doves and roses. In London the Nordoff Robbins Musical Therapy School in Lissenden Gardens, designed by Douglas Binnie and built in 1990, has an enigmatic terracotta figure of a boy beating a drum on the facade, and in Chester Timothy Clapcott created a series of square terracotta relief tiles in 1995 for the exterior of the Forum Shopping Centre, which has an iconographic theme based on the 'culture of shopping' showing figures clutching consumer goods (fig. 310).

But it is not only in Britain where this trend can be observed. An unusual example of terracotta figurative decoration can be seen in the United States on the exterior of the Gutman Library which is now part of Philadelphia University. This scheme was undertaken by the American artist Syma in 1991–2 when she was commissioned to create terracotta portraits of selected staff and students set in elaborate decorative frames that were placed above and between the windows of the library's exterior. The portraits were taken from live models with the aid of plaster bandages from which moulds were made, which in turn were used for press moulding the final

ABOVE LEFT [fig. 310] Hand-sculpted tile with the face a cook squeezing a garlic press on the exterior of the Forum Shopping Centre, Chester, England, by Timothy Clapton in 1995. It is part of series of large terracotta tiles celebrating the culture of shopping and the modern consumer society.

ABOVE RIGHT [fig. 311] Panel with a human head cast from life set in a decorative border frame on the exterior of the Gutman Library, Philadelphia University, United States, by the American ceramic artist Syma in 1991–2. It is part of a series of terracotta panels depicting past staff and students.

portraits using red clay. They were placed in separate terracotta frames that feature items and objects relating to various university departments and in this way the terracotta reliefs became an index of university life and people immortalized in fired clay (fig. 311).

Tiles made for public spaces are not just the preserve of the professional artist but can also be community projects by non-specialists under the guidance of dedicated professionals. Tile-making schemes are carried out by children or sometimes by senior citizens to decorate a school or community hall or in response to major world concerns or catastrophic events. Examples include the 'Tiles for Peace' project made by children under the direction of Teena Gould for Swiss Cottage Square, London in 1987 (fig. 312). Children were given red tiles covered with white slip, and scratched images and text into it revealing the underlying red body of the clay. These were then assembled together on a brick wall.

America has the emotionally moving Wall of Remembrance (Children's Tile Wall) in the Holocaust Museum in Washington, completed in 1993 to remember the 1.5 million Jewish children who perished in the Holocaust. School children painted more than three thousand tiles that line the wall showing images and messages that call for peace, hope and remembrance. American children, families and senior groups were also involved in the 'Tiles for America' project in 2001 to mark the 9/11 attack on the World Trade Center in New York in which thousands lost their lives (fig. 313). The tile project was started by the potter Lorrie Veasy who put hundreds of tiles with angels and American flags on a chain link fence on the corner of 7th Avenue and Greenwich Avenue. Soon many hundreds of tiles were added, made by children, families and senior groups throughout America with messages expressing thoughts of sadness as well as hope. Projects like this show that the medium of tiles can be used with great effect by people with a wide range of artistic abilities across all age ranges, and that tiles are a democratic medium open to everybody.

ABOVE LEFT [fig. 312] Tiles made by children under the direction of the ceramic artist Teena Gould for a community project 'Tiles for Peace' at Swiss Cottage Square, London, 1987. The incised line technique (sgraffito) is well-suited to enable children to express their ideas.

ABOVE RIGHT [fig. 313] 'Tiles for America', a scheme that commemorated the 9/11 Twin Towers disaster in New York in 2001. Until 2012 hundreds of tiles made by children and senior groups hung on a chain link on the corner of 7th Avenue and Greenwich Avenue, New York.

OPPOSITE [fig. 314] Composite panel of glazed tiles with hand-painted images of musicians and musical instruments by the Dutch ceramic artist Marieke Bouman on the facade of the KNA music centre, Lunteren, The Netherlands, 2010.

Tiles as public art can also be the result of creative communal enterprise. A good example is the so-called 'tile route' in the small town of Lunteren in Holland, where tile panels have been installed on the facades of local buildings as the result of a partnership between local artists, Lunteren Parish Council and the National Tile Museum in nearby Otterlo. The panels have all been designed and made for the facades of specific buildings, either shops, houses or public buildings, and mark and celebrate the activity carried out there or draw attention to the history of selected buildings in the town (fig. 314). The scheme was initiated in 2010 by the artist Marieke Bouman who with a group of local artists created fifteen tile panels for various locations in Lunteren. This has since expanded to thirty-eight tile panels and the project is still on going, actively supported by the local population. The involvement of many different artists ensures a variety of different stylistic approaches which give this tile scheme great breadth and diversity of subject matter, form and colour. Visitors follow the trail using the printed tile guides which are now available and which lead them through the town on a walking tour of tile discovery.

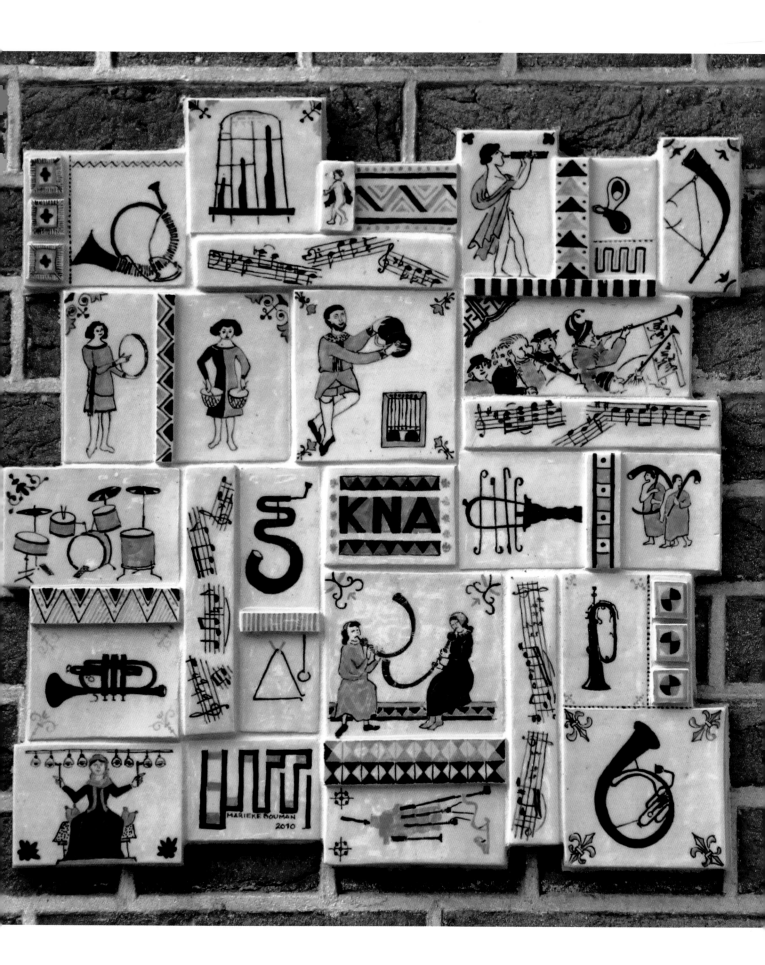

TILE ARTISTS AND DESIGNERS TODAY

... and for many the simple reason is that ceramic materials and processes have unique qualities in providing an amazing material for drawing, and outstanding palette of glaze, colour and light unobtainable in other media.

Paul Scott

Painted Clay, 2001

OPPOSITE [fig. 315] *Cabbage Butterflies* by Frouwien Soenveld, The Netherlands, 2004. Handmade earthenware tiles decorated with coloured glazes. Each tile: 13 x 13 cm.

There are many reasons why contemporary artists and designers are drawn into working with tiles. Firstly, there is the permanency of the medium because clay, ceramic pigments and glazes are transformed by fire into something that does not erode, disintegrate or fade. Secondly, there are the infinite ways in which the clay body of the tile and the variously coloured pigments and glazes can be manipulated as part of the creative process. Thirdly, the finished tile creations always have to go through a final physical transformation process in the kiln where, during the firing, all kinds of unexpected things can happen for better or sometimes for worse. There is always a moment of great anticipation when the kiln door is opened and the tiles are 'drawn' as it is not until then that the tile maker will know how things have turned out. Seeing and holding the fired tiles for the first time is always a revelatory experience not normally encountered in other artistic media.

More artists than ever are drawn to tiles as an expressive medium. Much of this can be attributed to the erosion of traditional boundaries between the so-called 'fine arts' and 'applied arts'. Decorative tiles may have previously been regarded as an 'applied' art form, but the breakdown of established demarcations in art has led to artists discovering tiles as a valuable medium offering limitless possibilities. Tiles have become a canvas on which they can freely express themselves using different clays, pigments and glazes.

The ways in which tile artists approach their medium varies greatly. Some want to be involved with and control the whole process of production and make their own tiles and glazes before grappling with the creative aspects of tile decoration. Others have opted to use ready-made industrial blanks and focus completely on image making, doing it by hand or carrying it out with the aid of transfer prints. There are

LEFT [fig. 316] *Mondnacht in Arieshén* by
Lothar Scholz, Germany, 2002. Dust-pressed
tiles painted with coloured glazes. Each tile:
15 x 15 cm.

also some artists who do not involve themselves directly with the physical tile
production and decorating processes but create designs which are then executed
by others. These different approaches have resulted in a very diverse contemporary
scene and are illustrated in the work of the following international tile artists.

Lothar Scholz

The German tile maker Lothar Scholz is a ceramic artist who began his career in
communist East Germany. Since the fall of the Berlin Wall in 1989 Scholz has been
living near Boizenburg in a converted farm house where he has his own tile studio.
He has successfully adapted from being a tile artist involved with state sponsored
commissions to the world of private enterprise and although he continues to
undertake tile murals for private patrons he is now also able to focus more on
personal small scale tile work. Since his farmhouse and studio are situated along
the scenic flat planes of the river Elbe, this has given him much inspiration for
landscape painting and capturing the various moods of the seasons and such
landscapes scenes have also found their way onto single tiles.

   This inspiration led to the creation of a series of polychrome landscape tiles
painted in an under glaze technique on single tiles under the name of 'Teldau
Landscapes' in 1991. Six years later in 1997 he re-visited this theme and began a
new more comprehensive series of Teldau landscapes and rivers scenes painted in

ABOVE [fig. 317] *Landscapes along the Elbe* by Lothar Scholz, Germany, 1997. A panel of thirty tin-glazed and dust-pressed tiles painted in an in-glaze technique. Each tile: 15 x 15 cm.

blue-and-white echoing the great tradition of Dutch delftware landscapes of the eighteenth century (fig. 317). In 2004 he undertook a series of polychrome romantic landscapes and river scenes which were painted on bigger tile blanks. The latter were sometimes rival oil-paintings in their detail and naturalism and in their directly observed weather conditions and how this affected the landscape in different seasons. Not one of the landscapes on his tiles is the same and this shows that the scenes along the river Elbe have provided him with endless inspiration over the years.

Scholz's landscape tiles are only one facet of his output and particularly over the past ten years he has been involved with many commissions executed in different styles ranging from completely abstract work to highly realistic representations. He also uses many different techniques such as under glaze and tin glaze. His subject matter covers the human figure, landscapes, animals and flowers executed with great dexterity and facility all based on a sound draughtsmanship, impeccable sense of colour and deep understanding of ceramic techniques. Scholz has also been a key figure in preserving Germany's tile heritage and he was instrumental in setting up the country's first dedicated tile museum which opened its doors in Boizenburg in 1998.

Eduardo Nery

The Portuguese artist and designer Eduardo Nery does not make or decorate his own tiles but creates designs that are executed as tile schemes in architectural settings. He is in the first instance a fine artist versed in various media such as painting, drawing, collage and photography, and since the late 1950s he has experimented with various styles such as Abstract Expressionism, Op Art, Kinetic Art and Metaphysical Painting. His most interesting work is done in the field of Op Art, the 1960s style of geometric abstract painting championed by artists like Bridget Riley and Victor Vasarely. It exploits optical illusion and visual ambiguity and this makes it an arresting and challenging visual experience for the viewer. Nery uses industrial square tiles as geometric abstract colour units in all-over patterns that challenge the eye. Although he started working in black and white, he soon became involved with colour. He has created numerous geometric abstract designs that are not only works of art in their own right but have also been translated into other media like tapestry and stained glass, but most of all using tiles.

ABOVE [fig. 318] *Tile Compositions* by Eduardo Nery, Portugal, 2003. Handmade and hand-painted earthenware tiles of the 18th century mixed with modern glazed tiles. 114 x 113.5 cm.

RIGHT [fig. 319] An abstact arrangement of coloured tiles by Eduardo Nery on the facade of the Municipal Museum of Modern Art in Tomar, Portugal, installed in 2004. H. 8 m.

Although much of his tile work is abstract, he has been involved with commissions using representational images such as the pictorial designs for the twenty-two giant support pillars of the Campo Grande Viaduct in Lisbon that reflect the life and history of the local area. These were carried out between 1983 and 1992. He also produced deconstructed images of steam locomotives for the Refer/CP railway station in Contumil, Oporto which were executed in 1992–94. The main thrust of his tile oeuvre, however, is concerned with the creation of abstract colour fields using differently coloured tiles. He generally makes carefully worked out designs that show each and every tile and their colour variations in position. This is then interpreted and executed by a commercial tile firm and the scheme is installed under his close supervision.

His numerous abstract tile schemes are conceived in widely different dimensions. Tiles for interior use on office walls are usually on a more human scale and these installations can consist of a mixture of recovered hand-painted eighteenth-century tiles and modern plain tiles carefully arranged either in chequerboard or diamond shape fashion, alternating new and old tiles, that look stunning from a distance and

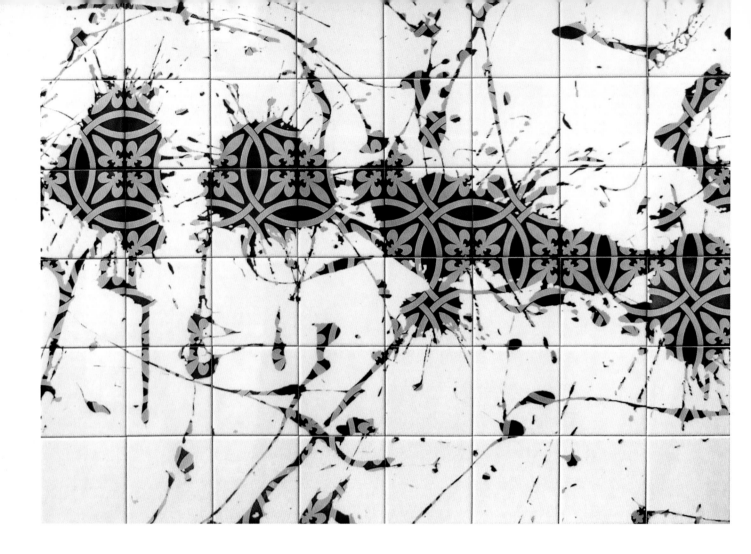

when scrutinized close up. This kind of tile art can be interpreted as homage to the great and illustrious history of Portuguese tiles. Nery's tile schemes for exterior use are often conceived on a monumental scale for a variety of buildings such as museums, banks, schools and water treatment plants, as well as for the walls of viaducts and underpasses. It is with these large tiled surface areas that Nery shows his absolute control over form and colour. For these schemes he uses tiles that are given a wide variety of differently coloured glazes according to his own design specifications. It is here that he exploits and makes creative use of colour juxtapositions, such as harmonious colours versus complementary colours and warm colours versus cool colours, arranged in horizontal, vertical and diagonal colour fields that challenge and delight the eye.

Robert Dawson

The British ceramic artist Robert Dawson is interested in the history of printed ceramics and tiles and he has made such historical works the source material for many of his ceramic creations. One of his basic intentions is: 'I want to make something that I hope will look good.' Whether something looks 'good' is always a matter of subjective judgement, but what he creates on his tile panels certainly looks intriguing. The panels draw you in optically whether you like it or not and make you look more actively and intently at his printed tile creations. He often uses traditional tile patterns as a starting point but then breaks up the design, fragments it, warps it

ABOVE [fig. 320] *Decorative Ceramic Wall Tiles with Sovereignty and Action* by Robert Dawson, UK, 2006. Transfer printed on glazed dust-pressed tiles. Each tile: 15 x 15 cm.

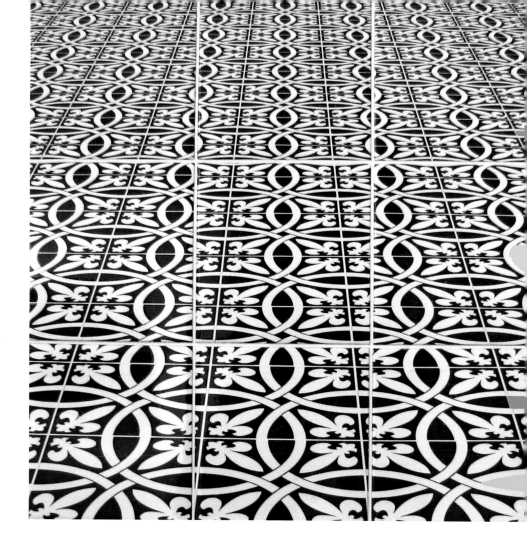

or makes it fade away. Spatial references are made deliberately ambiguous so that normal rules of pictorial space are subverted and then impel the observer to make visual sense of it.

Decorative Ceramic Wall Tiles with Sovereignty and Action, made in 2006 (fig. 320), consists of square machine-made tiles on which he printed fragmented sections of a Victorian floor tile design with interlacing circles and fleur-de-lis corner motifs. The original design is an arresting pattern but Dawson has 'etched' much of it away in an irregular fashion. In the middle of the panels some sections of the design have been preserved and they form a kind of haphazard horizontal design, while the rest of the pattern leaches away to virtually nothing at the top and bottom. What is left seems to be accidental leftovers of a once strong design scattered across the surface, and is reminiscent of the spattered effects created by Jackson Pollock in his action paintings. The final result is a residue of a bold tile pattern erratically eroded away into a ghost of its former self.

The work *Floored* created in 2008 (fig. 321) plays a very different game with the onlooker. It consists of a panel of nine square tiles that uses the same pattern employed in *Decorative Ceramic Wall Tiles with Sovereignty and Action* but now the tile design is shown in its entirety from a low viewpoint in extreme perspective that makes the design diminish acutely into the far distance. This sets up tensions and distortions with the real flat surfaces of the nine tiles on which the receding floor patterns have been printed. The original tile pattern used was made to be seen on a

LEFT [fig. 322] *Cabbage Butterflies* by
Frouwien Soenveld, The Netherlands, 2004.
Handmade earthenware tiles decorated with
coloured glazes. Each tile: 13 x 13 cm.

single tile, but is now seen as multiple design units distorted by linear perspective,
and the vertical and horizontal white grout lines of the actual tile panel clash with
the white grout lines of the tiles in the printed image that converge into the distance.
These visual ambiguities play with our perceptions of real and virtual space and
make us question and challenge what we see.

Frouwien Soenveld

The Dutch tile maker Frouwien Soenveld is interested in the nature of ceramic
materials and what can be achieved with them technically and aesthetically.
She makes her own tiles, clay slips and glazes, using a gritty type of red firing clay for
all her tiles that she feels provides a 'warm' basis for her matt opaque glazes. Patterns
and repeating designs are one of the main characteristics of her work but the tiles
themselves are not fixed units in a repeating pattern that can be extended over large
areas. She creates the pattern first and then imposes the square tile grid on it in such
a way that each tile when seen on its own is slightly different from any other and
therefore unique in the overall tile layout.

A major theme in her tile work of the past ten years has been the world of insects,
inspired by the designs of the Frenchman Eugène Alain Séguy who was a noted
early twentieth-century designer. As a result she has created tile panels showing
butterflies, ladybirds, wasps, bees and flies bringing out the peculiar forms of each
insect with sensitive outlines and finely coloured matt glazes. Usually the insects

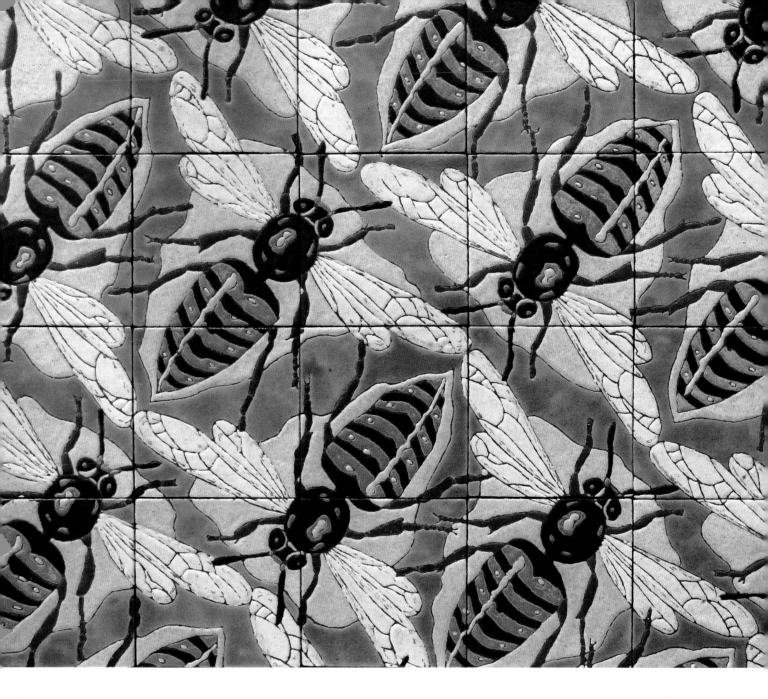

ABOVE [fig. 323] *Wasps* by Frouwien Soenveld, The Netherlands, 2005. Handmade earthenware tiles decorated with coloured glazes. Each tile: 13 x 13 cm.

have been depicted from above showing the most characteristic outlines of the body, wings and antennae but occasionally, as is the case with some butterfly patterns, they are shown at an oblique angle making them and the flowers on which they sit more three dimensional (fig. 322).

For her insect panels she has developed special techniques to keep the different coloured glazes used in her designs separate from each other (fig. 323). First she traces the design on her tiles with the aid of carbon paper and then re-traces the pattern with a pencil several times, building up graphite lines that will act as barriers between the glazes when they are fired. During the firing the graphite lines burn away and reveal the red body of the clay. Although the glazes may run very slightly the lines are not completely obliterated and are still clearly visible after firing, showing a diverse and playful network of lines. Soenveld's insect tile panels are visually arresting and seduce the eye with their striking shapes and colours.

OPPOSITE [fig. 324] *Porcelana y Lino* by Manolo Sales, Spain, 2008. Thin and light porcelain body stained with ceramic pigments. 35 x 40 cm.

Manolo Sales

The Spanish artist Manolo Sales has been interested in ceramics since he was a young boy. He used to make marbles from clay which were fired for him by a local potter whose clay products and smoking kiln stoked by brushwood left a lasting impression on him. Now as a mature artist he experiments incessantly with clay bodies, ceramic pigments and glazes and he has specialized in making ultra-thin porcelain plaques which he uses as a canvas for his minimalist abstract paintings.

His plaques are made by mixing cellulose (from paper or flax fibres) with porcelain paste. The cellulose burns away at 600 Celsius and then the pieces continue to be fired up to a temperature of around 1,250 Celsius when they vitrify into a white semi-translucent material. The final result is a thin fragile-looking textured ceramic body which has the appearance of handmade paper of exquisite lightness. Before the plaque is fired it can be decorated with ceramic pigments or sometimes the surface is scratched or slashed. The paint marks are usually small minimalist abstract squares or lines that seem to float on the white porcelain surface. The plaques have an air of transience and an almost ethereal quality that invites quiet contemplation: links have been made between Sales' ceramic work and Japanese Haiku poetry. He sees himself not primarily as a ceramic artist but as a painter who uses ceramics as a support, and by doing so he breaks down the boundaries between ceramics and fine art.

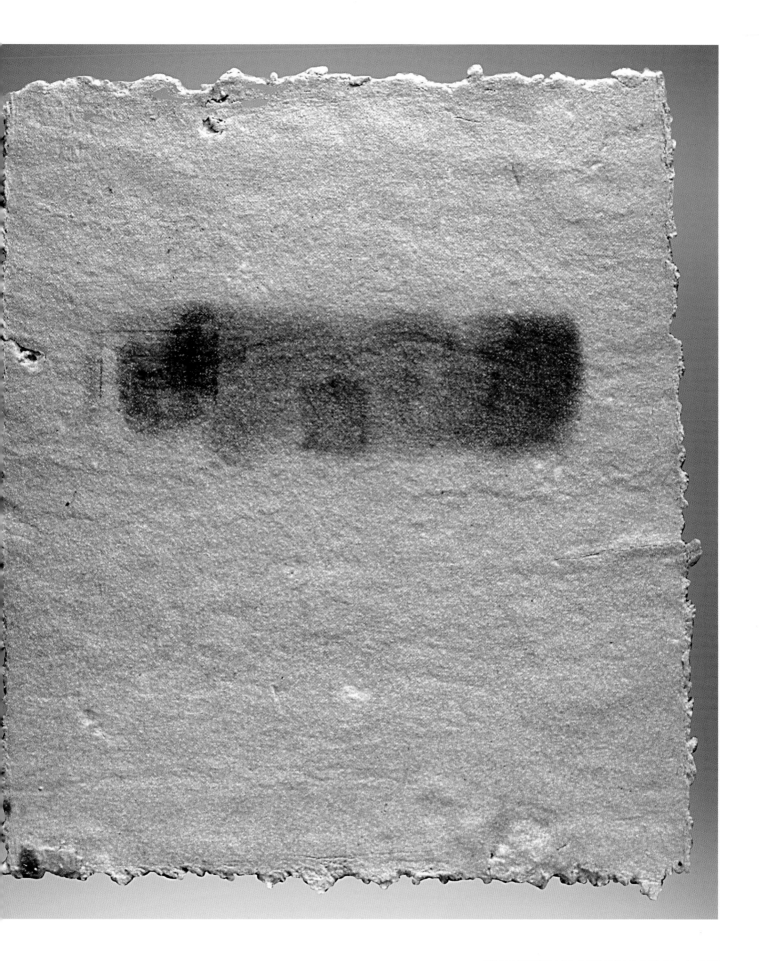

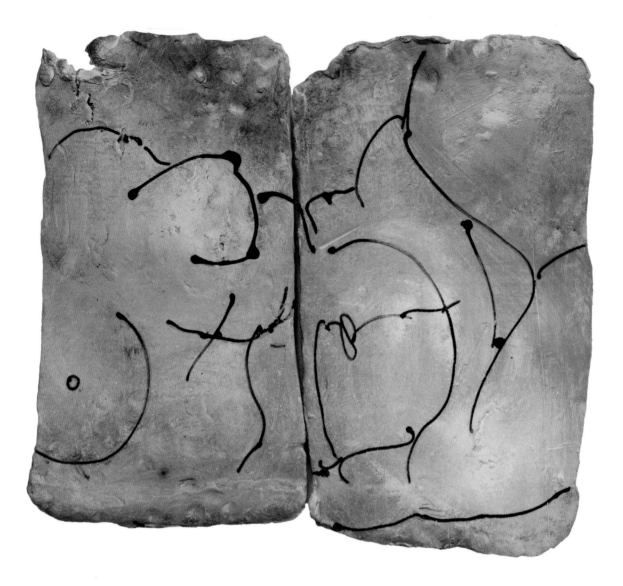

Bronwyn Williams-Ellis

Bronwyn Williams-Ellis is an established British tile maker who tries to reconcile her passion for drawing with her passion for making tiles – balancing art with craftsmanship as she calls it. She makes bold and fluent lines on ceramic surfaces and she has developed a special technique for this purpose, adapting a traditional Asian *tjanting* tool that is normally used for batik work. Instead of dye she uses finely ground manganese oxide dissolved in molten wax, in conjunction with water-based glazes that are kept apart in the firing when the wax burns away leaving a slightly sunken line as in the Spanish *cuerda seca* technique. Her art training exposed her to life drawing, and the nude has been a constant theme in her tile work, appearing in the form of complete male and female figures, as torsos (fig. 325) or sometimes just as a hand or a foot. Her line work is bold, direct and fluent with little dots at the beginning or end of lines which is a characteristic of her style of drawing. She often works on commercial tile blanks but also makes her own tiles that are cut from plastic clay and made into plaques of irregular sizes. These are stained with oxides but otherwise left unglazed. She then creates figure drawings which are permanently fixed on clay using her *tjanting* tool.

ABOVE [fig. 325] *Torso 7* by Bronwyn Williams-Ellis, UK, 2007. Two hand-shaped earthenware slabs brush-painted with coloured slips with lines drawn in dark manganese oxide using a traditional *tjanting* tool. 34 x 39 cm.

RIGHT [fig. 326] *THREE times THREE* by Susan Tunick, USA, 2002. Detail from a tiled wall at the Firefighter Christopher A. Santora School for young children, New York. Handmade glazed tiles have been combined with recycled industrially-made tiles.

Susan Tunick

The American artist Susan Tunick not only runs a tile studio in New York, but is also a noted tile historian who has published widely, and her deep understanding of tile history has enriched her creative tile work. She has undertaken commissions for tile murals in subway stations and schools, but also makes free-standing ceramic tile sculptures for specific sites. She produces her own tiles and develops her own glazes and is particularly interested in colour and texture as part of the ceramic process.

One of her tile projects for schools was carried out in 2002 for the Firefighter Christopher A. Santora School in New York. In this commission Tunick designed a tile installation suitable for an early learning centre for children while also creating a visually interesting tile design of mesmerizing quality in its own right. The tile creation is called *THREE times THREE* (fig. 326) and consists of three wall sections decorated with geometric shapes: three triangles, three circles and three hexagons. The intention was to interest the very young children attending this school in the three themes presented on the three walls: the blue wall shows ocean imagery, the salmon coloured wall incorporates the poem 'Now We Are Six' by A. A. Milne, and the green wall presents the geometry and activity of bumble bees. The three circular shapes are particularly rich in smaller round decorative elements and designs. In the outer borders of the circles she incorporated recycled tiles salvaged from buildings that stress the link between her work and the rich tile legacy of the past.

A more recent project, completed in 2010, was called *Mountain Top Trio: Vert, Violet et Rouge* and is a site specific installation on the land of a Vermont farm (fig. 327). It consists of three cedar and ceramic tile sculptures that are placed in an alley of apple trees and that accentuate the colours and forms of the surrounding countryside. The shapes of the sculptures were inspired by round bales of hay seen in the countryside. Tunick says: 'I didn't want the shapes to be so symmetrical. Thus, I felt that adding curves and some type of opening in the center could work well.' Coloured tiles cover both sides of each sculpture and create delicate nuances of colour and surface texture. Great pains were taken to get the shapes of the tiles and colour combinations right. Tiles were cut by hand from plastic clay and were then fitted in their exact place in the circular layout before the glazing processes took place. This was accomplished in stages by taking some biscuit tiles out and then glazing and firing them before returning them to the exact spot they came from. This process was then repeated with the other tiles until all the colour ranges were completed. The whole thing involved up to eight stages. The consequence of the sculptures being situated out of doors is that the different times of day and the changing seasons constantly change the way the three tile sculptures appear.

ABOVE [fig. 327] *Mountain Top Trio: Vert, Violet et Rouge* by Susan Tunick, USA, 2010. View of 'Vert, side 1', one of three sculptures out in the open air at Rutland, Vermont, USA. Handmade relief tiles covered with a wide variety of coloured glazes encased in cedar wood.

ABOVE [fig. 328] *Gateshead in a Box* by Paul Scott, UK, 2011. A printer's tray box with multiple compartments filled with various ceramic items and small screen printed blue-and-white tiles. 83 x 72 cm.

Paul Scott

The British ceramic artist Paul Scott often works in blue and white, or 'Cumbrian Blue' as he calls it because he lives and works in the county of Cumbria. Since the mid-1980s he has undertaken many commissions for schools, museums and hospitals as well as commercial and private institutions. In many instances he has abandoned the square tile in favour of irregularly shaped pieces which make his work look dynamic and he often paints and prints under the glaze on porcelain tiles. He, like Susan Tunick, is also an author and has published two groundbreaking books on the history of ceramics and print and on the contemporary history of painted clay surfaces. This wide understanding of the history of ceramics informs his own work in its choice of subject matter and technique and his own creations are strongly anchored in painted and printed visual imagery. Much of his pictorial repertoire is based on his observations and interpretations of the physical and political environment in which he lives. Since 2000 he has undertaken commissions which are designed for specific locations. This requires close study of the environment in which the work is placed so that it reflects the history as well as the contemporary concerns of the area and its inhabitants.

OPPOSITE [fig. 329] *Ponteland Cows and Sheep* by Paul Scott, UK, 2006. A detail of a tile installation showing cows and sheep printed on to white brick-shaped tiles forming part of a boundary wall of a housing estate at Ponteland, Northumberland.

Ponteland Cows and Sheep, made in 2006 (fig. 329), is such a commission and was executed for a new housing development in Ponteland, Northumberland. The site was an old lairage – the place where sheep and cattle were rested after travelling to market and before their sale. The new housing estate was separated from a still functioning abattoir by a high brick wall and it was thought appropriate that the new residents of the site were reminded of the older ones. This resulted in images of life-size cows and sheep printed in blue on white brick-shaped porcelain tiles. The foliage on which the cows and sheep lie and graze was generated by digitally cloning and collaging details from Thomas Bewick's engraving *The Kyloe Ox* from Cherryburn, Bewick's birthplace in Northumberland.

A departure from Scott's earlier work is *Gateshead in a Box* which was commissioned for Shipley Art Gallery and completed in 2011 (fig. 328). It consists of a printer's tray box, the compartments of which are filled with various items such as a piece of a Gateshead brick and a fragment of a clay pipe, as well as specially created ceramic objects with digital and screen printed in-glaze decals and impressed text that relate to local places, people and industries. It is the first object in the Contemporary Craft Collection that specifically refers to Gateshead, and was produced as a result of independent artistic research and community consultation. It seeks to distil something of Gateshead's past, present and future into a domestic sized object, suitable for gallery display.

Making and decorating tiles goes back thousands of years and this long history provides any contemporary tile artist or designer with innumerable examples. These can range from small individually created tiles to huge monumental schemes, with a vast range of uses, technical innovations, different ceramic techniques, styles and individual methods of working. It can be daunting to be at the end of such a long line but also immensely exciting and stimulating to be shaping a new future for tiles and trying to leave one's own mark. All of these tile artists acknowledge the past and strive to emulate it while at the same time creating their own legacy, but how they achieve this varies enormously. Whether they take a completely hands-on or a more distant approach, what all these artists have in common is their love of tiles as a medium and the seemingly endless different ways in which they can use tiles to interest and delight us.

TECHNICAL GLOSSARY

Acroterion: A terracotta ornament at the top or side angle of a roof pediment, common in Greek, Etruscan and Roman architecture.

Adobe: A sun-dried brick made from river mud and straw.

Alkaline glaze: A relatively low-fired glaze with a high concentration of alkali elements, such as wood or plant ash, in its composition. Alkaline glazes were used extensively in ancient Egypt and are known for their bright colours, but the glaze crazes easily and can be brittle.

Antefix: A terracotta ornament concealing the ends of roof tiles common in Greek, Etruscan and Roman architecture.

Architectural ceramics: Term for all kinds of moulded architectural ceramic ornament, whether glazed or unglazed.

Arista: Spanish for 'ridge'. The design is formed by ridges on the tile. Coloured glazes are then put into each space and are kept apart by the ridges (see CUENCA).

Art tile: A name used in the second half of the 19th century for tiles showing the influence of the design movements of the day, and often having a special aesthetic quality.

Azulejos: Spanish and Portuguese word for 'tiles'.

Barbotine: Tiles painted with a coloured slip and covered with transparent glaze.

Bat: A gelatine pad sometimes used in the process of TRANSFER PRINTING.

Bianco-sopra-bianco: Italian for 'white-on-white'. Found on TIN-GLAZED tiles, particularly those made in Bristol and Liverpool in Britain during the 18th century.

Biscuit: A tile that has been fired once and yet to be glazed and decorated.

Body: Main structure of a tile as distinct from its decoration and glaze.

Bottle kiln: A large type of INTERMITTENT KILN, usually coal-fired, formerly used in the large scale production of pottery and tiles. It has an inner kiln surrounded by a tall brick hovel in the shape of a bottle.

Chinoiserie: A style reflecting the fanciful perceptions of Chinese life and art held by the Europeans from the 17th century onwards.

Cobalt: A metal, the oxide of which produces a strong blue colour and a stable ceramic pigment that can be used at a wide range of different temperatures. Much used in the decoration of TIN-GLAZED tiles and later printed blue-and-white tiles.

Coperta: An Italian technique of adding an extra coat of transparent lead glaze to the already applied white tin glaze and painted decoration. When fired this helps to create a more glossy and hard-wearing surface.

Cuenca: Spanish for 'bowl'. Another term for ARISTA.

Cuerda seca: Spanish for 'dry cord'. A decorative process where the design is first painted in outlines using a compound of iron or manganese oxide and grease. Colours are then added but these do not cross the greasy lines. After firing, these outlines appear as matt dark sunken lines separating areas of glossy colour. The earliest form of the technique involved the use of a thin cord, impregnated with the iron/manganese and grease mixture which was carefully placed on the surface of the tile to create the outlines of the design.

Delftware: Tile which has been dipped in white TIN GLAZE at the BISCUIT stage and then painted by hand. This decoration is called 'IN-GLAZE' because it sinks into the GLAZE during the second firing. The term is derived from the Dutch town of Delft and is generally applied to tin-glazed tiles made in The Netherlands and Britain.

Dust clay: Finely powdered clay with a low moisture content.

Dust pressing: Describes the machine compression of powdered clay into metal moulds to form tiles.

Earthenware: Object made of ordinary clay then fired at about 1000 Celsius. Earthenware remains porous unlike STONEWARE or PORCELAIN.

Efflorescence: A natural process whereby salts move to the surface of the clay during the drying process forming a powdery crust of salt that turns into a GLAZE when fired.

Egyptian faience: Non-clay based ceramic composed of crushed quartz or sand, with small amounts of calcite lime and a mixture of alkalis. Used for making small glazed objects and tiles, it is called 'Egyptian faience' to distinguish it from tin-glazed ware and glazed architectural ceramics.

Émaux ombrants: From the French for 'shadow enamels'. A decorative process in which a tile with relief decorations is covered with a TRANSLUCENT GLAZE. Pooling of the glaze in the hollows produces gradations of light and dark of great delicacy.

Enamel: A ceramic pigment which can be painted on to a glazed tile and permanently fixed to it by low-temperature firing in a MUFFLE KILN.

Encaustic: A ceramic tile where the design is INLAID in coloured clays into the main BODY of the tile.

Faience: From the Italian town of Faenza. Originally a term for tin-glazed ware, but during the 19th century it was used to describe moulded and glazed ARCHITECTURAL CERAMICS. In France it was used for fine quality EARTHENWARE while in America it refers to tiles with a handmade look decorated with matt glazes.

Fettling: The process of removing the rough edges from a DUST-PRESSED tile after pressing.

Flux: An agent added to a GLAZE to help lower the melting point so that it adheres more easily to the clay BODY.

Glaze: Glassy substance used to cover tiles in order to make them impervious to water, as well as for decoration. Glazes can be TRANSPARENT, TRANSLUCENT, OPAQUE, glossy or matt. They are applied to a BISCUIT tile by dipping, painting or spraying, and then the tile is fired for a second time.

Goutou: A round glazed EARTHENWARE ornament concealing the ends of glazed Chinese roof tiles.

Hispano-Moresque: A term used for pottery and tiles produced in Spain (in places such as Malaga and Valencia) during the 14th and 15th centuries under Moorish influence. It is characterized by the use of LUSTRE often combined with COBALT blue on a white TIN GLAZE.

Imbrex: Latin word for a curved Roman roof tile which fitted over the raised flanges of TEGULAE.

In-glaze: Decoration painted on to an unfired tin-glazed surface. During the firing the decoration sinks into the TIN GLAZE and fuses with it.

Inlaid: A type of design formed by inserting different coloured clays into the surface of the tile (see ENCAUSTIC).

Intaglio: RELIEF in reverse or design stamped into the surface.

Intermittent kiln: A KILN in which the ware is set, fired, cooled and then drawn.

Kiln: Oven in which pottery and tiles are fired.

Lead glaze: Glassy, TRANSPARENT glaze made from lead oxide since ancient times. It is highly poisonous in its unfired state.

Lithography: A method of surface printing – from a specially prepared flat stone. The process is based on the antipathy of grease and water. The design is created with the aid of greasy ink or crayon, applied to the stone which is porous and readily accepts water The stone is first made wet after which it is rolled with greasy ink. The ink is accepted by the greasy design but repelled by the wet stone. Paper is then placed over the stone and put through a roller press which transfers the design to the paper.

Lock back: A special feature of DUST-PRESSED tiles that have under-cut indentations on the back to aid adherence to mortar or cement.

Lustre: A ceramic pigment usually derived from copper or silver which turns into a thin layer of metal on objects in the kiln when smoke or reduction gases are introduced. This produces iridescent metallic effects.

Maiolica/majolica: Originally EARTHENWARE with white TIN GLAZE, painted in bright colours and produced in Italy and Spain. The term 'majolica' was applied in the 19th century to RELIEF tiles with colourful OPAQUE glazes.

Manganese: A metal, the oxide of which produces a purple GLAZE much used on Dutch and English TIN-GLAZED tiles.

Mosaic: Small pieces of glass, stone or fired clay, known as *tesserae*, arranged to make a pattern or picture and set in plaster, mortar or cement.

Mudéjar: A term in design history which refers to a style of architecture and design that is a mixture of Islamic and Gothic styles. The style was particularly prevalent in Spain between the 13th and 15th centuries when Muslim craftsmen worked for Christian masters.

Muffle kiln: A relatively low-temperature KILN with an interior chamber totally enclosed and separated from the main kiln which shields the ware from the direct flames and combustion gases.

On-glaze: Decoration executed on already fired GLAZE with ENAMELS. Because on-glaze enamels can be fired at lower temperatures, a more varied range of colours is available than with UNDER-GLAZE decoration.

Opaque glazes: Coloured GLAZES that cover the tile without allowing the BODY to show through. They are made by adding coloured oxides and other opacifiers to TRANSPARENT GLAZES.

Opus sectile: A Latin term for pieces of tile cut into shapes that follow the outlines of the picture or pattern.

Pâte-sur-pâte: French term for 'paste-on-paste'. A delicate form of low-relief decoration built up by adding layer on layer of white SLIP on a contrasting ground.

Plastic clay: Ordinary wet clay.

Porcelain: A vitreous (glassy) ceramic material characterized by a dense, fine grained and smooth BODY.

Pounce: Small cloth bag filled with charcoal powder. The bag is patted over a piece of paper with a design marked by pinpricks allowing the charcoal to drop through and create an outline of the design on a tile.

Relief: Raised decoration moulded on to the surface of a tile.

Saggar: A fireclay box in which pottery and tiles can be set in a KILN to shield them from direct contact with kiln gases and flames.

Salt glazing: A process whereby the ware is glazed in the KILN. At the height of the firing, salt is thrown into the kiln. This vaporizes and reacts with the clay to form a GLAZE on the surface of the ware.

Sgraffito: From the Italian for 'scratching'. The technique of scratching through the top layer of a tile with two layers of clay to reveal the colour of the bottom layer.

Silk-screen printing: A decoration method for pottery and tiles. The simplest silk-screen equipment consists of a frame with a stretched silk cloth. A stencil is placed on the screen and varnish applied to fill in those parts of the screen not covered by the stencil. Ceramic colour dispersed in oil is rolled or squeezed through the screen on to the ceramic surface.

Slip: Thin liquid clay.

Stencil: A piece of paper, card or metal with a design cut out of it, allowing colour to be applied through the cutaway areas.

Stoneware: Tiles fired to a temperature of 1250 Celsius resulting in a VITRIFIED body which is both water and frost proof and therefore suitable for use on the exterior of buildings.

Tegula: Latin word for a flat roof tile with upturned flanges along the long sides.

Terracotta: Italian for 'fired earth'. Generally used to describe unglazed architectural ceramics except in America where it is applied to all kinds of glazed and unglazed architectural ceramic decoration.

Tile blank: A formed tile before any kind of decoration has been applied.

Tin glaze: A glaze made by adding tin to a LEAD GLAZE which becomes an opaque white when fired.

Transfer printing: A method of transferring designs and images from engraved copperplates or LITHOGRAPHIC stones to ceramic surfaces, with the aid of a thin paper tissue or gelatine BAT.

Translucent glazes: TRANSPARENT GLAZES to which small amounts of ceramic colour have been added, allowing the printed or RELIEF moulded design of the tile to show through.

Transparent glazes: Clear GLAZES used to cover tiles to make them impervious to water or dirt and to provide a protective covering for painted and printed decoration.

Tube lining: The piping of delicate lines of SLIP on to pottery and tiles to form raised lines that separate areas of coloured GLAZES.

Tunnel kiln: A continuous KILN fired by gas, oil or electricity in which ware passes through a stationary firing zone in the centre of the kiln. The ware is placed on the refractory lined decks of a series of cars that move slowly through a long straight tunnel.

Under-glaze: Decoration painted or printed on to the ceramic surface prior to the application of a GLAZE.

Up-draught kiln: An INTERMITTENT KILN in which the combustion gases pass from the fire box at the bottom through the firing chamber and then through one or more openings in the roof.

Vitrification: The progressive fusion of clay in the firing when the BODY becomes harder, denser and less porous the higher the temperature.

Zillij: Arab word for a smooth or slippery tile and used in Morocco, especially as a generic term for glazed tile MOSAIC.

BIBLIOGRAPHY

In a book such as this which covers the whole history of tiles, obviously only a selection of the main bibliographic sources can be listed. Research into the history of tiles is constantly expanding into new areas and the results of this work are often published in articles in specialist journals. This applies particularly to the material covered in the final chapter. The Tiles and Architectural Ceramics Society in Great Britain (www.tilesoc.org.uk), The Tile Heritage Foundation in the United States (www.tileheritage.org), and The Friends of the Dutch Tile Museum, Otterlo in The Netherlands (www.nederlandstegelmuseum.nl), are three non-profit-making tile organizations which specialize in the study of tiles and architectural ceramics. Over the years they have published a vast amount of material on the history of tiles in their annual magazines and journals. The subjects dealt with are too numerous to list but can be accessed online at the web addresses listed above.

Introduction
Berendsen, Anne (1967), *Tiles: A General History*, London, Faber and Faber

Graves, Alun (2002), *Tiles and Tilework of Europe*, London, V&A Publishing

Herbert, Tony and Huggins, Kathy (1995), *The Decorative Tile in Architecture and Interiors*, London, Phaidon

Lemmen, Hans van (1993), *Tiles in Architecture*, London, Laurence King Publishing

Lemmen, Hans van and Malam, John, (eds) (1991), *Fired Earth: 1000 Years of Tiles in Europe*, Shepton Beauchamp, Richard Dennis Publications

Pearson, Lynn (2005), *Tile Gazetteer: A Guide to British Tile and Architectural Ceramics Locations*, Shepton Beauchamp, Richard Dennis Publications

Riley, Noel (1987), *Tile Art: A History of Decorative Ceramic Tiles*, London, Quintet Publishing

Chapter One: Ancient Beginnings
Adam, Jean-Pierre (1994), *Roman Building: Materials and Techniques*, London, Batsford

Campbell, James and Pryce, Will (2003), *Brick: A World History*, London, Thames & Hudson

Clunas, Craig (2009), *Art in China*, Oxford, Oxford University Press

Kriwaczek, Paul (2010), *Babylon: Mesopotamia and the Birth of Civilization*, London, Atlantic Books

Friedman, F. D. (1998), *Gifts of the Nile: Ancient Egyptian Faience*, London, Thames & Hudson

Marzahn, Joachim (1992), *The Ishtar Gate: The Processional Way – The New Year Festival of Babylon*, Berlin, Staatliche Museen zu Berlin

Middleton, Andrew (1997), 'Tiles in Roman Britain', in Freestone, Ian and Gaimster, David (eds) (1997), *Pottery in the Making*, London, The British Museum Press

Rawson, Jessica (1992), *The British Museum Book of Chinese Art*, London, The British Museum Press

Rhodes, Daniel (1998), *Clay and Glazes for the Potter*, London, A & C Black

Seymour, Michael J. and Finkel, Irvin L. (2008), *Babylon: Myth and Reality*, London, The British Museum Press

Spencer, A. J. (ed.) (2007), *The British Museum Book of Ancient Egypt*, London, The British Museum Press

Tomlinson, R. A. (1995), *Greek and Roman Architecture*, London, The British Museum Press

Chapter Two: Islamic Designs
Atashoy, Nurhan and Raby, Julian (1987), *Iznik: The Pottery of Ottoman Turkey*, London, Alexandria Press in Association with Laurence King Publishing

Baer, Eva (1998), *Islamic Ornament*, Edinburgh, Edinburgh University Press

Barrucand, Marianne and Bednorz, Achim (1992), *Moorish Architecture in Andalusia*, Cologne, Taschen

Caiger-Smith, Alan (1973), *Tin-Glazed Pottery in Europe and the Islamic World*, London, Faber and Faber

Caiger-Smith, Alan (1985), *Lustre Pottery: Technique, Tradition and Innovation in Islam and the Western World*, London, Faber and Faber

Canby, Sheila R. 'Islamic lustreware', in Freestone, Ian and Gaimster, David (eds) (1997), *Pottery in the Making*, London, The British Museum Press

Carboni, Stefano and Masuja Tomoko (1993), *Persian Tiles*, New York, The Metropolitan Museum of Art

Carswell, John (1998), *Iznik Pottery*, London, The British Museum Press

Carswell, John and C. J. F. Dowsett (1972), *Kütahya Tiles and Pottery from the Armenian Cathedral of St James, Jerusalem*, 2 vols, Oxford, Oxford University Press

Degeorge, Gerard and Porter, Yves (2002), *The Art of the Islamic Tile*, Paris, Flammarion

Goowin, Godfrey (1971), *A History of Ottoman Architecture*, London, Thames & Hudson

Hedgecoe, John and Damluji, Salma Samar (1992), *Zil, the Art of Moroccan Ceramics*, Reading, Garnet Publishing

Öney, Gönül (1987), *Ceramic Tiles in Islamic Architecture*, Istanbul, Ada Press

Pickett, Douglas (1997), *Early Persian Tilework: The Medieval Flowering of Kāshī*, London, Associated University Presses

Porter, Venetia (1995), *Islamic Tiles*, London, The British Museum Press

Porter, Venetia (2012), *The Art of Hajj*, London, The British Museum Press

Chapter Three: Medieval Magnificence
Eames, Elizabeth S. (1980), *Catalogue of Medieval Lead-Glazed Earthenware Tiles*, 2 vols, London, The British Museum Press

Eames, Elizabeth S. (1992), *English Tilers*, London, The British Museum Press

Eames, Elizabeth S. and Fanning, Thomas (1988), *Irish Medieval Tiles*, Dublin, Royal Irish Academy

France, J. (1998), *The Cistercians in Medieval Art*, Gloucestershire, Sutton Publishing

Foster, Richard (1991), *Patterns of Thought: The Hidden Meaning of the Great Pavement of Westminster Abbey*, London, Jonathan Cape

Klijn, E. M. Ch. F. (1995), *Lead-Glazed Earthenware in The Netherlands*, Arnhem, Nederlands Openluchtmuseum

Lägers, Hans (2006), *Hersteen en Cronement: Haardstenen uit de zestiende en zeventiende eeuw*, Utrecht, Gemeente Utrecht

Landgraf, Eleonore (1993), *Ornamentierte Bodenfliesen des Mittelalters in Süd – und Westdeutschland 1150 bis 1550*, 3 vols, Stuttgart, Theiss

Lane, Arthur (1939), *Victoria and Albert Museum: Guide to the Collection of Tiles*, London, HMSO

Lemmen, Hans van, (2000), *Medieval Tiles*, Princes Risborough, Shire Publications

Lewis, J. M. (1999), *The Medieval Tiles of Wales*, National Museums and Galleries of Wales

Norton, Christopher (1992), *Carreaux de Pavement du Moyen Age et de la Renaissance*, Paris, Musée Carnavalet

Norton, Christopher and Park, David (eds) (1986), *Cistercian Art and Architecture in the British Isles*, Cambridge, Cambridge University Press

Rodwell, Warwick and Mortimer, Richard (eds) (2010), *Westminster Abbey Chapter House: The History, Art and Architecture of 'a chapter house beyond compare'*, London, Society of Antiquaries

Santi, Bruno (1982), *The Marble Pavement of the Cathedral of Siena*, Florence, Scala

Stopford, J. (2005), *Medieval Floor Tiles of Northern England*, Oxford, Oxbow Books

Chapter Four: Renaissance and Baroque Splendour

Archer, Michael (1997), *Delftware: The Tin-Glazed Earthenware of the British Isles*, London, V&A The Stationary Office

Betts, Ian M. and Weinstein, Rosemary I. (2010), *Tin-Glazed Tiles from London*, London, Museum of London

Dam, Jan Daniel van and others (1984), *Dutch Tiles in the Philadelphia Museum of Art*, Philadelpia, Philadelpia Museum of Art

Dawson, Aileen (2010), *English and Irish Delftware 1570–1840*, London, The British Museum Press

Domestici, Fiamma (1995), *I Della Robbia a Pistoia*, Florence, Octavo

Estall i Poles, Vicent (2010), *The History, Art and Tradition of the Tiles of Valencia: The Collections of the Tile Museum of Onda*, Boizenburg, Erstes Deutsches Fliesenmuseum Boizenburg and Museo del Azulejo Onda

Frothingham, Alice W. (1969), *The Tile Panels of Spain 1500–1650*, New York, The Hispanic Society of America

González Martí, Manuel (1952), *Cerámica del Levante Español: Siglos Medievales*, 3 vols, Barcelona, Labor

Gschnitzer, Hans and Menardi, Herlinde (1986), *Stuben-Öfen-Hausmodelle*, Innsbruck, Haymon Verlag

Guidotti, Carmen Ravanelli (1988), *Il Pavimento Della Cappella Vaselli*, Bologna, Grafis Edizioni

Horne, Jonathan (1989), *English Tin-Glazed Tiles*, London, Jonathan Horne

Lemmen, Hans van (1997), *Delftware Tiles*, London, Laurence King Publishing

Meco, José (1988), *The Art of Azulejo in Portugal*, Amadora, Bertrand

Pluis, Jan (1997), *The Dutch Tile: Designs and Names*, Leiden, Primavera Pers

Quinterio, Francesco (1990), *Maiolica Nell' Architettura del Rinascimento Italiano*, Florence, Cantini

Rackham, Bernard (1926), *Early Netherlands Maiolica with Special Reference to the Tiles at The Vyne in Hampshire*, London, Geoffrey Bless

Ray, Anthony (1973), *English Delftware Tiles*, London, Faber and Faber

Ray, Anthony (2000), *Spanish Pottery 1248–1898*, V&A Publishing

Schaap, Ella B. (1994), *Dutch Floral Tiles of the Golden Age and their Botanical Prints*, Haarlem, Becht

Stahl, Siefried (1977), *Deutsche Fliesen: Fayencefliesen des 18 Jahrhunderts*, Braunsweig, Klinkhardt and Bierman

Wilson, Timothy (1987), *Ceramic Art of the Italian Renaissance*, London, The British Museum Press

Chapter Five: From Industry to Art

Atterbury, Paul and Wainwright, Clive (eds) (1994), *Pugin: A Gothic Passion*, New Haven and London, Yale University Press and The Victoria and Albert Museum

Atterbury, Paul, and Irvine, Louise (eds) (1979), *The Doulton Story*, Stoke-upon-Trent, Royal Doulton Tableware Ltd

Austwick, J & B (1980), *The Decorated Tile: An Illustrated History of English Tile-making and Design*, London, Pitman Publishing

Barnard, J. (1972), *Victorian Ceramic Tiles*, London, Studio Vista

Beaulah, Kenneth and Lemmen, Hans van (2001), *Church Tiles of the Nineteenth Century*, Princes Risborough, Shire Publications

Catleugh, Jon (1983), *William De Morgan Tiles*, London, Trefoil Books

Chalmers, Meg, and Young, Judy (2005), *The Saturday Evening Girls: Paul Revere Pottery*, Atglen, Schiffer Publishing

Cross, A. J. (1980), *Pilkington's Royal Lancastrian Pottery and Tiles*, London, Richard Dennis Publications

Drakard, David and Holdway, Paul (1983), *Spode Printed Ware*, London, Longman

Durant, Stuart (1993), *Christopher Dresser*, London, Academy Editions

Furnival, W. J. (1904), *Leadless Decorative Tiles, Faience, and Mosaic*, Stone, W. J. Furnival

Greenwood, Martin (1989), *The Designs of William De Morgan*, Shepton Beauchamp, Richard Dennis and William E. Wiltshire III

Hansen, Joan Maria (2007), *Lewis Foreman Day (1845–1910): Unity in Design and Industry*, Woodbridge, Antique Collectors' Club

Jones, Joan (1993), *Minton: The First Two Hundred Years of Design & Production*, Shrewsbury, Swan Hill Press

Kamermans, Johan and Lemmen, Hans van (eds) (2004), *Industrial Tiles 1840–1940*, Otterlo, Nederlands Tegelmuseum

Karlson, Norman (2005), *The Encyclopedia of American Art Tiles*, 3 vols, Atglen, Schiffer Publishing

Koehler, Vance, A. (1994), 'American decorative tiles 1880–1950', in *American Art Tiles 1880–1950*, Lambertville, David Rago Arts & Crafts Movement Gallery

Lambourne, Lionel (1996), *The Aesthetic Movement*, London, Phaidon

Lemmen, Hans van (2000), *Victorian Tiles*, Princes Risborough, Shire Publications

Locket, Terrence (1979), *Collecting Victorian Tiles*, Woodbridge, Antique Collectors' Club

Myers, Richard and Hilary (1996), *William Morris Tiles*, Shepton Beauchamp, Richard Dennis Publications

Parry, Linda (ed.) (1996), *William Morris*, London, Philip Wilson Publishers in association with The Victoria and Albert Museum

Pennington, Richard (2010), *Low Art Tile: John Gardner Low and the Artists of Boston's Gilded Age*, Charleston, South Carolina, CreateSpace.

Pisano, Ronald G. (1999), *The Tile Club and the Aesthetic Movement in America*, New York, Abrams

Reed, Cleota (1980), *Henry Chapman Mercer and the Moravian Pottery and Tile Works*, Philadelphia, University of Pennsylvania Press

Sigafoose, Dick (1997), *American Art Pottery*, Paducah, Kentucky, Collector Books

Skinner, D. S. and Lemmen, Hans van (eds) (1984), *Minton Tiles 1835–1935*, Stoke-upon-Trent, City of Stoke-upon-Trent Museum and Art Gallery

Stapleton, Annamarie (2002), *John Moyr Smith 1839–1912: A Victorian Designer*, Shepton Beauchamp, Richard Dennis Publications

Whiteway, Michael (2001), *Christopher Dresser 1834–1904*, Milan, Skira

Chapter Six: The Century of Design

Anscombe, Isabelle (1993), *Omega and after: Bloomsbury and the Decorative Arts*, London, Thames & Hudson

Artucio Urioste, Alejandro (2004), *El Azulejo en la Arquitectura Uruguaya: Siglos XVIII, XIX y XX*, Montevideo, Linardi y Risso

Augustine, Betsy and Halkin, Barry (1999), *Philadelphia's Magic Gardens: The Art of Isaiah Zagar*, Philadelphia, Open Eyes Press

Baeck, Mario and Verbrugge, Bart (1996), *De Belgische Art Nouveau en Art Deco wandtegels 1880–1940*, Brussels, Ministerie van de Vlaamse Gemeenschap

Barros Veloso, A. J. and Almasqué, Isabel (2000), *Portuguese Tiles and Art Nouveau*, Lisbon, Inapa

Blanchett, Chris (2006), *20th Century Decorative British Tiles*, 3 vols, Atglen, Schiffer Publishing

Carandell, Josep M. and Vivas, Pere (2005) *Park Güell: Gaudí's Utopia*, Barcelona, Triangle Postals

Corbett, Angela and Barry (2013), *Pilkington's Tiles 1891–2010*, Lancaster, Pilkington's Lancastrian Pottery Society

Giorgini, Frank (1994), *Handmade Tiles: Designing-Making-Decorating*, Asheville, Lark Books

Greene, John (1987), *Brightening the Long Days: Hospital Tile Pictures*, Gloucester, Tiles and Architectural Ceramics Society

Hayward, Leslie (2011), *Poole Pottery: Carter & Company and their Successors 1873–2011*, Shepton Beauchamp, Richard Dennis Publications

Kessler-Slotta, Elisabeth (1985), *Max Laeuger 1864–1952*, Saarbrücken, Saarbrücker Druckerei und Verlag

König, Wolfgang and Weichselbaum, Rudolf (2006), *Carl Sigmund Luber: His Life and Work as Artist for the Art Nouveau Ceramics of Johann von Schwarz 1896–1906*, Einbeck, König-Weichselbaum Verlag

Lemmen, Hans van (2012), *Art Deco Tiles*, Oxford, Shire Publications

Lemmen, Hans van and Blanchett, Chris (1999), *20th Century Tiles*, Princes Risborough, Shire Publications

Lemmen, Hans van and Verbrugge, Bart (1999), *Art Nouveau Tiles*, London, Laurence King Publishing

Muthesius, Angelika (1999), *Hundertwasser Architecture: For a more Human Architecture in Harmony with Nature*, Cologne, Taschen

Pearson, Lynn (2006), *Public Art since 1950*, Princes Risborough, Shire Publications

Pluis, Jan (2008), *Nederlandse Tegels 1900–2000*, Leiden, Primavera Pers

Saporiti, Teresa (2000), *Decorative Tiles of Eduardo Nery*, Lisbon, Museu National do Azulejo

Scott, Paul (2001), *Painted Clay: Graphic Arts and the Ceramic Surface*, London, A & C Black

Stratton, Michael (1993), *The Terracotta Revival: Building Innovation and the Image of the Industrial City in Britain and North America*, London, Gollancz

Tunick, Susan (1997), *Terra-Cotta Skyline*, New York, Princeton Architectural Press

Weisser, Michael (1983), *Jugendstilfliesen*, Frankfurt, Fricke Verlag

PICTURE CREDITS

Frontispiece *see* 258
2 Courtesy of Museo de Cerámica de Manises
4 Courtesy of Henk Nijenhuis
5 Courtesy of Lothar Scholz
6 © bpk / Vorderasiatisches Museum, SMB / Olaf M.Teßmer
7 Courtesy of Wikimedia Commons (Photo: Soare)
13 Photo: akg-images / Erich Lessing
17 © 2013. Image copyright The Metropolitan Museum of Art/Art Resource/Scala, Florence
38 Courtesy of the author
44 Courtesy of the author
46 Courtesy of the author
47 Courtesy of the author
48 Courtesy of the author
49 Courtesy of the author
50 Courtesy of the author
53 Courtesy of the author
60 Courtesy of the author
61 Courtesy of the author
68 Courtesy of the author
70 Courtesy of the author
75 Courtesy of the author
76 Courtesy of the author
77 Courtesy of the author
78 Courtesy of the author
79 Photo: John Land
80 Photo: John Land
81 Drawn by Jim Farrant after Kenneth Beaulah; © The Trustees of the British Museum
85 Courtesy of Nederlands Tegelmuseum, Otterlo
87 Courtesy of Thelma Shepley
90 ©iStockphoto.com
92 Courtesy of the author
93 Courtesy of the author
94 Courtesy of the author
99 Courtesy of Nederlands Tegelmusuem, Otterlo
102 Courtesy of Abdijmuseum Ten Duinen, Koksijde
103 © Groeningemuseum, Bruges, Belgium / The Bridgeman Art Library
107 Courtesy of the author
108 Courtesy of the author
114 Courtesy of Nederlands Tegelmuseum, Otterlo
115 Courtesy of Museo del Azulejo, Onda
116 Courtesy of Nederlands Tegelmuseum, Otterlo
117 Courtesy of Museo del Azulejo, Onda
119 Courtesy of Museo del Azulejo, Onda
120 Courtesy of Nederlands Tegelmuseum, Otterlo
121 Courtesy of the author
130 Inv. 18869 Museo Internazionale delle Ceramiche in Faenza
136 Courtesy of the author
137 Courtesy of the author
138 Courtesy of the author
139 Courtesy of the author
140 Courtesy of the author
141 Courtesy of the author
142 Courtesy of Museo del Azulejo, Onda
143 Courtesy of the author
144 Courtesy of the author
145 Courtesy of the author
146 Courtesy of the author
147 Courtesy of the author
148 Courtesy of the author
149 Courtesy of the author
156 Inv. 21365 Museo Internazionale delle Ceramiche in Faenza
157 ©National Trust Images/Andreas von Einsiedel
158 © Royal Museums of Art and History, Brussels

159 Courtesy of Nederlands Tegelmuseum, Otterlo
161 Courtesy of Nederlands Tegelmuseum, Otterlo
162 Courtesy of Nederlands Tegelmuseum, Otterlo
163 Courtesy of Nederlands Tegelmuseum, Otterlo
164 Courtesy of Nederlands Tegelmuseum, Otterlo
165 Courtesy of Nederlands Tegelmuseum, Otterlo
168 Courtesy of the author
169 Courtesy of Nederlands Tegelmuseum, Otterlo
173 Courtesy of the author
174 Courtesy of the author
175 © Victoria and Albert Museum, London
176 Courtesy of the author
177 Courtesy of the author
178 Courtesy of the author
181 Courtesy of the author
182 Courtesy of the author
190 Courtesy of the author
193 Courtesy of the author
194 Courtesy of the author
195 Courtesy of the author
196 Courtesy of the author
198 Courtesy of the author
200 Courtesy of the author
201 Courtesy of Roger Hensman
202 Courtesy of the author
203 Courtesy of the author
204 Courtesy of the author
205 Courtesy of the author
206 Courtesy of Mario Baeck
207 Courtesy of the author
208 Courtesy of Nederlands Tegelmuseum, Otterlo
209 © Victoria and Albert Museum, London
211 Courtesy of the author
217 Courtesy of the author
218 Courtesy of the author
219 Courtesy of the author
223 Courtesy of Adrian Grater
226 Courtesy of Ironbridge Gorge Museum Trust
230 Courtesy of the author
231 Courtesy of Smithsonian Institution, Washington, DC
232 Courtesy of Smithsonian Institution, Washington, DC
233 Courtesy of Smithsonian Institution, Washington, DC
234 Courtesy of Smithsonian Institution, Washington, DC
235 Courtesy of Smithsonian Institution, Washington, DC
236 Courtesy of the author
237 Courtesy of the author
238 Courtesy of the author
239 Courtesy of Cooper-Hewitt National Design Museum, New York
240 Courtesy of Cooper-Hewitt National Design Museum, New York
241 Courtesy of Smithsonian Institution, Washington, DC
242 Courtesy of Cooper-Hewitt National Design Museum, New York
243 Courtesy of Smithsonian Institution, Washington, DC
244 Courtesy of Cooper-Hewitt National Design Museum, New York
245 Courtesy of John Scott
248 Courtesy of the author
249 Courtesy of the author
251 Courtesy of the author
252 Courtesy of the author
253 Courtesy of the author

254 Courtesy of Mario Baeck
255 Courtesy of the author
256 Courtesy of Nederlands Tegelmuseum, Otterlo
257 Courtesy of Wolfgang König
258 Courtesy of Nederlands Tegelmuseum, Otterlo
259 Courtesy of the author
260 Courtesy of the author
261 Courtesy of John Scott
264 Courtesy of the author
268 Courtesy of the author
269 Courtesy of the author
270 Courtesy of the author
271 Courtesy of the author
272 Courtesy of the author
273 Courtesy of Douglas van der Horst
274 Courtesy of the author
275 Courtesy of the author
276 Courtesy of the author
277 Courtesy of Smithsonian Institution, Washington, DC
278 Courtesy of Roger Hensmen
279 Courtesy of the author
280 Courtesy of Mario Baeck
282 Courtesy of the author
283 Courtesy of the author
284 Courtesy of the author
285 Courtesy of Roger Hensmen
286 Courtesy of the author
288 Courtesy of Fielding Auctioneers Ltd
289 ©Victoria and Albert Museum, London
291 © Victoria and Albert Museum, London
292 Courtesy of the author
293 Courtesy of Ineke Ganzinotti-Bart
294 Courtesy of Museo del Azulejo, Onda
295 Courtesy of the author
296 Courtesy of Adrian Grater
297 Courtesy of the author
298 Courtesy of Penny Beckett
299 Courtesy of Chris Blanchett
300 Inv. 24502 Museo Internazionale delle Ceramiche in Faenza
301 Courtesy of Robert Jones
302 Courtesy of the author
303 Courtesy of Stephen Cocker
304 Courtesy of the author
305 Courtesy of the author
306 Courtesy of Lothar Scholz
307 Courtesy of the author
308 Courtesy of the author
309 Courtesy of Paul Rothery
310 Courtesy of the author
311 Courtesy of Syma (photo: Randy Schaeffer)
312 Courtesy of the author
313 Courtesy of Susan Tunick
314 Courtesy of the author
315 Courtesy of Frouwien Soenveld
316 Courtesy of Lothar Scholz
317 Courtesy of Lothar Scholz
318 Courtesy of Eduardo Nery
319 Courtesy of Eduardo Nery
320 Courtesy of Robert Dawson
321 Courtesy of Robert Dawson
322 Courtesy of Frouwien Soenveld
323 Courtesy of Frouwien Soenveld
324 Courtesy of Manolo Sales
325 Courtesy of Bronwyn Williams-Ellis
326 Courtesy of Susan Tunick
327 Courtesy of Susan Tunick
328 Courtesy of Paul Scott
329 Courtesy of Paul Scott

INDEX

Page numbers in **bold** refer to information contained in captions.

ACKNOWLEDGEMENTS

This book would not have been possible without the assistance of many people throughout the tile world in Britain and abroad who checked information for captions, answered small queries, supplied translations and kindly provided images. I would like to thank the following:

Sandra Barry, Richard Byrn, Frans Caignie, Bonnie Campbell Lilienfeld, Angela and Barry Corbett, Robert Dawson, Jan Daan van Dam, Vicent Estall, Adrian Grater, Roger Hensman, Douglas van der Horst, Wilhelm Joliet, Robert Jones, Johan Kamermans, Vance Koehler, Wolfgang König, Susan Montgomery, Eduardo Nery, Richard Pennington, Ger de Ree, Cleota Reed, Paul Rothery, Judy Rudoe, Manolo Sales, Lothar Scholz, John Scott, Paul Scott, Thelma Shepley, Mike Sims, Frouwien Soenveld, Syma, Alan Swale, Joe Taylor, Susan Tunick, John Turner, Dirk Vanclooster, Bronwyn Williams-Ellis, and Maria Yamul.

Special thanks are due to Mario Baeck, Penny Beckett, Ian Betts, Chris Blanchett, Aileen Dawson, Dora Thornton, Jessica Harrison-Hall, Peter Higgs, Venetia Porter and Alan Swale for their kind and valuable help in reading and commenting on sections of the manuscript. Any mistakes or omissions are my own.

Also many thanks to the curatorial staff at the British Museum and the editors at the British Museum Press for their help and support during the writing of this book. The biggest thank you is owed to my wife Patsy who, as a trained historian, always read and commented on any draft text before it left my desk.